Better Homes and Gardens.

gardening
made
simple

The complete step-by-step guide to gardening

WILEY

John Wiley & Sons, Inc.

Better Homes and Gardens®
Gardening Made SImple

Contributing Writer and Project Editor: Kate Carter Frederick
Contributing Designers: Ken Carlson, Bruce Yang; Waterbury Publications, Inc.
Editor, Garden Books: Denny Schrock
Editorial Assistant: Heather Knowles
Contributing Copy Editor: Fran Gardner
Contributing Proofreaders: Fern Marshall Bradley, M. Peg Smith
Contributing Indexer: Ellen Sherron
Photographers: Marty Baldwin, Dean Schoeppner
Contributing Photographers: Adam Albright, Matthew Benson, Rob Cardillo, Susan Gilmore, Doug Hetherington, Graham Jimerson, Lynn Karlin, Pete Krumhardt, Scott Little, Blaine Moats, Kritsada Panichgul, Denny Schrock, Joe Schulte, Bill Stites, Jay Wilde

Meredith® Books
Editorial Director: Gregory H. Kayko
Editor in Chief, Garden: Doug Jimerson
Art Director: Tim Alexander
Managing Editor: Doug Kouma
Executive Director, Sales: Ken Zagor
Director, Operations: George A. Susral
Director, Production: Douglas M. Johnston
Business Director: Janice Croat
Imaging Center Operator: Randy Manning

John Wiley & Sons, Inc.
Publisher: Natalie Chapman
Associate Publisher: Jessica Goodman
Executive Editor: Anne Ficklen
Assistant Editor: Charleen Barila, Meaghan McDonnell
Production Director: Diana Cisek
Manufacturing Manager: Tom Hyland

This book is printed on acid-free paper.

Note to Reader: Due to differing conditions, tools, and individual skills, Meredith Corporation assumes no responsibility for any damages, injuries suffered, or losses incurred as a result of following the information published in this book. Before beginning any project, review the instructions carefully, and if any doubts or questions remain, consult local experts or authorities. Because codes and regulations vary greatly, you should always check with authorities to ensure that your project complies with all applicable local codes and regulations. Always read and observe all the safety precautions provided by manufacturers of any tools, equipment, or supplies, and follow all accepted safety procedures.

***Better Homes and Gardens*® Magazine**
Editor in Chief: Gayle Goodson Butler

Meredith Publishing Group
President: Tom Harty
Executive Vice President: Doug Olson

Meredith Corporation
Chairman of the Board: William T. Kerr
President and Chief Executive Officer: Stephen M. Lacy

In Memoriam: E. T. Meredith III (1933–2003)

For general information on our other products and services or for technical support, please contact our Customer Care Department within the United States at (800) 762-2974, outside the United States at (317) 572-3993 or fax (317) 572-4002.

Wiley also publishes its books in a variety of electronic formats. Some content that appears in print may not be available in electronic books. For more information about Wiley products, visit our website at www.wiley.com.

Library of Congress Cataloging-in-Publication Data

Better homes and gardens gardening made simple : complete step-by-step guide to gardening.
    p. cm.
Includes index.
ISBN 978-0-470-63854-5 (pbk.)
1. Gardening--Handbooks, manuals, etc. I. Better homes and gardens. II. Title: Gardening made simple.
SB453.B474 2011   635--dc23   2011030365

Printed in the United States of America

10 9 8 7 6 5 4 3 2 1

CONTENTS

SIMPLER IS BETTER

Generations of gardeners have acquired knowledge by digging into soil at the heels of a grandparent or parent. The tradition of gardening continues with as much need and desire as ever, but today's gardener can also access a world of information in an instant. Sorting through this information and finding what's useful and accurate can be an overwhelming feat. And who knows if it will really help you save time, effort, and money.

This is where *Gardening Made Simple* comes in. It gives you all the information you'll need to plant and maintain your garden. We know that you want gardening to be easy, fun, and, most of all, doable in your yard. So we made this book to help you accomplish the basics along with enjoyable and affordable options. A wealth of useful, garden-tested tips and techniques are here, along with detailed photographs to make the process of gardening simple.

In the midst of busy challenging lives, there is widespread longing for simplicity that takes us into the garden. There, and on the pages ahead, you will find down-to-earth ways to cultivate knowledge and work with nature to create something beautiful and delicious. No matter your age, your level of gardening experience, or the state of your garden, *Gardening Made Simple* encourages you to experiment and grow with us. From the Better Homes and Gardens Test Garden® to your garden, best wishes for happy gardening!

KATE CARTER FREDERICK
Editor, *Better Homes and Gardens®, Gardening Made Simple*

TEST GARDEN TIP

SHAPELY BEDS Edging helps a garden bed retain its shape. Whether edging is set flush with the ground or raised, it can take a straight or curved course. The length of an edger affects the shape of the curve. It's easier to lay smooth curves with short edgers and straight courses with longer edgers *(page 79)*.

HOW TO USE THIS BOOK

Turn to this reference whenever you need answers to your gardening questions. Use it as a tool, a source for tips, and a way to generate ideas.

This book was designed as a complete go-to guide to gardening that covers the most relevant subjects, from choosing tools to solving pest problems. It provides the information and advice you will need to master the basics, adapt the project ideas to your yard, and be inspired to experiment with techniques. Created to serve you with a simplified approach, the book's step-by-step instructions plus hundreds of detailed photos will help you make and improve your garden. Get garden plans that meet your specific needs here: bhg.com/gardenplans.

TEST GARDEN TIP

Find insights and proven practices in these hints from the Better Homes and Gardens Test Garden®.

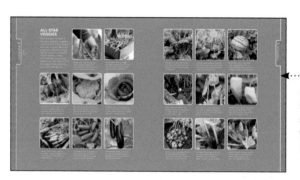

PLANT GALLERY

Simplify your plant selections by starting with these reliable performers.

IDEA GALLERY

Gather inspiration for a better garden and make gardening easier.

HOW TO Use the step-by-step guides to ensure the success of your projects.

ASK THE GARDEN DOCTOR

Get answers to your gardening questions from the editors of *Better Homes and Gardens®:* bhg.com/gardendoctor.

ASK THE GARDEN DOCTOR

WHAT KIND OF STONE SHOULD I USE TO EDGE MY GARDEN? Tumbled fieldstone enhances a casual garden in a rustic setting. Uniform cut stone, laid end to end, makes a tidy statement with a more clearly defined sense of formal organization. The stone's color may complement or contrast with a setting *(page 78)*.

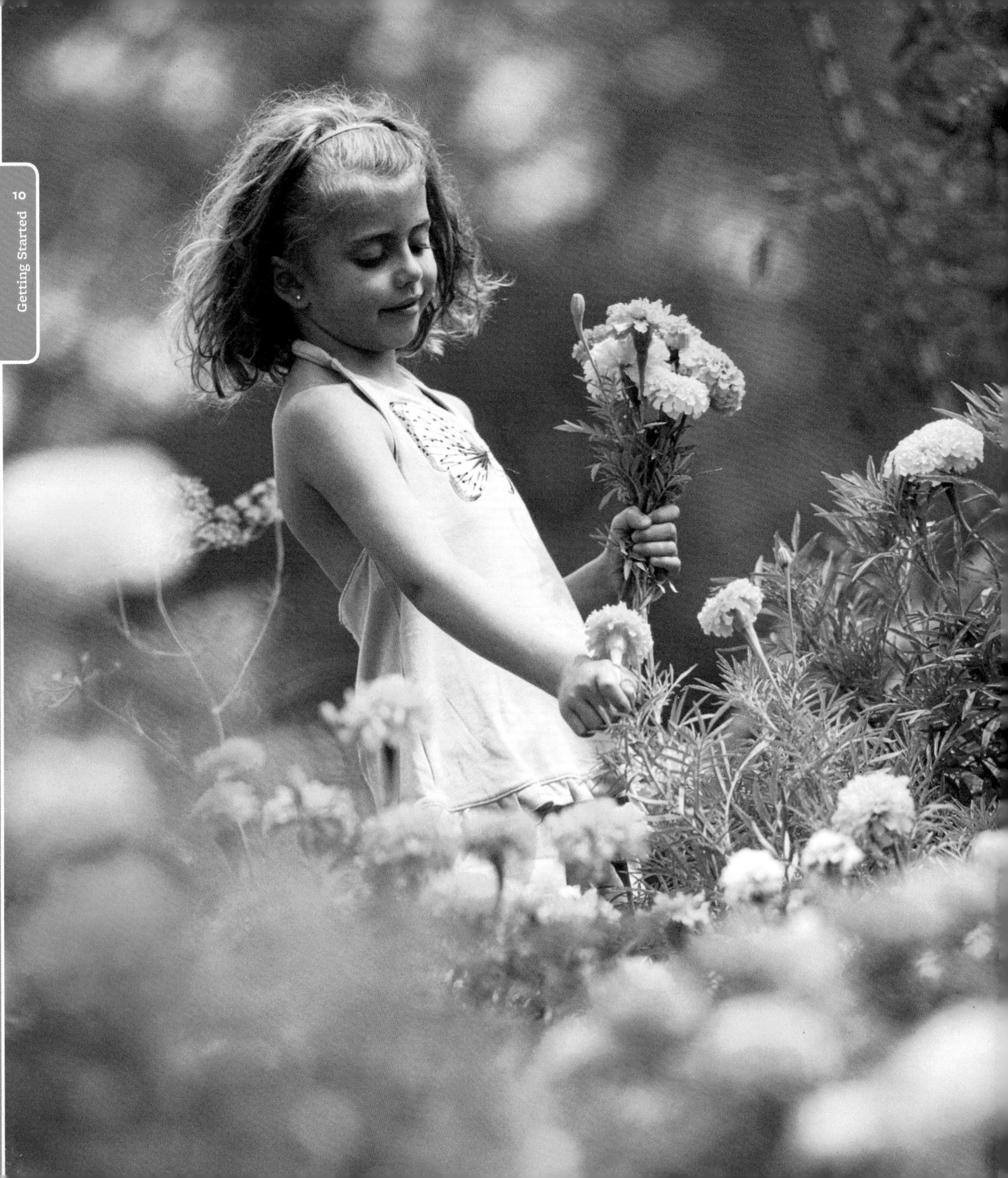

CHAPTER 1

GETTING STARTED

Gardening is an adventure and a lifelong learning process. Start here to create a beautiful, enjoyable garden.

WHAT'S IN IT FOR YOU?

What's so good about gardening? Pretty much everything!

The rewards of gardening are as pleasantly surprising as they are varied. Most gardeners say they garden for fun, relaxation, fresh air, or some form of therapy. Plants—and flowers, especially—lift spirits. You enjoy the process as well as the results. Beginning each day with a ritual walk in the garden brings comfort.

Throughout history, gardens have provided places of wonder and refuge, capable of promoting the well-being of all who entered. Modern research bears it out: Gardening improves health. Just strolling through a garden relieves stress. What's more, the bending, digging, and lifting are good exercise.

Gardening makes bones strong and joints supple. It lowers blood pressure, burns calories, and more.

For many, the garden is also a source of nutrition. Growing your own organic food yields the freshest produce. It also promotes the practice of putting pesticide- and additive-free food on the table. Besides, gardening is one of the ultimate earth-friendly activities. Yes, adopting green gardening habits saves resources, but it saves money and time too.

Gardening bolsters families and communities. It links generations and neighbors—whose hands reach into soil, poke seeds into earth, and pluck juicy tomatoes—growing and learning together.

WHAT GROWS IN A GARDEN?

All sorts of possibilities grow in a garden. A garden provides a place for people of all ages to nurture budding interests.

Gardens are not just places of planting and weeding, they are also places of exploration and delight. When kids are encouraged to dig into gardening, they develop a lifelong interest in plants and wildlife. Gardening awakens a child's senses as he sniffs lemon basil, touches soft earthworms, tastes radishes that he grew. Curiosity grows in a garden. Learning comes from digging holes and picking produce. Sooner or later, gardeners develop a taste for the vegetables they grow.

Once you get over the notion of gardening as work, it becomes just the opposite: a source of stress relief and relaxation. When you are focused on a gardening task, especially something repetitive or tedious, it can become meditative. Interacting with plants and nature bolsters the spirit and promotes mental health. Everyone needs to take a break from the daily grind—and many find the most refreshing place to do that is in their garden.

PURPOSE A garden gives many people a reason to head outdoors and soak up sunshine and fresh air.

TRADITION Generations of gardeners have passed along their knowledge of techniques and wisdom of experience, inspiring those who follow.

WONDER Nature entertains those who pause to look, listen, and discover—from the fascination of ants toting grains of soil to the drama of fall foliage color.

CONFIDENCE Anyone who gardens can learn more and become a better gardener—there's always room for growth.

PEACE Gardening teaches patience and respect for nature. Gardening gives many rewards, especially serenity.

GARDENING WHERE YOU LIVE

Working with nature and understanding how your garden experiences the local climate helps ensure plants' success as well as their survival.

Many factors influence plants' survivability. Cold hardiness and heat tolerance, which are affected by local climate, come to bear in particular. When choosing plants for your garden, it's useful to start with the Hardiness Zone Map, developed by the U.S. Department of Agriculture (USDA). The map divides North America into zones based on the lowest recorded temperatures. Zone 1 is the coldest area and Zone 11 is the warmest.

Plants thrive in specific climates. What grows well in one region may not grow well in another. In terms of zone hardiness, plants have traditionally been classified by the coldest temperature they can endure. For example, plants hardy to Zone 3 survive where winter temperatures drop to –30°F. Plants hardy to Zone 7 would die before it gets that cold. Plants rated for a range of hardiness (Zones 3–7), usually survive winter in the coldest region as well as tolerate the summer heat of the warmest one.

The map is easy to use. Find your location on the map and determine your zone based on the color assigned to the area where you live. Plants now have USDA Heat Zone ratings too.

A plant's ability to survive winter is also affected by other factors, including soil conditions, sun and shade, wind, freeze-thaw cycles, and snow cover. When you find a plant that thrives in your garden, look for other species in the same family to try. For extra protection, move down a zone. If your garden is Zone 5, for example, try varieties that have a hardiness rating to Zone 4.

HOW'S THE WEATHER? Has an increase in average temperatures affected gardening in your region? Do you know which plants will fare best in unusually hot, dry summers?

TO EVERY SEASON In your region, if the growing season is short (90 days or so) and limited by cold weather, fall comes as early as September. Make gardening plans according to the season.

ASK THE GARDEN DOCTOR **HOW DO I KNOW HOW LONG THE GROWING SEASON LASTS IN MY AREA?** The growing season is the period of time that occurs in your region between the average date for the last spring frost and the first fall frost. Do you know how cold it gets in your garden in winter and how much rain it receives on average each year? This information will help you make good plant choices.

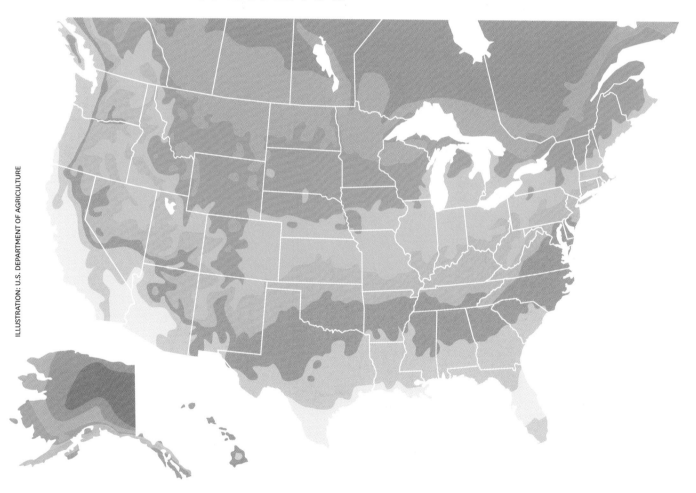

TEST GARDEN TIP

PROTECTING PLANTS Although you cannot control the weather, there is much you can do to protect your plants from weather extremes and even extend the growing season where you live. You will find tips and techniques throughout the pages ahead for nurturing plants.

USDA HARDINESS ZONE MAP

ILLUSTRATION: U.S. DEPARTMENT OF AGRICULTURE

Range of Average Annual Minimum Temperatures for Each Hardiness Zone

Zone 1: below –50°F (below –45.6°C)
Zone 2: –50 to –40°F (-45 to –40°C)
Zone 3: –40 to –30°F (-40 to –35°C)
Zone 4: –30 to –20°F (-34 to –29°C)

Zone 5: -20 to -10°F (–29 to –23°C)
Zone 6: -10 to 0°F (–23 to –18°C)
Zone 7: 0 to 10°F (–18 to –12°C)
Zone 8: 10 to 20°F (–12 to –7°C)

Zone 9: 20 to 30°F (–7 to –1°C)
Zone 10: 30 to 40°F (–1 to 4°C)
Zone 11: 40°F and above (4.5 C and above)

WHAT'S YOUR ZONE?

Climate affects how plants grow and how you garden.

The climate in your area consists of differing weather patterns: temperature, wind, sunlight, frost, rain, snow, and humidity. The effects of the climate on your garden are complex and different from those in gardens across your state and beyond.

Gardeners have a love-hate relationship with weather; gardens don't grow without light, rain, and heat. In spring, the morning sun on a rain-soaked garden is a welcome bringer of blooms. But in a summer drought, the sun seems cruel when it cracks earth, scorches petals, and wilts leaves.

Gardening Where It Isn't Easy

Every gardener faces climate challenges. Some locations have inherently extreme weather. Savvy gardeners adapt and look for ways to overcome the obstacles. Dry desert gardens require conservative water use and native plants. In cold-winter areas, mulch helps plants survive the dramatic temperature swings of freeze-thaw cycles.

As gardeners, we know we cannot change the weather, so we strive to understand, gauge, and prepare for it. We turn to high-tech weather wizards and data, hoping for insights that will help us help our plants. We check the rain gauge, keep an ear out for frost warnings, and figure out how to shield evergreens from drying winter winds.

In the end, the best tool for the weather-conscious gardener is a well-adjusted attitude with sharpened senses of awe, humor, and defiance. Knowing that the weather is an ally and a threat keeps climate from dampening the gardening spirit.

SPRING Gardeners dream of spring, envisioning tulips gleaming in the sun and streams of grape hyacinths popping up in the yard.

SUMMER The season of long, hot days brings waves of flowers and produce as the garden reaches its peak of activity.

FALL The autumn garden transforms into a kaleidoscope of colors. The gardener gets busy with a long to-do list.

WINTER Ongoing snow cover works like a blanket, insulating the ground from freeze-thaw cycles and bolstering plants' survivability in cold climates.

ASK THE GARDEN DOCTOR **HOW CAN I FIND THE MICROCLIMATES IN MY YARD?** Notice the places where children and pets most likely go—protected from wind. Do the plants there bloom earlier or later than other plants in the yard? Is it always sunny or shaded there? Is there an impermeable surface (driveway or sidewalk) next to the area that captures heat? These are signs of sheltered spots that may offer ideal conditions for particular plants.

A GOOD MATCH
Suiting plants to place translates into minimum future maintenance. This rooftop garden holds climbing hydrangea, daylilies, and ornamental grasses.

WHAT IS A MICROCLIMATE?

Every garden has opportunities and limitations within a range of climates and conditions.

Within your yard, there are unique pockets where surface features (buildings, large rock forms, mature tree groups) and elevations (hills, valleys, plains) alter the effects of atmospheric conditions, such as moisture and temperature. The climate in that area may be warmer or colder than surrounding areas.

Areas on the south or west sides of a house are typically warmer than constantly shaded areas exposed to wind. Fences, walls, and large rocks can protect plants from wind and radiate heat, creating sheltered spots. Paved surfaces (patios, driveways, sidewalks) can absorb heat during the day and radiate it into the landscape, moderating nighttime temperatures. Balconies and rooftops provide aerial microclimates subject to drying winds.

Every garden has limitations and opportunities, with a range of climates and conditions. Getting to know your circumstances will help you discover optimal places for specific plants.

WHAT'S YOUR GARDEN STYLE?

The best and most interesting gardens have a strong sense of place that reflects where and how you live.

Garden design trends come and go, but gardens that honor regional climates transform with the seasons. Adapting styles to suit the realities of climate and site is vital to a garden's health and appearance. This is easier if you choose native plants that have already adapted and experiment with others that need help adjusting. For instance, incorporating local stone into a garden ties it into the surroundings naturally.

Your Ideal Garden

Create your garden according to a specific style or focus on qualities that reflect the character of your home, your personality, and your lifestyle. Ideally, a sense of style unifies house and garden, providing an outlet for personal expression. What do you see in the garden of your dreams? Does it match the view outside your windows? When you make your garden as a place for you and your family and friends, it can serve whatever purpose you desire. Private refuge, relaxing room, play place, food source, or wildlife haven—it's your call.

As you make or remake your garden, consider how your garden can work for you by solving a problem. Let a living fence replace a wooden one and continual painting chores; let easy-care grasses disguise an unsightly air conditioner. Look for ways to add comfort, convenience, energy efficiency, property value, privacy, and living space—plants and gardens can do all that and more. Above all, gardens are places of transcendent beauty that give meaning to our lives.

COTTAGE STYLE A penchant for plants shows in dense plantings: favorite flowers and shrubs mix informally with practical edibles and structures.

EASY-CARE STYLE Taking a simplified approach yields a garden where less is more: Water-wise perennials team with shrubs and trees.

CASUAL STYLE A sleek and eco-chic design works with nature, using native plants that need no pampering and little water.

FORMAL STYLE An urban lifestyle calls for bold architectural plants that provide artful elements in containers and limited space.

? ASK THE GARDEN DOCTOR **WHERE DO I START TO MAKE A KITCHEN GARDEN?** How do you plan to use your garden? Besides raising fresh produce within steps of the kitchen door, do you want to include a place to serve meals, grill, or store tools? Form a plan, then gather ideas for structures and planting that will help make good use of the space.

MAKING PLANS FOR YOUR GARDEN

Rough out a plan and use it to determine the number of plants you will need.

Putting a garden plan on paper makes sense. It puts you in the position of looking at your yard from a bird's-eye view. Instead of getting bogged down with details, you can play with possibilities.

A simple sketch and a few measurements on paper will do. Whether you're planning a container garden, a bed, or an entire yard, a plan provides a useful reference. Take it with you to the nursery when you select new plants. Let it tell you how much mulch you'll need to order. Your garden plan will help you log progress and decide about changes as your garden grows and evolves.

Before You Dig

Plan before planting. Rough out a planting scheme and use it to determine the size and quantity of plants you will need. Then refer to the plan when adding plants to the garden. It will give you a future reference as well.

Take inventory and consider your garden's existing features. What works and doesn't work in the current scheme? Has a tree matured and turned a once full-sun area into a place that needs more plants for dry shade?

Best-Laid Plans

You might save time and money in the long run by hiring a landscape designer to develop a garden plan. Many nurseries offer a free service to customers who agree to purchase the plants from them. A good designer translates your wishes into a plan that you can bring to life.

CALL BEFORE YOU DIG Call 811 before you dig and request the free service that will mark your underground utility locations. Prevent costly damage to natural gas, cable service, or phone lines with a quick call.

TAKING TIME FOR GARDENING

You can create and maintain a beautiful garden and still have plenty of time to enjoy it.

Gardening smarter instead of harder enables you to have the garden you want without straining yourself to achieve it. In this busy, busy world, gardening offers a respite and an opportunity for relaxing—even in the midst of weeding or mowing.

Swap part of any hectic day for a little quality time in the garden. "Not enough time" often really means too much hassle or effort. Instead of focusing on time constraints, look for ways to make that chore easier, more efficient, and less demanding. Choose gardening as daily or weekly me-time, as essential to your well-being as exercise. Garden for exercise and double your pleasure. The goal is not to have a perfect garden, but an enjoyable one.

Time-Saving Strategies

No garden is care-free, but a low-maintenance garden can be yours. Time- and money-saving tips appear throughout this book to help you reduce the work and expense and enjoy your garden more. Get started with these tips:

Focus on developing one or two key garden areas that offer impact, rather than placing multiple beds and borders in all corners of your property.

Group plants according to their needs. Clustering containers simplifies watering, plus it allows pots to shade one another, which reduces watering. Grouping acid-loving plants means you can acidify the soil more efficiently.

Choose easy-care plants, including shrubs, groundcovers, and perennials that grow well in your area and practically take care of themselves. These are the plants that bring color and character to the garden throughout the growing season and maybe even year 'round.

Do little and often, making gardening part of your routine and keeping up with what needs doing. Water houseplants every Friday morning, for instance. Regularly doing part of bigger jobs—weeding, pruning, mulching—minimizes them.

GARDEN SHORTCUT

At the top of your gardening to-do list, keep these words: Enjoy the garden. The hottest days of summer are among the best times to put up your feet and just relax. Set the tools aside and savor what you have accomplished. Take time to figure out a game plan for fall.

ASK THE GARDEN DOCTOR **WHERE CAN I FIND INSPIRATION FOR MY GARDEN?** If you have not gardened before, look for design and planting ideas in public gardens, garden center displays, magazines, books, and blogs. Take local garden tours. Focus on a theme, a collection, a vacation spot, or works of a favorite garden writer as a jumping-off point for your garden design.

BUDGET MATERIALS
Concrete blocks, gravel, pressure-treated wood, inexpensive pavers, and terra-cotta pots are among the materials that fit tight budgets.

SPENDING AND SAVING

Gardeners have a reputation as a thrifty and resourceful lot—and they enjoy living up to it.

Gardening presents countless ways to spend money on new plants, gleaming tools, must-have doodads, and other supplies. Of course, you can spend tons of money on a garden, but most gardeners do the opposite. Frugality is a watchword among gardeners.

Many gardeners continually look for ways to stretch dollars, planting seeds to grow food, or waiting until the end of the season to snap up deals on leftover fertilizer and broken bags of soil. Only gardeners could show you how they repurpose milk jugs into umpteen garden helpers, from plant tags to season-extending cloches.

Thrifty Gardening Tips

Invest in your soil. Improve and build soil with compost and other amendments. Ensure the money for plants is well spent by putting your time, energy, and dollars into making great soil. It will show in your garden's success.

Propagate your own plants. Start plants from seeds and cuttings. Divide and replant perennials you already have before running out to buy more.

Go green to save green. Recycle kitchen and yard waste into gardeners' gold—compost—free soil enrichment. A rain barrel, a rain garden, and irrigation conserve water and shrink your water bill.

Divide and conquer. Share skills, time, tools, space, and other resources with other gardeners in your community. Share the fun and the bounty.

Reduce your energy bills. Plant shade trees. Consider investing in a single tree rather than spending the same money on annuals and perennials. Trees also increase property values.

GOOD QUESTION!

In an age of a global communication network, gardeners exchange information and ideas faster than ever before.

You won't need to look far for more information about any aspect of gardening covered in this book. Since most of us live and work on the Internet, some of the easiest answers are within reach of a keyboard. Blogs, plant societies, growers, suppliers—you'll find horticultural experts of all kinds in cyberspace.

Closer to home, advice is free from your extension service, master gardeners, nurseries, and garden centers. Garden tours, home and garden shows, and classes offer additional learning opportunities. Garden mentors and coaches are easy to find.

GOOD BOOKS Books like the one you are holding are made to help you. Learning about gardening is an ongoing process.

BHG.COM Tap into websites and explore treasure troves of gardening information, designs, and plant sources.

VISIT GARDENS Botanical gardens and arboretums serve as living laboratories, testing plants suited to your region's climate. Visit the demonstration gardens and stroll the grounds to gather ideas and information.

EVER WONDERED?
· What's the difference between a shovel and a spade?
· Why are there holes in my hosta leaves?
· Where is the best place to plant a new tree?

ASK THE GARDEN DOCTOR **WE NEED HELP FIGURING OUT A PLAN FOR OUR YARD. SHOULD WE HIRE A LANDSCAPE DESIGNER?** You may save time and money in the long run by hiring a pro to develop a garden plan for you. Many nurseries offer a free design service when you agree to purchase plants from them. A good designer will transplant your wishes into a plan that you can bring to life.

SHARING PLANTS WITH FRIENDS

Gardeners love to talk over the garden fence, sharing stories and advice about what works for them.

One of the best resources for gardeners is other gardeners. Neighbors, friends, and experienced green thumbs in your community will share knowledge and skills as well as plants, tools, harvest, and more (often without being asked). There's a kindred spirit among gardeners.

Buy, Sell, or Swap

Plant exchanges and sales are a spring tradition. You and your garden can benefit from the abundance of plants tried-and-true in your zone. The events typically benefit a charity or group. For experienced gardeners, they are a chance to find unusual and interesting plants, plus get tips for growing them. If there isn't a sale or exchange in your community, organize one.

GARDEN PARTY Invite your gardening friends for a plant swap at the beginning or end of the garden season. Set guidelines for sharing seeds, seedlings, and favorite-plant divisions. Ask that all plants be identified and labeled.

SPRING EVENTS Plant sales hosted by botanical centers, arboretums, garden clubs, and community gardens offer plants not typically found at commercial nurseries or garden centers.

CHAPTER 2

UNDERSTANDING PLANTS

Providing what a plant needs is essential to making a garden.

FLOWERS Their color, fragrance, and form are nature's way of attracting pollinators. Flowers help some plants reproduce by producing seeds.

LEAVES They convert light, carbon dioxide, and water into food for the plant. Plants also lose water through their leaves.

STEMS As the framework of many plants, stems hold up leaves and flowers to help them receive light or be pollinated.

ROOTS These anchor plants and take up water and nutrients from the soil or air.

WELCOME TO THE WORLD OF PLANTS

Gardening allows you to observe nature and participate in an enthralling, exquisite process of life on Earth. If you understand a bit about the nature of plants, you can help provide what they need to survive and thrive.

Among the many pleasures of gardening is watching plants develop and change with the seasons and over the years. By and by, plants grow from tender sprouts to magnificent mature specimens.

In between the beginning and end of plants' lives, they do their work and reach stage after stage. If plants get what they need in the process, they'll perform admirably and fulfill their purpose. An annual blooms colorfully for a single growing season; a tree can grace the lives of generations.

All plants require various nutrients for growth. They absorb carbon dioxide, nitrogen, and oxygen from air and water. From soil, they draw other nutrients: nitrogen, phosphorus, potassium, and more. Plants use these elements to fuel their energy-making process called photosynthesis.

It's a gardener's job to assist nature in providing plants with the essentials, especially during their formative stages. Although much of what plants do is invisible, the gardener keeps on—willing to make mistakes and learn.

UNDERSTANDING PLANT GROUPS

Different types of plants provide gardeners with a garden's most essential materials. It helps to understand the terms used to describe plants. You'll make informed choices of plants when you're aware of what each one adds to a garden and how it behaves.

SHRUB As an essential part of a garden, shrubs work as accents and hedges. Deciduous or evergreen shrubs offer seasonal appeal and long-term interest.

ANNUAL An annual such as viola completes its life cycle in a year. The plant begins life developing from a seed, then focuses its energy into flowering and setting seeds.

PERENNIAL Garden mainstays, this huge array of plants (including Japanese iris) fills beds with shapes, colors, textures, and fragrances. They often die down to the ground during winter, but live on for years.

BULB Hardy bulbs such as tulips stay in the ground year 'round. Tender bulbs must be dug in freezing climates. Plant spring-flowering bulbs in fall, summer-flowering bulbs in fall or spring.

TURFGRASS North American lawns include cool- and warm-climate plants that need repeated cutting. Practical and pretty lawns should include a blend of suitable grass types.

TREE Evergreen or deciduous (shedding foliage) trees bring height, shape, and a long-lived framework to a yard. Trees add shade, shelter, and large-scale seasonal beauty.

CLIMBER OR VINE Annual or perennial, these versatile plants climb, sprawl, and cling. Whether fast- or slow-growing plants, they add verticality to the garden.

GLOBAL GARDENING

Never before have gardeners had so many planting options. Plants hailing from distant lands match the conditions in your garden and create healthy, sustainable diversity.

Our gardens combine plants from every continent. Anyone can grow Mediterranean plants, such as lavender and dianthus, by echoing their native conditions of very well-draining soil and full sun. Plants adapt to the conditions of their habitat to survive. They have deep roots, fine hairy foliage, thick roots, or other characteristics that have evolved as means of survival. Gardeners look for plants with enhanced capabilities to survive heat, drought, wet places, shade, and salty soil.

Native or indigenous plants have adapted to the climate and soil of prairie, forest, desert, meadow, woodland, or seacoast. They can naturalize in similar conditions and grow as if in their wild habitat. They're typically hardier and less demanding than introduced plants or exotic, nonnative species.

Your Growing Garden

You'll always find intriguing new plants to spark your creative spirit. These plants may be newly developed and introduced to commerce or merely unfamiliar to you. Some plants are not appropriate choices if they behave aggressively or invasively.

CONTROLLING AN ASSERTIVE PLANT

Mint has desirable qualities—delicious fragrance and flavor—but it quickly becomes weedy and wreaks havoc in gardens. Control it from the start if you want to grow mint without headaches.

1 CORRAL IT Cut out the bottom of a large nursery pot and wiggle it down into the planting hole. Keep the pot's rim above soil level.

2 BOTTOMLESS POT Partially fill the bottomless nursery pot with soil, then set the new plant on that soil.

3 FILL IN Add soil, leaving the rim of the buried nursery pot just above the soil level. The pot will prevent the mint's roots from running astray.

? ASK THE GARDEN DOCTOR **HOW DO I KNOW IF A PLANT MIGHT BE INVASIVE?** Any plant can become weedy by growing where it shouldn't. Nonnative invasive plants compete with other plants, cause problems in native habitats, and resist elimination. Some invasives prove problematic in one region but not in another. Recognize and prevent invasives. Consult your county extension service and Internet sites such as *www.invasivespeciesinfo.gov* for lists of undesirable plants in your region.

LIGHT How much sun or shade does the site receive? How much light does the plant need?

RIGHT PLANT, RIGHT PLACE

No matter how much you love a plant, it won't thrive in your garden if it isn't suited to the conditions.

Matching plants to the growing conditions of your site is key to creating a beautiful garden with low-maintenance plants. If your garden poses problematic areas—dense shade, slope, boggy spots, hot and dry places—find plants that can cope with the challenge. In the long run, unsuitable plants only mean more work for you.

Consider these practical factors when you choose plant varieties and make sure they are appropriate: size, soil, hardiness, heat, and humidity.

SIZE How big will the plant be at maturity? How much space is needed between it and adjacent plants for growth and adequate air circulation?

SOIL Does the soil contain the air, nutrients, and water needed by plants to grow and thrive? Can the plant tolerate a wet or dry site?

HARDINESS Is the plant rated for your hardiness zone? (See the USDA Hardiness Zone Map on page 15.)

HEAT AND HUMIDITY Can the plant withstand these added challenges? Will it continue to bloom or fruit?

THE FACTS OF LIGHT

The growing requirements of plants are expressed in terms of full sun, part sun (or shade), and full shade. Once you assess your site's sun and shade patterns, you can match plants to those places.

FULL SUN = at least 6 hours of direct sun daily.
PART SUN/PART SHADE = 3 to 6 hours of sun daily; also sites that receive filtered or dappled light.
FULL SHADE = less than 3 hours of sun daily.

PAINTING WITH PLANTS

Every gardener is an artist. What you do with your garden is free expression. Above all, make it what you want and enjoy the process.

Few gardeners dig into their ground with a master plan in mind. Instead, the garden evolves as plants come and go. Mistakes are made along with choices. In time, you discover which plant colors, growth habits, and foliage textures appeal most to you.

A few guidelines help simplify the process of selecting plants and deciding where to plant them.

Start big and plan for mature size. Think of trees and shrubs as the foundation of your garden. If you underestimate their full size they can outgrow the location and cause other problems.

Plant size includes height and width or spread, and depends on growing conditions. Keep mature plant size in mind as a parameter in planning.

Choose plants with year-round interest. Depend on outstanding plants that offer aesthetic value in every season. You might choose a shrub such as spring-flowering viburnum that continues into summer with lush foliage followed by bright berries in fall and showy bark in winter.

Group plants. You might put herbs in an herb garden for the simplest approach to garden design. Or take a more eclectic approach: Combine herbs with shrubs and perennials for lasting effects, add annuals for color, and complete the scheme with a few ornamental edibles.

Aim for small groupings. Start with an evergreen shrub, a deciduous shrub or two, and a few perennials. Stick with a few plants that go well together and repeat the combination.

Start with a single color. Green is a given, but you'll discover hues of green from chartreuse to gray- and blue-green. Use green as a canvas and contrast your other color choice against it.

Choose plants in the same color family. The easiest garden is a monochromatic one. White is a

strong, elegant, and serene color. Yellows are warm and cheerful; blues are cool and relaxed; pinks work well with neutral house colors and offer abundant plant choices.

Every color has character, but mixing them all together ends up looking scattered. You can't go wrong with a single-color scheme. Eventually, add one other color to update your garden.

ASK THE GARDEN DOCTOR

MALE FEMALE

WHY DO PLANTS HAVE FLOWERS? Flowers exist to help plants reproduce. Fruit and nut trees, berries, and vegetables need help from bees and other pollinators to complete the process, especially when they have male and female flowers (such as the squash blossoms, *left*).

NAME THAT PLANT

Getting a handle on the plants available to you is a name game—literally.

A challenging aspect of gardening is its large vocabulary, including botanical plant names. Every plant has a scientific name and one or more common names. Sorting out and remembering them is important when you want to acquire a specific plant.

Common names are popular. They frequently vary from one part of the country to another. They're also incorrect at times and often become confusing.

Botanical names are given to all plants. Each is a precise, organized means of sorting out the vast, diverse, and continually changing world of plants. With so many plants—sizes, forms, and colors—from which to choose, the prospect of gardening becomes exciting yet staggering.

A Plant by Any Other Name

Each plant is categorized within a long list of classifications. You might like to know that plants are grouped in families on the basis of similar characteristics. From there, the references become more refined and relevant.

The Latin two-name system includes a plant's genus and its species. The genus name of some plants is also used as the common name: zinnia or coreopsis, for example.

Plant hybridizers select outstanding qualities and breed new cultivated varieties known as cultivars. Cultivar names are written enclosed in single quotes. When breeders cross species to produce hybrids, the botanical name includes an ×.

Something Old, Something New

Familiarize yourself with heirloom plants and you can become a time traveler. Grow the rose favored by your great-grandmother, the corn eaten by Incas, or the annuals treasured by Victorian gardeners. Robust, time-tested heirlooms have enduring virtues—unique flavor, pure fragrance, disease resistance, regional adaptability—that make them keepsakes in almost any garden.

A PLANT FAMILY TREE

FAMILY
ASTERACEAE
SUNFLOWER OR DAISY
Plants are grouped in families as the result of their evolutionary history and shared characteristics. A shared trait of this family: ray flowers.

GENUS
ECHINACEA (CONEFLOWER)
The genus includes closely related plants. Think of it as a surname that passes to the next generation.

SPECIES
PURPUREA
(PURPLE CONEFLOWER)
This more-specific name distinguishes the plant from all other plants in the genus.

CULTIVAR
E. PURPUREA 'MAGNUS'
Assigned by the plant breeder, the name refers to a cultivated variety within a species that has distinct characteristics.

HYBRID
E. PURPUREA × ORANGE MEADOWBRITE 'ART'S PRIDE'
The result of crossing two or more unrelated plants, combining the parents' most desirable traits.

HOW PLANTS ARE SOLD

Plants come in a confusing range of sizes, containers, and prices. But if you understand the differences between plant materials, you can simplify your choices.

Start your garden right, with plants suited to your garden and the way you garden. If you choose to start plants from seeds, you'll gain confidence from raising your plants and saving money. At the other end of the spectrum, you'll find container-grown perennials, shrubs, and trees readily transplantable from a nursery for instant impact.

You'll also find flats of annual bedding plants (flowers or foliage) for planting big displays. Choose plants for sun or shade, color, and mature size.

SEEDS OR SEEDLINGS? Seeds save money; seedlings save effort. Many annuals and vegetables are easier to grow from seeds; perennials grow easier from seedlings.

PLUGS Baby plants (such as groundcovers or turfgrasses) are sold in flats of small cells. This is an affordable way to purchase young plants for filling in a large area.

SEEDLINGS Started from seeds, transplants are an economical choice for annuals, perennials, or vegetables. Keep them growing until they reach garden-ready size.

BULBS Hardy or tender bulbs and bulblike roots, including tubers, rhizomes, and corms, supply the flowering plant-to-be inside them with food year after year.

POTTED PLANTS Most plants are sold in some type of container. It's a convenient way to transport and plant nursery stock. Container sizes range from 2-inch-diameter to 5-gallon pots.

BALLED-AND-BURLAPPED Trees and shrubs may be dug with a soil ball around their roots that is wrapped in burlap. This provides a safe way to move the large plants without damaging their roots.

TEST GARDEN TIP

STORING NEW PLANTS It's best to plant within a few days of purchasing plants. Wet ground, cold weather, or a busy schedule may keep you from planting, but your new plant materials need to be stored carefully in the meantime to keep them in top shape.

RECEIVING MAIL-ORDER PLANTS

Turn to plant specialists if you're unable to find particular plants locally. Or mail order your selections in advance of the proper planting time (spring or fall).

SEEDLINGS OR CONTAINER-GROWN PLANTS Keep them in a somewhat shaded place. Water daily if rain doesn't come.

BULBS Store bulbs in paper bags or boxes and keep them cool and dry until planting time. Do not let them freeze.

MAIL-ORDER PLANTS Unpack plants as soon as they arrive. Remove any broken plant parts, replace any soil spilled from containers, and water well.

BARE ROOT SHRUB OR TREE Soak roots overnight in a bucket of water. If possible, plant them when they're received. Plant in a permanent location as soon as possible.

BARE ROOT Perennials, trees, roses, and other shrubs are lifted from a nursery bed and sold in a dormant (not actively growing) state. If necessary, plant the roots temporarily and keep the soil damp.

BUYING PLANTS

Instead of just picking the most eye-catching plants, take time to read labels and research plants before you buy. Then be choosy: Get the healthiest plants at reasonable prices.

When to Shop

Sales are highest during spring—peak planting season. By the end of June or early July, seasonal garden centers close. Shop early for the best choices, but be prepared for full prices and crowds. Garden centers stock up on weekdays. Get the best selection and quality by shopping before the weekend rush leaves behind only picked-over goods. If you prefer to hold out for bargains, wait until late June or late summer, when nurseries typically slash prices.

Where to Shop

Local garden centers range from seasonal outlets in parking lots, which buy plants from wholesalers, to nurseries and greenhouses that grow their own selections. Specialized nurseries offer plants you might not find elsewhere.

Catalogs and websites expand your plant choices, especially for unusual plants and seeds, roses, trees, and shrubs. Settle on a few good sources to save on shipping costs. Avoid getting caught up in the allure of catalog or online descriptions. Make your wish list, set it aside for a few days, and edit before placing your order.

Reputable garden centers dedicated to long-term care of plants guarantee purchases. If the plant fails within a year, they will replace it or refund your purchase (depending on their policy) with your proof of purchase. Save plant tags with receipts.

What to Buy

You'll find generic versions of plants and patent-protected varieties. Patented varieties may cost a little more, but they're a good buy if you get better winter hardiness, disease resistance, or a space-saving form. Generic plants may vary in appearance, while named varieties have consistent characteristics.

KEEP TABS ON TAGS Plant tags include information that will help you choose suitable plants. Read tags and note a plant's hardiness, potential size, needs for light and water, and other care advice.

MIX, MATCH, BUY Put together eye-catching plant combinations in your shopping cart. Coordinate colors and textures, trying different groupings, until you get a look you like, such as sedge, hosta, and coral bells.

IS BIGGER BETTER? Plants in economical cell packs or small pots ultimately provide plenty of flower power within a season or two. Larger plants give more impact sooner.

CHOOSING HEALTHY PLANTS

Use these guidelines when plant shopping and you'll achieve quality control.

- Opt for plants with buds over those with flowers.
- Check roots by gently removing the pot. Extremely dense, tangled, or dark roots are not desirable.
- Avoid stressed plants with stretched-out stems, yellow or brown leaves, or roots growing out of the bottom of the pot.
- Forgo sickly clearance plants. They are not a bargain if they have withered, are mushy, or have disease-spotted leaves.
- Choose firm bulbs, tubers, and rhizomes; avoid ones that are soft or dried up.
- Choose a shrub that is dense and well balanced.
- Look for a tree with a strong, upright leading shoot and a full crown.

Maximize Your Budget

- Resist the urge to buy plants just because they are inexpensive or appealing.
- Stick to a budget by shopping with a wish list and following a planting plan.
- Shop cooperatively. Buy bulbs in bulk and annuals in flats, for instance, and split them with other gardeners. Combine online or mail orders with friends and share shipping costs.
- Research trees, shrubs, and other big purchases before you buy. Prevent costly mistakes by being aware of a plant's strengths and weaknesses before you add it to your garden.
- Buy trees, shrubs, and perennials deeply discounted in late summer. The plants still have time to settle into the garden and root before winter. But there is a trade-off: Nurseries usually sell plants as is at the end of the season, with no guarantee.
- Keep in mind that new varieties, brand names, and collector's specimens come at a premium price. Prices for new varieties usually drop after a few years when supply catches up with demand.

COMPARE PLANTS Look for lush, vigorous plants at the nursery.

CONSIDER OVERALL APPEARANCE Look for balanced top growth and root mass.

INSPECT PLANTS Look under leaves and poke soil to check for insects.

PEEK AT ROOTS Look for smooth, pale roots.

CHAPTER 3

CHOOSING AND USING TOOLS

The best implements make gardening easier and more pleasurable.

THE GARDENER'S TOOLBOX

Most gardeners get by with a few basic tools, but an increasing array of options promise more efficiency.

Good tools are designed to help you tackle specific jobs efficiently and comfortably. As you become more familiar with what a tool can do, you'll find more uses for it. A multipurpose tool such as a spade handles various chores effectively and earns its keep quickly.

It pays to get the best-quality implements that you can afford. Price often reflects quality, but not always. Sometimes inexpensive tools are perfectly good ones. Other times, there is more cost than value in replacing cheap tools. If you keep your tools handy and in good shape, they will serve you well for years.

The Best Tools for You

Ask any gardener, "What is your favorite tool?" and the answer will vary because the choice is personal, based on the gardener's temperament and gardening style. Tool choices are guided by one's age, strength, flexibility, balance, and experience.

The right tool suits your size and weight as well as your garden's workload. A short shovel proves handy enough for a petite gardener who periodically tucks in a few plants, while a more burly digger with a large rocky plot is better off using an extra-sturdy shovel with a long solid-wood handle.

Most gardeners get by with a few basic hand tools. But anyone can save time and effort with a high-quality spade, a large-yet-lightweight watering can, and a durable wheelbarrow.

A continually expanding array of specialized implements promises greater efficiency. New generations of gas- and electric-powered tools offer speed and maneuverability. If you're unsure of a tool's efficacy, borrow or rent one for a trial run.

DIGGING

Breaking ground and turning soil mark the rituals that bring plants to life.

Digging is among the most basic of gardening tasks. In general, you can depend on pointed or curved blades for digging; flat-edge blades for cutting; and deeply curved, spoonlike blades for scooping. Wide-blade tools move a lot of material swiftly. Use a narrower or smaller blade to dig in tight spaces.

❶ SPADE Typically, a spade has a long, flat rectangular blade with a straight profile and digging edge. Combined with a compact handle, the blade's precision lets you dig up a perennial or shrub while keeping the root ball and surrounding soil intact. Use a spade to slice out planting holes, shape beds and borders, cut through sod, divide root masses, and break up soil.

❷ HAND WEEDER The Cape Cod weeder shown works like a sharp bent finger and reaches into the tightest spots to dig out weeds. The best weeders are forged of steel and have sharp blades that pry, slice, or yank weeds out of the ground root and all. You'll find short- and long-handled weeders.

❸ TROWEL Made to work as an extension of a gardener's hand, a good trowel digs small holes, cultivates soil, scoops soil into pots and amendments into planting holes, and pries out weeds. A longer handle provides greater leverage.

❹ SHORT SHOVEL The pint-size version of a shovel works like a giant trowel. It is well suited to smaller gardeners and those who prefer to work while kneeling or sitting.

❺ SHOVEL Indispensible for digging, this versatile tool is also made to lift, carry, and throw soil, sand, gravel, compost, mulch, and such. The curved blade helps hold the load and prevents spilling until you're ready to distribute the material.

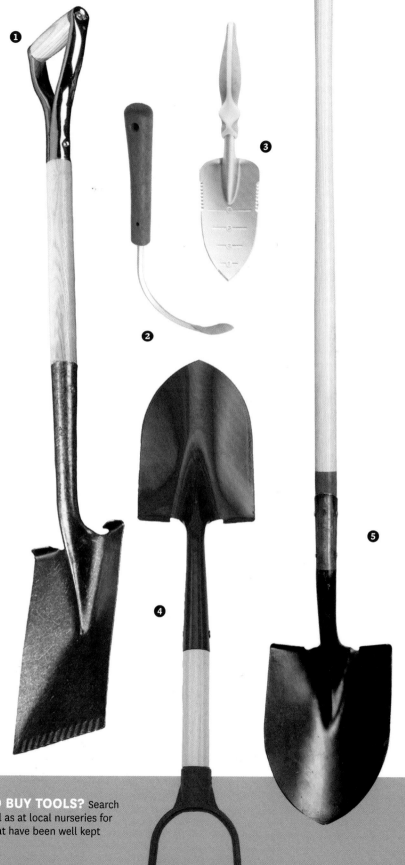

ASK THE GARDEN DOCTOR

WHAT IS THE BEST PLACE TO BUY TOOLS? Search online and in mail-order catalogs as well as at local nurseries for high-quality tools. Secondhand tools that have been well kept can be just as good as new ones.

CULTIVATING

Getting soil ready for planting requires cultivating—using a tool to dig and turn over soil, stir it up, and break clumps into pieces.

Working soil is essential to preparing new beds or planting areas and removing weeds. Cultivating involves digging and turning soil. The process aerates the soil and makes it easier to plant. It also breaks up a crusted soil surface and uproots weeds.

Rely on tools to ease the laborious chores of loosening soil, making furrows for planting, mounding soil, mixing in an amendment or fertilizer, and even uprooting weeds. Various long- and short-handled tools feature different blades for specific purposes—all can be categorized as cultivators. Beware: Your toolbox can quickly become overwhelmed with cultivators. The basic ones include a garden rake, garden hoe, and hand cultivator.

Once soil has been tilled or turned over, it is easier to refine with a hand cultivator of some sort. If you are cultivating an area prior to planting, or are working around widely spaced plants, you can cover more ground with a tool that has a wider head and more tines, such as a garden rake or a garden fork.

HOE A basic hoe carves furrows, chops, grades, and weeds effectively. You may prefer another hoe with an angled, pointed, or swiveling blade and more refined uses.

GARDEN FORK Nothing beats this tined tool for loosening compacted soil and mixing in compost. Use a fork with more than four tines to lift and move loose materials, such as compost and mulch.

HAND CULTIVATOR This short-tined, handheld tool allows you to work in the soil between plants without disturbing roots.

ASK THE GARDEN DOCTOR **HOW SHOULD I CULTIVATE MY GARDEN?** Prepare your garden for planting annuals or vegetables each year by turning the soil to loosen it. Work the soil when it is dry or damp—not wet—to avoid damaging the soil's structure.

TEST GARDEN TIP

KEEPING TRACK OF TOOLS Paint tool handles red or yellow. Tools with bright color handles are less likely to disappear when you set them down during a gardening spree. Put tools away in the same place after every use. Keep gloves and a few hand tools in a bucket where they will be most handy.

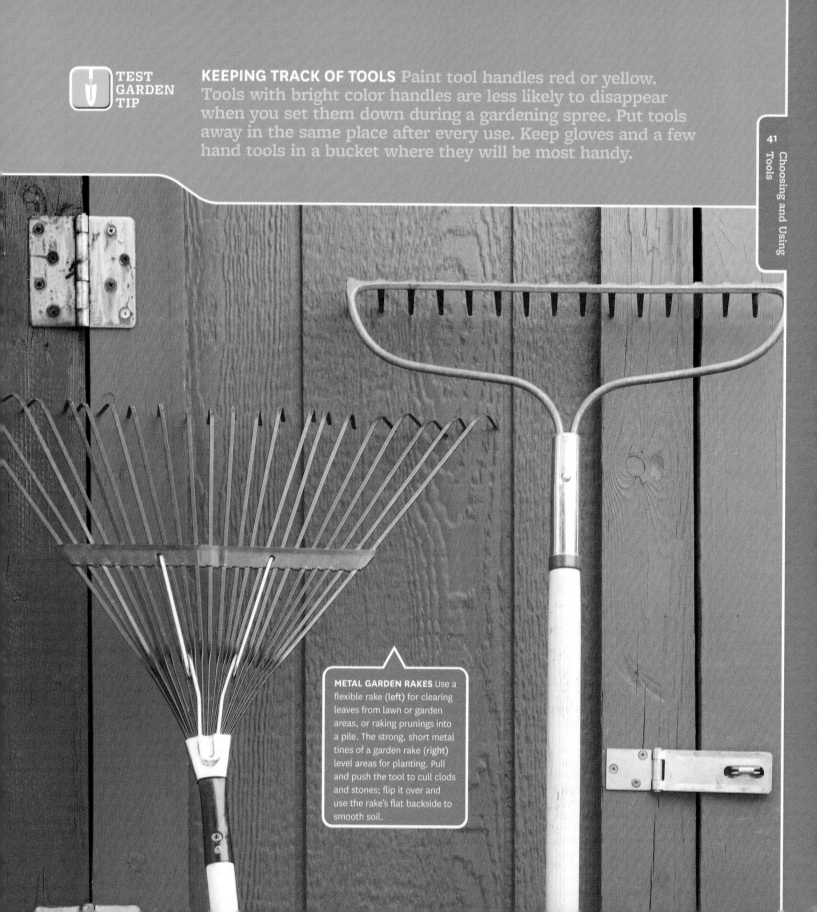

METAL GARDEN RAKES Use a flexible rake (left) for clearing leaves from lawn or garden areas, or raking prunings into a pile. The strong, short metal tines of a garden rake (right) level areas for planting. Pull and push the tool to cull clods and stones; flip it over and use the rake's flat backside to smooth soil.

CUTTING

Take some of the guesswork out of any cutting task: Start with the most-fitting tools.

Every time you cut a stem or branch of a plant, you are pruning it. Having the right tool that's sharp and up to the task is the first step in pruning successfully.

Choose a tool that fits in your hand so well you forget that you're holding it. Hand shears should not open wider than your hand can extend comfortably. Find a left-handed tool if need be.

Also look for these features when choosing quality cutting tools: Well-cushioned and lightweight (aluminum or carbon composite) handles contribute to comfortable use. Coated blades reduce friction, which keeps blades sharper and minimizes effort. Shock-absorbing cushion bumpers reduce fatigue. Replaceable steel blades are part of an ideal tool that can be taken apart for thorough cleaning. A safety latch that keeps the tool closed when not in use should be easy to flip with your thumb.

What You'll Need

Outfit your toolbox with three types of cutting tools: hand pruners, loppers, and a pruning saw. If you have a hedge or lots of shrubs, add hedge shears to your collection.

You'll find two types of hand shears and may want to have both: Bypass pruners, the most indispensible cutting tool for gardeners, feature two precision-fit blades that slide past each other in a scissorlike action. Anvil pruners pinch a branch between a straight blade and flat edge (anvil).

Pruning saws are the next step up from loppers, handling branches 3 inches or more in diameter. Most saws consist of a long blade with a handle at the end. The blade cuts on the pull stroke. The thicker the branch, the longer the blade should be and the fewer, deeper teeth per inch it should have.

HEDGE SHEARS allow you to trim big and small twigs at the same time and produce a surface of dense, healthy growth. Choose an electric- or gas-powered version for large hedges or shrubs that must be trimmed frequently.

ANVIL PRUNERS are best for cutting deadwood branches up to ⅝ inch in diameter. Bypass pruners are best for making clean, close cuts on live stems up to 1 inch in diameter.

LOPPERS work the same as pruners, but their long handles provide the torque to slice cleanly through green branches. Use them to cut through a branch up to 1½ inches in diameter in a single firm motion. If this doesn't work, sharpen the blade or switch to a pruning saw.

TEST GARDEN TIP

REACH OUT Tools with telescoping (extendable) handles give you extra reach for cutting without extra effort. A lightweight pole with nonslip grips eases strain on arms and hands.

POLE PRUNERS This tool has a bypass pruner or saw blade at the end of a long pole. Most extend to prune branches within a 12-foot reach and have changeable attachments.

BOW SAW This saw has a narrow blade that cuts on both push and pull strokes. Use it on branches narrower than the width of the bow.

STRAIGHT SAW The saw's handle provides a comfortable grip. This one has a sheath for storage. Its small teeth are best for hardwood or dead branches.

FOLDING SAW The design makes this tool convenient and safe. The molded handle makes it comfortable to hold. This one has large teeth for cutting green (live) wood.

HOLDING AND HAULING

Lighten your loads and protect your back by using containers that are easy to fill, lift, carry, and empty.

There's always something that needs to be carried to or from the garden. When it comes to bulky or heavy loads, an efficient container helps a lot. Try similar holders, such as a bucket, a bushel basket, a lidded bin, and you'll likely find diverse uses for each of them. You'll need heavy-duty storage containers, for instance, which will keep birdseed and organic fertilizers away from mice. Opt for sturdiness over prettiness. Any good holder or hauler must be able to endure rough use.

Harvest Basket

Lightweight but strong, durable, and exceedingly portable, the best harvest basket or trug makes it easy to carry any garden pickings. A flat bottom makes the basket stable.

Wheelbarrow

Balance a spacious container on a wheel or two, add a lever, and you have a nifty invention that functions deftly. Four wheels make it a garden cart. Use either to tote many plants or rocks at once or to move loads of other heavy stuff, from compost to concrete.

Tub

A flexible plastic tub serves as the modern version of a bushel basket. This multipurpose container is equally able to hold soil or water, sticks or stones, fruit or flowers, tools or plants. It's also sturdy and washable.

USING TOOLS PROPERLY

Most tools don't come with instruction manuals. Avoid accidents and damaged tools by using implements for their intended purposes. If you find you're using your spade as a pry bar, maybe it's time to get a pry bar.

Gardening tools have been designed and improved over the centuries through the natural movements of their users. Momentum powers most tools, but brute force often results in strain and pain. Every gardening tool has the potential to perform a job well without causing you discomfort or injury as long as you use the tool correctly. Be aware of how you hold a tool as well as how you stand or sit when you use it. If you relax and enjoy the process of using tools properly, gardening can be more satisfying.

Take It Easier

Gardening is an intense, whole-body activity. Ease into the season and avoid charging into chores to prevent injury. Avoid sore muscles by using your body and tools properly. Always use your legs and arms—not your back—to bear the brunt of any load. Bend your knees when lifting. Vary tasks, pace yourself, and take frequent breaks to minimize stiffness. During repetitive jobs, switch the tool from one hand or side of your body to the other.

❶ CORRECT DIGGING Use a shovel appropriately by pushing the blade straight down into the soil. Keep your back upright but relaxed.

❷ USE YOUR WEIGHT Place your foot firmly on the shovel's tread (the flat or rolled edges at the back of the blade) and press down.

CAN YOU DIG IT?

Protect your back when digging, lifting, and taking on other weight-bearing chores.

RHYTHM IN MOTION The right way to lift: Bend at the knees and use your legs and arms—not your back—to lift a load. Scoop lighter loads to strike an efficient rhythm.

GET A GRIP Use short-handled tools for leverage tasks, such as scooping, scraping, and digging. Keep your grip light, letting the tool handle twist and turn, as you put your weight behind the push. Shift your weight with the movement of the tool.

ROCK AND ROLL Use long-handled tools for reaching tasks, such as raking and hoeing. A relaxed stance, with your body bent over the tool, allows your weight to shift and rock with the tool's motion—forward and back—and power the dance.

IT TAKES TWO An adjustable pot lifter turns the chore of hoisting a hefty pot or rock into a quick, easy task for two.

WATERING

Nothing waters a garden better than a slow, steady rain. But delivering water to plants is a matter of life and death when rainfall doesn't do the job for you.

A few reliable tools help you to get water to the place where plants need it most: at root level. For the most basic hand-watering, a garden hose or watering can works best. For more sophisticated and efficient watering, drip irrigation systems make watering easy on you and the environment. Read more about watering methods in Chapter 12, page 248.

Long, Cool Drinks

It's easy to waste money buying more watering tools than needed and gadgets that don't quite work. Avoid these common mistakes by starting with the highest-quality vinyl or rubber hose you can afford. Choose a hose made with five or six layers or piles and brass connectors for the longest life.

Extend the life of your watering devices—like any tools—by storing them properly. Hoses are especially notorious for deteriorating when left outdoors exposed to weather season after season. No tool is made to spend the winter outdoors in a frigid climate.

It's handy to keep the watering can full and at-the-ready in season. But watering tools should be drained and put away where they will not freeze. This prevents bursting and cracking caused by swelling ice.

WATERING CAN This shapely vessel, whether metal or lightweight plastic, enables you to tote and dispense water. It gently showers transplants and seedlings, and saturates a few potted plants. The sprinkling end, called a rose, is attached to the spout.

SPRAYER/SPRAY BOTTLE Use a hand pump, hose-end sprayer, or pressurized tank to mist plants with liquid fertilizers, insecticides, herbicides, and other solutions. Plastic versions are lighter weight than metal ones, but they can absorb chemicals. Label the contents of any spray bottle.

RAIN BARREL Collecting rainwater in a durable tank keeps it handy for watering when needed. The practice reduces your water bill and conserves a vital resource. A spacious rain barrel with a built-in spigot proves practical.

GARDEN HOSE A variety of attachments make any garden hose more convenient (with a shutoff valve), useful (with gentle or forceful spray patterns), and maneuverable (with a reach extension or pivoting head).

ASK THE GARDEN DOCTOR **HOW CAN I FIX A LEAKY HOSE?** If a hose or its attachment leaks, first tighten the connections. If the leak persists, replace the rubber or plastic washer (ring) inside the hose-end fitting. If the hose itself leaks, replace it or cut a new end at the leak and replace the coupling.

GARDEN CLEANUP

The list of must-have tools for cleaning up the garden is short: willingness, elbow grease, and patience.

Cleaning the garden, especially at the beginning and end of the growing season, is an essential part of the annual maintenance regimen.

Early spring prompts gardeners to get out there to pick up fallen branches and clear debris from beds. It's time to reach into beds with pruners in hand and cut back a plant's remaining old growth before it gets tangled in new growth.

Throughout the growing season, tidying gives the garden a well-kept appearance. Regularly removing and disposing of diseased, infested, or spent plant parts promotes a healthy garden.

Breaking a large cleanup job into smaller tasks will make it more manageable and less overwhelming. Accomplish the mission in a weekend or two instead of pushing to finish in a day.

Autumn's Gold

The biggest cleaning job—dealing with autumn leaves—is necessary. Left on the lawn, whole leaves form a mat that can smother the grass and create bare spots by next spring. Instead, put leaves to work for your lawn and garden.

Leaves contribute free organic material for composting and mulching. Shredding leaves with a mulching mower is a lot less work than raking and bagging. Plus, you can let the pieces fall. They will break down and feed the lawn. If you prefer, rake chopped or whole leaves into a pile where they can be left to decompose over winter. Decayed leaves are ideal for improving soil.

Your choice of tools can take the aches and blisters out of dealing with leaves. Use a rake with an ergonomic or padded handle, for instance.

LEAF COLLECTORS Pair a lawn or leaf rake with a large-capacity flat-bottom bag and you'll be ready for fall cleanup. Choose a wide, flexible-tine rake made of bamboo, plastic, or metal.

STRAP-ON HOLDER New tools come along regularly with promises to make gardening easier. The Gardener's Hollow Leg fulfills its potential as a hands-free bag for holding debris or harvest.

LEAF BLOWER The powerful airstream of a leaf blower clears a leaf-covered lawn swiftly. Use a gas- or electric-powered blower to clean areas that are difficult to reach with a rake. Wear ear plugs and safety goggles to protect yourself.

BRISTLE BRUSH Scrub pots with a stiff brush at season's end to remove soil, mineral deposits, and stains. Clean pots promote healthy plants. Besides, you'll be ready to grow with clean pots in the spring.

BASIC TOOLS ARE BEST Reach for a simple set of tried-and-true tools rather than fancy high-tech gadgets for cleaning, watering, or other gardening activity. A few tools that serve various purposes will be used reliably over and over.

HEALTHY GARDENING

Gardening yields a bumper crop of benefits. What other activity improves your strength and endurance, reduces stress, aids relaxation, and produces nutritious food?

Gardening is such a pleasure for most people that it comes as a bonus that this moderate aerobic activity is comparable to brisk walking. Good for your heart and your figure, gardening burns an average of 265 calories an hour.

Just as you must protect your plants or lose them to the ravages of pests or harsh weather, you can maximize the benefits of gardening by caring for yourself in the process. First and foremost, dress appropriately by donning shoes, gloves, and a hat.

Helping Hands

Protect your finest of all gardening tools—your hands—whether you like wearing gloves or not.

Bacteria, fungi, and parasites live in soil, and any cut, puncture, or other irritation can develop into a serious infection. Stock several pairs of comfortable gloves, and wash them periodically.

Protect your skin. The same sunlight that nourishes plants can cause wrinkling, premature aging, and skin cancer. Apply a SPF 30 sunscreen with UVA and UVB protection at least 30 minutes before you head outdoors, even on a cloudy day. If you prefer, wear a long-sleeved shirt and pants to shield your skin from sun, as well as from thorns, branches, and insects. Take breaks in the shade and drink plenty of water.

All of these practices will help ensure that gardening continues to be good for you.

GLOVES Protect your hands from injury. Stretchy fabric ensures dexterity. A rubberized grip and reinforced fingertips make gloves durable. Waterproof or insulated; lightweight or washable; cotton, rubber, vinyl, or leather—get different kinds and be ready for any job.

GAUNTLET GLOVES These extra-long gloves shield your hands and forearms from thorns, brambles, and branches. Heavy-duty leather or other materials make the gloves more protective.

HAT There's no hiding from the sun's damaging rays, but a hat helps. Choose one with a 3-inch-wide or wider brim all the way around that will shade your face and neck.

KNEELER Cushion knees from the strain placed on them. If you prefer to work on your knees, keep a straight back and stand up periodically to straighten your legs. Instead of kneeling, sit while weeding.

? ASK THE GARDEN DOCTOR **WHAT'S THE BEST WAY TO CLEAN MY HANDS AFTER GARDENING?** Scrub with soap and water, using a pinch of sugar as a gently cleansing grit. Use an old toothbrush to remove soil from under fingernails. Rub a freshly cut lemon over stains to erase them and leave hands smelling fresh.

BE PREPARED Standard gear for a well-equipped gardening routine includes sunscreen, insect repellant, gloves, and sunglasses or safety goggles. Top off your provisions with a hat and a bottle of water.

GARDEN TIP Update your tetanus booster every 10 years to guard against infection with the dreadful disease of which gardeners are at high risk.

CLEANING YOUR TOOLS

Protect your investment in quality tools by taking care of them. In return, your tools will aid you year after year.

Tools deteriorate when left outdoors exposed to weather. Prevent rust and other damage by cleaning tools and putting them away after every use. Clean off soil and plant debris. Spraying a tool with a hose or soaking it briefly in water helps remove stubborn muck. Dry tools thoroughly before storing them.

CLEANING TOOLS: METHOD 1

1 WATER WORKS Spray soil with a hose to loosen and dislodge it.

2 SCRUB THE TOOL Use a stiff brush to remove stubborn soil and any debris.

CLEANING TOOLS: METHOD 2

1 REMOVE RUST If a tool has begun to rust, rub the metal briskly using a wire brush.

2 PREVENT RUST Finish with several drops of lubricating oil and a piece of steel wool.

KEEPING IT CLEAN

Use a small bucket for hand tools (a larger bucket for long-handled tools). Fill the bucket with coarse sand, then pour half a quart of clean motor oil over it (use more oil in a larger bucket). Plunge clean tools into the oiled sand—even store them there—to keep the implements primed and ready to work.

SHARPENING TOOLS

Sharp tools work most efficiently, giving you more time to enjoy your garden.

When gardening tools have well-honed edges, they'll make any task easier for you. Sharp tools cause fewer injuries to their users. Dull cutting tools injure plants by tearing them.

Sharpen tools when the fall chores are done. Use a bastard file for annual sharpening. If heavy use dulls or nicks a tool during the gardening season, touch up the blade's edge using a simple sharpening steel. Anvil-type pruners should be sharpened on both sides of the blade.

Take your tools to a professional for sharpening, if you prefer. Ask about sharpening services at a local hardware store or tool supplier.

When you're done sharpening tools, apply clean motor oil or lubricating oil to the blades, using a clean cloth. Also rub tung oil or boiled linseed oil into wooden handles to prevent them from drying and splintering.

TOOL SHARPENERS Use a fine-grade flat (bastard) file to sharpen tools annually. A sharpening steel enables periodic touchups.

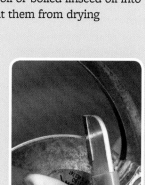

FLAT FILE File from the blade's outer edge, working to its center. Holding the file at an angle, push it down and away from you.

SHARPENING STEEL Drag the edge of the sharpening tool along the blade, following the beveled or angled edge.

TOUCH UP Several swipes with a pocket-size blade sharpening tool quickly enhance the edge of a tool.

CORRECT ANGLE Restore a blade's sharpness by following the angle of its existing bevel with the file.

TEST FOR SHARPNESS Touch the beveled edge of a blade against the top of your thumbnail. You will feel resistance if the blade is sharp. A dull blade feels smooth.

HANDY TOOL STORAGE

Every gardener needs a place within steps of the garden where tools can be kept easily accessible.

You can depend on your tools to make every task simpler if you store the implements where they will remain clean, sharp, and ready for the next use. Taking care of your tools saves you the cost of replacing them.

A garage, toolshed, or garden house provides convenient year-round storage for all things garden. Make your storage space as multipurpose and efficient as possible by including a potting bench, wall space for hanging long-handled tools, and shelves for storing bins or flat sturdy baskets full of accessories. Fit in the lawn mower, wheelbarrow, hoses, bins for potting mixes and amendments, and watering cans. Ideally, you'll have room to work in the shelter and to move around comfortably to access your gardening gear.

Where space is limited and you must store tools in a corner or closet, explore your options. Corral tools in a portable caddy that can go to the garden with you. Turn the back of a door into a storage rack by fitting it with a sheet of lattice and hanging tools from S-hooks or broom clamps. Use a 5-gallon bucket as one of the handiest tool totes around. Top it with a cushioned lid, and it becomes a garden seat.

When storing long-handled tools in a garage, garden shed, or similar situation, try hanging up tools to keep them handy and uncluttered. What's more, hanging tools helps to keep the ends sharp.

HANG ON Put the walls of a garage or shed to work by installing an organization system. This one features rails anchored to studs and movable sleeves with clip-on hooks for tools.

DOUBLE DUTY Where there is no room for conventional storage, think outside in the box—a bench, that is, for stowing garden gear.

CLEVER SOLUTIONS A potting bench offers storage and work space. Heavy-duty metal shelving keeps fertilizers and chemicals high, dry, and safely out of reach of kids and pets.

SPECIAL DELIVERY If you've ever wished for a place in the garden to tuck a few tools and a pair of gloves, a mailbox may be the answer.

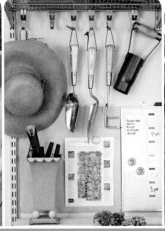

ASK THE GARDEN DOCTOR **HOW CAN I SAVE ENDLESS TRIPS TO THE GARAGE TO GRAB MY GARDENING TOOLS?** Outfit a 5-gallon bucket with a convenient tool belt and use it as a portable toolbox. It will easily house your most essential hand tools as well as gloves, plant labels, and other practical items.

TEST GARDEN TIP

GIVE 'EM SHELTER Customize a ready-made shed for an attractive workspace that also helps you organize and access all your lawn and garden implements.

STORAGE STATION Put walls and doors to work for easily accessible storage. Adjustable, multipurpose hooks make it possible to rearrange as needed.

CHAPTER 4

PREPARING AND IMPROVING SOIL

Build healthy soil. This is a gardener's most important task.

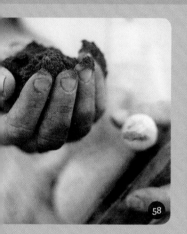

SOIL: THE KEY TO SUCCESS

The secret to every plant's health and any garden's vitality is in the soil.

Soil provides the key to your garden's success. It really is that simple. Healthy soil holds enough water, air, and nutrients to sustain plant life and help it thrive. Healthy soil also teems with beneficial microorganisms. It holds the sun's warmth and nurtures helpful earthworms.

More Than Dirt

The soil of our Earth is not inert dirt but a balanced system of layers, from a foundation of bedrock to mineral-rich subsoil and living topsoil. In an endless spiral of life, plant and animal debris break down over time, enriching the soil with organic material called humus.

Soil consists mostly of silt, sand, and clay particles plus organic matter, water, and air. The proportions of the particles determine the type and texture of soil in your garden. There are thousands of kinds of soil, with highly varied composition. You may have rocky clay soil that is almost impossible to dig or cultivate. The mucky clay soil found in some wet low-lying areas holds water and supports few crops.

In addition to sandy, silty, or clay soil, there is peaty soil, which contains mostly decomposed organic matter. It is acidic and tends to hold too much moisture and not enough nutrients. Chalky soil is stony, dry, and alkaline. It needs a lot of improvement in order to support plant life.

Evaluating Soil Texture

Ideal soil or loam is a rich balance of humus, silt, sand, and clay. Dark, crumbly, and easy to work, loam is the goal of most gardeners.

Feel your soil by rubbing a pea-size bit of it between your fingers. Or smear a generous pinch of it on stone, paper, or the backside of a spade. The type and quality of your garden's soil affects how much time you'll spend working to improve it.

SILTY SOIL FEELS COARSE It is composed of minerals and organic material. Easy to work, it can hold moisture and nutrients, but it compacts easily.

CLAY SOIL FEELS STICKY This heavy stuff holds water and nutrients, but compacts easily and is difficult to work when dried out. It turns slick when wet and sticks to a spade when you dig into it.

SANDY SOIL FEELS GRITTY Sandy soil doesn't hold nutrients because it drains and dries out quickly. On the plus side: Sandy soil is easy to work.

TEST GARDEN TIP

LIVING SOIL Healthy soil teems with life, from easy-to-see earthworms and helpful insects to invisible microbes, such as beneficial fungi, nematodes, and bacteria. Apply compost annually to keep these microorganisms well fed.

IT'S A SIGN Turn over a shovelful of earth and count: At least three or four earthworms indicate healthy soil.

IMPROVING SOIL

Nurturing soil is the best thing you can
do for your garden to enable its health
and productivity.

Most soils fall short of the ideal—loose, rich in
organic matter, and drainable—that is key to healthy
plant growth. But adding organic materials, such as
compost and shredded leaves, improves any soil.

Well-draining soil is another ideal. Drainage
describes the way water and air move through soil
and plants' root zones. In soil that is either too wet
or too dry, plants grow poorly.

Adding organic matter to soil enhances its ability
to soak up the water plants need and drain away the
excess. You can also improve drainage by building
raised beds.

Contrary to common sense, adding sand to clay
soil creates a concretelike result—the opposite of
improved drainage. Instead, loosen clay soil by
working in loads of organic matter.

**ASK THE
GARDEN
DOCTOR** **HOW DO I KNOW IF MY SOIL DRAINS PROPERLY?** If puddles remain a day or two after a soaking rain, you have poorly
draining soil. Grab a handful of soil and squeeze it. Well-draining soil crumbles as you squeeze. Sandy soil does not hold
moisture and will feel gritty and dry.

EVALUATING YOUR SOIL

A soil analysis gives you valuable
information about your soil to help
you make it better.

Getting your soil tested is a worthwhile process.
Before planting, go online or contact a county
extension service or garden center to get directions
for submitting a soil sample to a nearby laboratory.
Home test kits are also available online and at
garden centers, but their generalized results have
limited accuracy.

Laboratory analysis of soil comes at a small fee.
The test will identify the soil texture (proportions
of sand, silt, and clay), nutrient content, and
amount of organic matter. A soil test also reveals
the pH level (acidity or alkalinity), which influences
nutrient availability.

Once you know your soil's components, you can
change the soil by amending it, or choose plants
adapted to the existing soil conditions. The analysis
will suggest how to correct any nutrient deficiencies
and adjust the pH.

SOIL TESTING Even if you
have gardened in the same
place for years, a soil
test will provide you with
information that is not readily
apparent. A test will take the
guesswork out of fertilizing
and amending soil.

WELCOME EARTHWORMS
Organic matter attracts
earthworms—nature's soil
builders—into your garden.
Earthworms turn organic
matter into humus, adding
their castings and boosting
the soil's fertility. Their
burrowing activity improves
aeration and drainage. The
more earthworms, the better
the soil.

LOVE THAT LOAM When
you improve the soil before
planting, you make a smart
investment that yields high
returns in healthier, sturdier,
easier-care plants.

BUYER'S GUIDE TO SOIL

All plants depend on good soil for their prosperity. But garden soils and potting soils or mixes differ and should not be used interchangeably.

Garden centers and landscape suppliers sell organic matter—including soils—in bags or bulk. Bagged products offer convenience, while bulk options prove more economical. Getting 2 or 3 cubic yards of compost (enough to fill a pickup truck) delivered for a new garden or other large project trades convenience for a small fee.

Packaged garden soil is specially designed to work in garden beds the same way potting mix works in pots. It typically includes a blend of topsoil, compost, and other amendments. You can usually count on it to be free of weed seeds.

When buying soil and soil amendments, it can be a challenge to determine how much you'll need for a project. These materials are usually sold by volume (cubic feet or cubic yards) or by weight (pounds or tons). A ton of soil or sand may seem like a lot, but it will fill up less than a cubic yard (27 cubic feet or a space 3 feet long, 3 feet wide, and 3 feet deep).

PERFECT MIX A raised bed offers the opportunity to fill your garden with compost and peat moss for a nutrient-rich, well-draining mix.

BAG A BARGAIN Garden centers usually mark down and clear out bagged soil and amendments at the end of the garden season. They also periodically discount damaged bags that may have lost some of their contents.

READY TO ROLL Save yourself repeated trips to the garden center by stocking up on bagged topsoil, compost, and potting mix early in the garden season. You'll have plenty on hand when you need it.

 **ASK THE GARDEN DOCTOR**

WHAT IS ORGANIC TOPSOIL ANYWAY? Read the product label for bagged potting soil and look for ingredients such as compost and composted leaves. If possible, look for a dry, screened soil that does not contain debris. If the package does not list ingredients, how can you be sure of what you're buying? Call the manufacturer and inquire.

POTTING SOIL AND MIXES

All potting mediums are not created equal. Container plants need porous soil that holds some moisture but also drains well and is rich in nutrients.

Garden soil is too heavy, compacts too easily, and drains poorly in containers. Experiment with potting soil mixes to discover which ones work best for your plants.

For potted plants outdoors or indoors, choose a fresh, high-quality mix labeled with ingredients such as peat, vermiculite, and composted bark. The package will tell you if it's a lightweight soilless mix (good for starting seeds) or an organic soil-based blend (good for growing herbs and other edibles). Potting soil alone is useful as the main ingredient in a mix, but some potting soils are nothing more than sterilized topsoil, which is too heavy for potted plants.

Premium specialty potting mixes ensure an appropriate balance of ingredients for optimum plant health. Some are blended for special types of plant, such as cacti or African violets. Other blends work for a particular purpose. A premium mix that contains slow-release fertilizer helps sustain long-term plantings such as shrubs and perennials. A mix that

BLEND YOUR OWN Make potting mix in a large lidded storage container or trash can that will also store the mix for you. Make a large batch and keep it where you have easy access to it for quick potting.

includes water-holding polymer crystals suits potted annuals and plants in hanging baskets.

Customize a potting mix by enriching it with compost, for instance. Improve the drainage with vermiculite. Or stir in polymer crystals to make a moisture-holding mix on the cheap.

DESERTLIKE POTTING MIX Purchase a ready-made soil mix designed for cacti and succulents that provides porous, easily draining conditions. Or mix the soil yourself, using equal parts sand, perlite, and potting soil.

ALL-PURPOSE POTTING MIX Read the product label for bagged potting mixes and be aware of what you purchase—or make your own mix with peat, compost, and coarse sand.

PREMIUM POTTING MIX Customize a potting mix by amending potting soil or pay for a premium product that has done the work for you. Added ingredients may include leaf mold, fertilizer, composted manure, and vermiculite or perlite.

HOW MUCH SOIL OR AMENDMENT WILL YOU BUY?

A cubic yard of soil, compost, or mulch fills about this much space:

2 inches deep = 160 square feet
3 inches deep = 110 square feet
To figure cubic yards, consider a 10×20-foot garden = 200 square feet, for example. Multiply the area by .33 (one-third of a foot to get cubic feet: 200 square feet × .33 = 66 cubic feet. Divide cubic feet by 27 to get cubic yards: 66 cubic feet / 27 = 2.44 cubic yards.

THE PH FACTOR

Soil pH is significant because it affects whether plants get essential nutrients.

Your garden's soil has a pH level that indicates its acidity or alkalinity. Checking pH is done simply as part of a soil test or using an inexpensive tool from a garden center. Plant preferences vary, but most plants prefer a slightly acidic (6.5–7.0) pH.

Acid-loving plants include azalea, rhododendron, camellia, holly, and blueberry. Unless you live in a rainy region where the soil is typically acidic, you'll need to acidify the soil to help acid-loving plants thrive.

If soil is too acidic, add ground limestone from a garden center or hardware store.

If you live in a particularly dry region or a place with soils on top of limestone, your soil will most likely be alkaline.

If soil is too alkaline, add powdered sulfur, iron sulfate, or an acidic fertilizer. Lower the pH over time by working in acidic organic material, including pine needles or peat moss.

WHAT ARE MICRONUTRIENTS?

Plants need at least 13 nutrients or elements for healthy growth. Only four of them are commonly applied as fertilizers: nitrogen, phosphorus, potassium, and calcium. Plants also use large amounts of carbon, hydrogen, and oxygen (elements available in air and water) as well as sulfur and magnesium.

The elements needed in smaller quantities include iron, copper, manganese, zinc, molybdenum, boron, and chlorine. These trace elements occur naturally in most soils, but in some regions, one or more of the elements may be deficient.

You can add mineral-rich ground rock to soil to gradually increase its fertility. Ground limestone, gypsum, and rock phosphate, for example, add minerals to the soil over time. Organic fertilizers such as greensand and bonemeal contain abundant nutrients; most synthetic fertilizers do not. Read more about mineral fertilizers in Chapter 11, page 234.

ACIDIFY SOIL Blueberry plants grow best in acidic soil (pH of 5 to 6). The plants benefit from regular soil amendments of pine needles, peat moss, or soil acidifier. These additions make the soil more acidic as they decompose.

TESTING, TESTING A pH soil meter or test kit, available from most garden suppliers, gives you a quick and accurate reading of your soil's pH level. Both methods measure pH on a scale from zero to 14, with 7 being neutral. Above 7 indicates alkaline soil; below 7 is acidic.

WORKING SOIL

To have a good planting bed, you must work the soil. Make it easier by lifting and turning small loads of soil at a time.

The initial preparation of a garden is the biggest workout. But routinely loosening soil before planting becomes easier each year as you continue to incorporate organic amendments in the process. Some gardeners dig ground by hand with a garden fork or spade. Others prefer to make the job easier using a power tiller.

Work soil only when it is damp or dry. Soil is workable when you squeeze a handful and it forms a clump that breaks apart when poked. If soil is wet, let it dry out before digging.

Compacting Soil

Working wet soil compacts it and causes rock-hard clods that will be difficult to break up. No matter how good the soil, if you subject it to traffic by people, pets, and vehicles, it will become compacted. In compacted soil, plant roots won't get the air and water they need. Compaction is probably the most common soil ailment. You can prevent compaction if you avoid walking and standing on beds and lawns when they are wet.

1 DIG IT If an area hasn't been worked much, prepare it for planting when the soil is not wet. Dig in with a garden fork and turn the soil. Break up any clods and level the surface.

2 ROCKIN' SOIL If the area has been worked before, thrust the fork into the ground and rock the tool back and forth to loosen the soil. Work your way across the area, breaking up any clods.

TO TILL, OR NOT TO TILL? Compared with digging by hand, rototilling is a faster, easier method of preparing a large bed or renovating a lawn. But some say tilling causes soil compaction and upsets the balance of microorganisms and humus.

AMENDING SOIL

Adding organic matter to soil helps create the best growing conditions for plants.

For long-term success, it's better to feed the soil than the plants. Even good soil benefits from regular additions of amendments. Organic amendments, such as rotted leaves (called leaf mold) and peat moss, improve the soil's fertility along with its ability to hold and drain moisture. Inorganic materials, such as gypsum and limestone, may improve soil structure or correct soil-mineral deficiencies.

Good Soil Nutrition

Improving soil is an ongoing process. Provide your garden soil with regular helpings of nourishing organic matter. Apply amendments individually or in combination at the beginning or end of the growing season, or both. Also add amendments whenever you tuck in or remove plants. Add at least a 2-inch layer of compost or another organic amendment to your garden annually. In existing beds, it's easiest to amend open areas before plants leaf out.

Find what's available, depending on where you live. In coastal regions, seaweed and composted fish additives are easy to come by. In the Southeast, cotton burr compost is widely available; in the Northwest, mushroom compost; in the Northeast, salt marsh hay.

❶ ADD COMPOST When amending areas among existing plantings, work carefully to avoid injuring plant roots.

❷ WORK IT Mix in the amendment using a garden fork. Stab, rock, and stir up the soil to about 6 inches deep.

AMENDING AN OPEN BED

❶ LOADS OF GOODNESS Improve the soil in a vacant bed by applying a 2-inch layer of compost or other amendment over the area.

❷ ADD FERTILIZER TOO Apply fertilizer to counteract temporary nitrogen loss while uncomposted organic matter decomposes.

❸ MIX WELL Use a garden fork to begin incorporating the amendment and fertilizer into the soil.

MAKING AMENDS In order to do its work, any soil amendment must be mixed into the soil from 3 to 12 inches deep.

 **ASK THE GARDEN DOCTOR**

HOW DO AMENDMENTS HELP SOIL? Amending soil with organic matter helps reduce compaction, making the soil easier to cultivate. Think of it as fluffing the soil, loosening it and incorporating air. All these processes make it easier for plant roots to find air and water and to grow.

ORGANIC SOIL AMENDMENTS

Turn to amendments whether you wish to generally improve soil or allay specific problems. Dependable amendments include:

LEAF MOLD Made of partially decomposed leaves, shredded or whole, it lightens soil and promotes healthy biological activity in soil. Not especially rich in nutrients, leaf mold may be slightly alkaline. For details about making leaf mold, see page 73.

COMPOST Decomposed organic matter comes free from your own compost pile or a commercial source. Made mostly from kitchen and yard waste, this premium soil conditioner adds nutrients and outperforms fertilizers. It is the richest and best amendment of all.

SPHAGNUM PEAT MOSS This partially decomposed plant material soaks up water and nutrients like a sponge. It lightens and acidifies soil. Peat moss is a limited resource. Use coir, made from coconut husks, as an earth-friendly alternative.

COMPOSTED MANURE If well rotted and broken down, the waste product of an animal provides nitrogen and stabilizes pH. It helps sandy soil retain moisture and loosens clay soil. Most manure comes from barnyard animals. Cat and dog excrement is unsafe for garden use.

VERMICULITE Flakes of mica (a mineral) expanded by heat absorb water, release it slowly, and keep container garden soil mixes more porous.

GYPSUM Add it to help leach salt out of soil. Add it to soil next to a street or sidewalk where plants suffer from winter salt applications. It can relieve aluminum toxicity and does not affect pH.

COARSE SAND Its tiny rock particles can help open up heavy soil and allow air to penetrate it, but sand can also make clay soil worse. It's especially helpful for growing some plants, such as cactus, succulents, carrots, and asparagus.

PERLITE These heat-expanded granules of volcanic ash do not absorb water, but they help potting soil drain and resist compaction.

ASK THE GARDEN DOCTOR

WHAT ARE WORM CASTINGS? The result of red worms or wigglers turning vegetable waste into nutrient-rich humus, this odorless stuff works efficiently when sprinkled into planting holes, seed rows, and pots. Castings improve soil fertility and drainage. The rich material also promotes plant health and vigor.

 **TEST GARDEN TIP**

GOOD MANURE Use only well-aged manure on the garden. Most fresh (hot) manure contains ammonia that can burn plants. Compost manure for at least one year before using it.

CHOICES, CHOICES The soil amendments you use will depend on what is readily available and practical. Try different amendments to see what works best for your garden.

MAKING COMPOST

Turn yard debris and kitchen scraps into nature's ideal soil amendment.

Gardeners call it "black gold" with good reason. The luxuriously humus-rich organic material is the stuff that fuels legendary gardens. Compost amounts to free fertilizer.

No matter where you garden or what you grow, added compost improves the soil. Besides making more air and water available to plants, compost slowly gives them nutrients. It also helps protect plants from diseases and pests. Compost attracts earthworms and microorganisms that build soil.

Goodness Grows

Composting is an easy way to go green and reduce your carbon footprint. You'll diminish your dependence on purchased fertilizers and amendments that require fossil fuels to make and distribute. Want to generate as much as one-third less garbage and save yourself from bagging all those leaves? You got it: Compost!

The easiest technique entails simply piling up yard and kitchen waste in a designated place, with or without a bin. If you like, start a new pile when you begin to harvest compost from your first pile. By alternating the heap-harvest cycle with each pile, you'll have a continual source of compost. Whichever composting technique you use, continue adding materials when they're available.

Expose a compost pile to the elements where some sun, rain, and other weather will help decomposition. But you can make compost indoors too.

COMPOST HAPPENS You need only layer organic waste from the yard and kitchen in a pile. Sunshine, rain, and nature do the rest.

WHAT GOES AROUND A two-bin composting system allows you to make compost in one bin and keep a supply of finished compost in the other.

ASK THE GARDEN DOCTOR **HOW LONG DOES IT TAKE TO MAKE COMPOST?** Using a bin system or an open pile, you'll have finished compost in two months to a year, depending on the weather and the mix of materials in the compost. If you live in a freezing climate, you can continue to add to the pile over winter, and let the debris break down as it will.

TEST GARDEN TIP

COMPOST ACTIVATOR A commercial inoculant (dormant microorganisms) or soil activator is not necessary to make compost. A nitrogen source such as leaves or grass clippings is typically enough to initiate the process.

BLACK GOLD
Nature's ideal plant food, finished compost is dark and crumbly—soillike. It has a pleasant earthy aroma.

COMPOSTING MADE EASY

Situate a compost bin or pile where it is most convenient for you.

Make your composting system simple or simpler. A bin, built or bought, encloses a compost pile and provides a tidy place to manage it. Numerous self-contained composting units are available to help you turn everyday stuff into garden gold.

Short on space? Keep a portable compost bin where it suits your lifestyle—on the back porch or in the kitchen, for instance. A bin allows compost to heat up and decompose faster. You'll find a variety of hard-working bins to help you accomplish your mission.

You can compost in something as unobtrusive as a plastic trash can by drilling air holes into it and cutting out the bottom. Partially bury it to put your compost in contact with the earth to introduce beneficial microbes and earthworms.

RED WIGGLERS These small redworms turn organic materials such as kitchen scraps into compost. Worm composting, or vermicomposting, in a plastic storage box is easy to do indoors, outdoors, or even at the office.

KITCHEN COMPOSTER This motorized appliance works indoors to compost kitchen waste quickly. It tumbles and heats the materials in the process.

COMPOST BUCKET Collect kitchen scraps in a lidded container and store it handily on the counter or under the sink. When it is full of food scraps, take the bucket outdoors and empty it on the compost pile.

STACKABLE COMPOSTER This unit allows you to add sections to it as materials pile up. The bottom section and lid have air-catching vents.

WHEELED TUMBLER Keep it near the backdoor for convenient loading; roll it to the garden to unload finished compost. Rotating composters can finish compost in weeks.

ASK THE GARDEN DOCTOR **DOESN'T COMPOST SMELL BAD?** No. Healthy compost smells like damp earth. If a bad smell arises from compost, it's a sign that the pile needs more air. Add dry leaves, twigs, or wood chips to the pile and turn it to incorporate the added carbon-rich material and air.

TIPS FOR SUCCESSFUL COMPOSTING

Get your compost off to the best start possible and keep it going.

■ Mix nitrogen-rich green materials (grass clippings, fresh garden debris, fruit and vegetable scraps, coffee grounds, and tea bags, plus calcium-rich eggshells) with carbon-loaded brown materials (chopped dry leaves and plant stalks, pine needles, small twigs, wood shavings, and shredded newspaper). Aim to compost about three times as many brown materials as green.

■ Avoid composting meat, bones, fat, dairy products, animal waste, branches, diseased plants, weeds with seedheads, and plants treated with herbicides or pesticides

■ Keep adding kitchen scraps to a compost pile over the winter in cold climates. They'll decompose when the weather warms.

■ When nature doesn't precipitate essential moisture for your compost pile, sprinkle it using the garden hose.

■ Turning a compost pile annually promotes decomposition, but is not necessary.

■ Although unusual, odor in a compost pile may indicate a lack of aeration. Turn the pile and add dry brown materials to increase air spaces.

■ You can add a limited amount of fireplace ashes to a compost pile no more than once a year. Ashes are highly alkaline and can change pH rapidly. Ash from a charcoal grill is unsuitable for composting.

■ When starting a compost pile, include a few shovelfuls of garden soil. The microbes in the soil will fire up decomposition. Compost activating products are unnecessary.

■ If you don't have space for a compost pile or leaf bin, pack leaves in bags available for municipal composting or yard waste programs—let someone else do the composting for you.

KITCHEN SCRAPS
This includes veggie and fruit waste, coffee grounds, tea bags, and eggshells.

LEAVES AND TWIGS Chopped materials break down faster.

GRASS CLIPPINGS Gather them as you mow, or rake afterward.

SOIL Starting a pile with a bit of soil introduces good bugs—the decomposers.

YARD WASTE Leave out any diseased plant materials. Include small twigs.

SCREENING BINS

Compost and leaf mold are beautiful things, but the process of making them isn't as pretty as other garden features. There are lots of ways to neaten a composting area.

Some people are averse to composting because they don't like the prospect of a pile of decomposing yard or kitchen waste in their yard. For others, it's a natural process, but they'd like to keep it out of view just the same.

There are various ways to screen the process, whether you simply pile up leaves to make leaf mold or add kitchen waste and make compost. If you tuck your pile into a dark corner, it won't get enough light or air to decompose adequately. Plantings, such as low shrubs or ornamental grasses, form a living screen for a compost pile.

Adding a low fence, lattice panels, or bamboo screening also works to disguise a compost pile. A fence with spaces between pickets or similar openings that allow air to circulate works best.

HIDE AND SEEK Plant cannas or other tall plants near your compost bin to form a leafy screen for the structure. Situate plants where they will not interfere with your access to the bin or shade the pile.

HOW TO SCREEN A COMPOST BIN

A super-simple compost bin is made with 4-foot-tall wire fencing and steel fence posts. Screen the bin using bamboo fencing that camouflages while allowing air circulation. If the posts are not anchored too deeply in the ground, the entire bin can be lifted to allow access to finished compost.

1 SIZE TO FIT Cut a length of bamboo fencing to fit around the wire, allowing a few inches to overlap.

2 WRAP AROUND Wrap the bamboo fencing around the wire bin and pull it taut. Use a length of heavy wire to lash the bamboo to the wire fencing at the top of the fencing.

3 TIE ENDS After securing the top ends of the bamboo fencing to the bin, use more wire to fasten it at the middle and bottom of the bin. Tuck in the wire ends safely.

TEST GARDEN TIP

MAKING LEAF MOLD By composting leaves you mimic what nature has been doing on forest floors for eons. The result of this process is called leaf mold, a humus-rich material. Transform leaves and grass clippings into leaf mold—or make compost—in an easy-to-make bin.

1 STAKE THE AREA Locate your bin in a sunny spot where there is easy access. Measure a 4-foot square. Post fencing stakes at each of the corners.

2 REMOVE WEEDS Clear the ground, removing any turfgrass and weeds that would grow into your compost pile and wreak havoc.

3 FENCE THE AREA Wrap wire fencing around the posts and shape a square bin. Overlap the ends of the fencing. Green vinyl-covered fencing blends easily with nearby plants.

4 HOLD IT Use strong wire to secure the wire fencing to each stake. Leave the open end loosely tied for easy access.

5 FILL IT Compost all kinds of yard and garden refuse or just leaves. Twigs and larger branches must be chopped or shredded in order to compost them.

6 PLANT A SCREEN Screen the bin from view, if you prefer, by planting a small ornamental shrub nearby.

MAKING BEDS

A new garden evolves, transforming an uncultivated area into a planting bed with no digging.

If the designated area for a new bed or border is covered with lawn, another groundcover, or weeds, you'll need to clear the area and prepare it for planting. There are several ways to accomplish this. One of the easiest methods harnesses sun, weather, and earthworms to turn turf into plantable earth.

When making a new bed and determining its size, keep in mind that any length will do, but limit the width to 3 or 4 feet across. This width enables you to reach the center of the bed from either side. If you make the bed wider than 4 feet, place a path or stepping-stones near the center of the bed so you can step across the garden without compacting the soil.

EASY OUTLINE If you use a garden hose to lay out an irregularly shaped bed, you can easily adjust the garden's size and shape.

① **STAKE OUT** First mow the area, cutting the grass as close to the ground as possible. Then outline the new border or bed using stakes and landscape tape. Adjust the size and outline of the bed as desired.

② **SMOTHER TURF** Cover the area with cardboard or a 6- to 12-sheet layer of newspaper. Saturate the paper using a garden hose. Moisture promotes decomposition and draws earthworms to help the process. The paper will break down and add organic material to the soil.

③ **LAYER COMPOST** Spread a 4- to 6-inch layer of compost on top of the paper. If you don't have enough compost, supplement it with high-quality topsoil or composted manure. Let the sun, weather, and earthworms work to decompose the layers.

④ **BE PATIENT** The layers will decompose completely within about 6 months. You can make a bed like this one in fall and it will be ready for planting by spring, for instance.

 **ASK THE GARDEN DOCTOR** **DO I HAVE TO WAIT TO PLANT A NEW NO-DIG BED?** You can plant in a bed recently made on top of existing turf by cutting through the layers of paper and turf to make planting holes. Otherwise, wait 6 months until the cardboard and turf decompose.

CONVERTING LAWN INTO GARDEN

As with any new garden, first determine a shape for your garden. Allow yourself plenty of time to complete this job, breaking it into small tasks.

This conventional method for clearing away turf is time tested. It involves digging and lifting sod, then digging compost into the soil to improve it. All told, it's a good workout.

Adding compost is essential when an area has been lawn for some time. The soil needs nourishing.

Ease the task of removing the sod by using a mechanical sod cutter, available at rental centers. Use a sod cutter to clear a large garden space lickety-split.

If the sod is good quality and not thickly infested with weeds, it can be replanted elsewhere. Once the sod is lifted, transplant it onto a bare area of your yard or share it with a neighbor. Once transplanted, keep the sod well-watered and it will quickly take root. Otherwise, compost the sod.

Another Way to Get Rid of Turf

Some gardeners use herbicide to kill the aboveground portion of turf and weeds. Nonselective herbicides such as those containing glyphosate may be applied almost any time the turf and weeds are growing, and they kill growth within a few weeks. If you need to eradicate perennial weeds, it's best to spray plants in late fall when the herbicide will most readily kill the underground portion of the plants.

❶ KILL TURF Spray the herbicide precisely as directed on the product label. Never spray on a windy day.

❷ DIG IN Dig and turn the dead grass into the new bed. Over time, the remains of the turf will deteriorate and add organic matter to the soil.

CLEARING TURF FOR A NEW BED

❶ MARK THE PERIMETER Outline the bed using chalk or flour. Use a spade to cut through the sod. Loosen sections of sod, sliding a spade an inch or two below the roots of the turf.

❷ REMOVE THE SOD Using the spade to cut the sod again, slice off a section that you can easily lift. Transplant sod by laying it on open ground, tamping the sod into place with your foot, and watering the area thoroughly.

❸ CLEAR THE AREA As you remove the turf, also dig up any weeds or other groundcovers to clear the area. Spread a 3- to 6-inch layer of compost over the cleared area and dig it into the soil.

❹ SMOOTH THE AREA Work methodically over the area until the amendment is well cultivated. Break up any clods and remove any stones and other debris as you level the area.

MAKING A RAISED BED

Save time and effort with another simple method for creating a new planting area. A raised bed solves common garden problems and brings benefits too.

Frame a bed with rot-resistant wood (cedar, cypress, or pressure-treated), stone, or concrete blocks. The frame prevents grass and weeds from creeping into the bed, meaning less maintenance. Make a raised bed of any size—a kit (available from mail order or online sources) simplifies the process. A 4×4-foot bed is perfect for a patio or other small space and is easily accessible from any of its sides. If you have room, create a grid of raised beds with paths in between them.

Benefits of Raised Beds

Raised beds dry out faster than conventional ones, so make yours at least 12 inches deep and customize it with drip irrigation. (This watering technique delivers water directly to plant roots; see page 256.) Beds elevated 24 inches or more eliminate bending and stooping.

A raised bed provides a solution to poor soil, such as clay or bedrock. Fill your raised bed with an ideal mix of compost, topsoil, and composted manure for guaranteed good drainage. Avoid stepping on the soil and compacting it. After planting, spread a 2-inch layer of mulch such as chopped leaves or cocoa shells to help preserve soil moisture.

Raised beds offer a wealth of other benefits too. The soil warms earlier in spring, giving you a head start on the growing season. The frame provides a place to sit, kneel, or stand and makes gardening more reachable. Raised beds give you affordable options, especially if you recycle materials such as concrete blocks for framing.

? ASK THE GARDEN DOCTOR **WHEN IS THE BEST TIME TO MAKE A RAISED BED?** Make a new bed in the spring when the threat of frost has passed, then plant as soon as the bed is ready. Or make the new bed in fall, let the soil sit over winter, and plant as soon as the weather allows in spring.

MULTIPLE BEDS Raised beds lend themselves to creative configurations. You can build beds side by side, make some deeper than others, form a grid of beds, leave a path between them—whatever your site and imagination suggest. Adjust the dimensions and materials to customize your design.

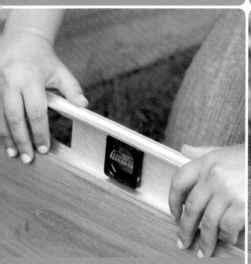

1 LAY OUT To make a two-tiered bed, cut 10 pieces of 1×4 lumber to 4-foot lengths. Lay the boards in place to preview the bed.

2 ADD COLOR Apply a premium water-base outdoor stain to enhance the bed's appearance and help blend the structure into the surroundings. This step is optional.

3 FASTEN CORNERS Connect the boards using six metal corner brackets, stainless steel screws, and four in-line connectors (available in a kit from a gardener's supply).

4 LEVEL BED Adjust the frame with shims if needed. Secure the frame using stakes included in the corner bracket kit and cover with plastic caps (also in the kit).

5 EXCAVATE SOD Unless the ground is already prepared, dig to a depth of 6 inches to make room for root growth. Remove sod from the shallower front tier; turn over sod in the deeper back tier.

6 ADD SOIL Fill beds with a good blend of two parts topsoil or garden soil and one part each mushroom compost, peat moss, and composted manure. Mix well before planting.

EDGING A GARDEN

A supreme multitasker, edging works hard to make the gardener's life a little easier.

Edging has a place in any garden. As a decorative element, it complements plantings and enhances your garden style. On the practical side, it keeps garden soil and mulch in, turf and weeds out.

You'll find a range of edging materials and designs. Widely used—if not the most attractive—prefabricated composite bender board or rimmed plastic get the job done. Designed to be partially buried, both types can pop out of the ground.

Use your imagination to come up with prettier edging. Stones, recycled glass bottles, or bent green-wood branches can be repurposed at the garden's edge. Quality edging is made to withstand the elements. Most edging works whether your garden is framed by lawn or a hard surface, such as a sidewalk or driveway.

Edging buried partway in the ground should be particularly resistant to moisture. Edging made of wood or metal can be well made and sturdy, but it won't last forever. Bricks or stones cost more than plastic or metal edging, and they last longer.

**ASK THE
GARDEN
DOCTOR**
WHAT KIND OF STONE SHOULD I USE TO EDGE MY GARDEN? Tumbled fieldstone enhances a casual garden in a rustic setting. Uniform cut stone, laid end to end, makes a tidy statement with a more clearly defined sense of formal organization. The stone's color may complement or contrast with a setting.

TEST GARDEN TIP

SHAPELY BEDS Edging helps a garden bed retain its shape. Whether edging is set flush with the ground or raised, it can take a straight or curved course. The length of an edger affects the shape of the curve. It's easier to lay smooth curves with short edgers and straight courses with longer edgers.

CUTTING EDGE Carve a neat edge in minutes using a half-moon edger, spade, or power edger. Among the simplest of edges, this option is effective at keeping lawn and garden separate.

DOWN AND DURABLE Bricks or pavers form a curved or straight edge that can be laid in various patterns. This version includes a strip to make mowing easier.

LIVING ON THE EDGE Compact and low-growing plants such as sweet alyssum 'Snow Princess' form ideal edging—easy care, budget-friendly, and quickly replaceable.

CASUAL CHARM When you finish pruning your trees and shrubs, transform the trimmings into a simply woven traditional edge called wattle.

PRETTY AND PRACTICAL Scalloped concrete edging (5×12 inches) is inexpensive and easy to install. It provides a neat decorative edge along a walkway.

DOUBLE DUTY Drip irrigation hides readily inside round-edged plastic edging. When the tubing is punctured, a drip emitter fits right into the edging and completes this creative approach to watering.

MAKING A MOWING STRIP

This quick, inexpensive, and satisfying project neatens your garden's appearance and saves you time mowing and trimming around the garden.

A 4- to 12-inch-wide strip, laid just above ground level between the edge of a garden and lawn, makes mowing more efficient. Mower wheels roll over the strip while the blade cuts freely without nicking any edging. No additional trimming needed. As a bonus, a mowing strip also keeps turf and weeds from creeping into the bed.

When preparing the area between the lawn and garden for your mowing strip, clear an area wide enough to accommodate the mowing strip material you choose.

MOWING STRIP OPTIONS

Concrete pavers come in several colors, including gray, terra-cotta, and brown. You'll also find them in various shapes and sizes—all excellent for mowing strips. Or choose another edging material that suits your garden or expresses your personality. Consider these materials for a mowing strip: brick, concrete, flagstone, or recycled rubber edging.

❶ BEFORE This garden will benefit from a mowing strip because its undefined edge merges with adjacent lawn. In the process of mowing, plants along the garden's edge can be damaged.

❷ EXCAVATE Use a spade to cut through the turf and form a crisp, well-defined edge. Clear a 5-inch-wide area between the garden and the lawn, removing any grass rhizomes and weeds, and loosening the soil.

❸ LAY THE PAVERS Place the edgers end to end along the edge of the bed. Snuggle the pavers into place until they lay flat about an inch above the soil's surface. Remove any excess soil and toss it into the garden.

❹ AFTER Once all the pavers have been set, tamp each one into place just above ground level with a mallet. You'll spend less time mowing and trimming around the garden.

ASK THE GARDEN DOCTOR **CAN I MAKE A MOWING STRIP WITHOUT ADDING PAVERS OR BRICKS?** Yes, you can excavate the area and leave the ground bare. You may need to weed the strip periodically or rein in garden plants that creep into the area.

MAKING A SIMPLE GARDEN PATH

Any bed wider than 3 feet benefits from the addition of a simple path.

A few stepping-stones or another path that cuts across a bed provides access to areas of the garden that you cannot easily reach from an outside edge. In addition, a path enables you to get from one side of the garden to the other without tramping on plants or compacting soil. It also offers sure footing and a place to set tools or a harvest basket. In a large garden, make the path wide enough to accommodate a wheelbarrow.

① SELECT MATERIALS
Round up newspaper, bark mulch, and concrete pavers or stepping-stones (one stepper for every 2½ feet of path). This 4-foot-wide path includes two steppers.

② USE PAPER Lay out the pathway using newspaper. Overlap the sheets of newspaper and stack them 6 to 10 deep. The paper will disintegrate eventually.

③ USE MULCH Spread a 3-inch layer of bark mulch on top of the newspaper. Over time this organic mulch will break down. It will need to be replaced along with the newspaper.

④ ADD PAVERS Take a walk across your new path. Watch where your feet land as you stride. Those are the spots where you will place the pavers or stepping-stones.

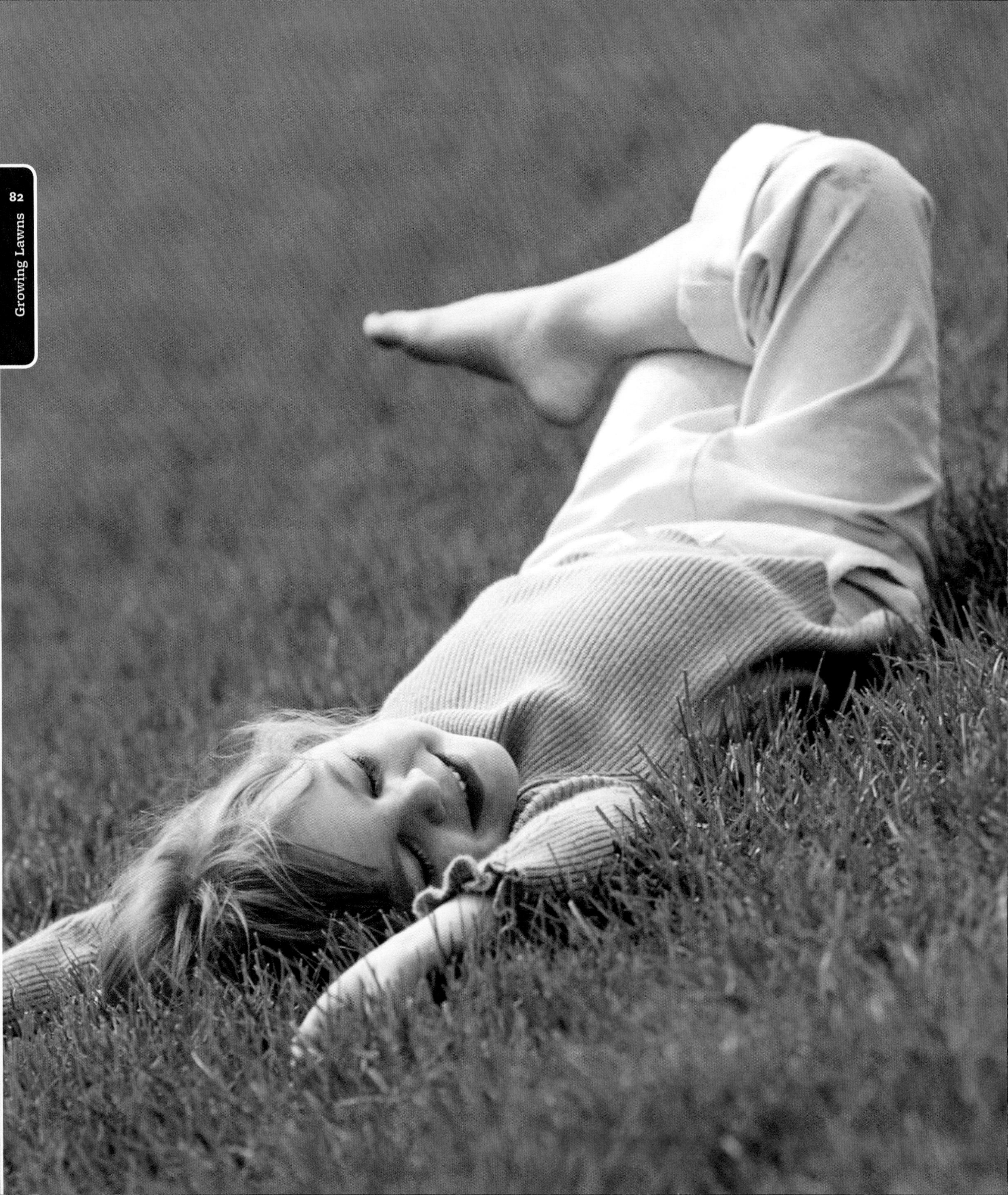

CHAPTER 5

GROWING LAWNS

You can have a beautiful lawn that works for you and the environment.

88

91

94

96

WHY LAWN?

A lawn enhances the enjoyment of your home. It also improves your property's value and your neighborhood's aesthetics.

A healthy lawn does more than you might realize. The millions of grass blades in a lawn work together and benefit your well-being in various ways. As turfgrass traps dust and pollution, it prevents soil erosion and produces oxygen. Lawn gives you a cushioned carpet for your outdoor rooms as well as a place to walk or play. It helps keep you cooler in the summer.

Your lawn should suit you and your lifestyle. Think about how you use your lawn and then consider whether it is the right size, shape, and type of lawn for you. You may decide to have only grass paths through your garden and a lush green sitting area in another part of the yard, for instance.

When grass is growing strong, caring for a lawn can be relaxing and enjoyable. Your efforts will have visible, tangible results.

Whatever its size and shape, a fitting lawn should be an integral part of an overall landscape design, rather than an afterthought that fills space between other elements.

RUN AROUND A circle of lawn forms an oasis in a small yard. This 14-foot-diameter island provides enough space for kids to turn cartwheels and somersaults.

ARTFUL APPROACH The simple-yet-creative arrangement of large (18- to 24-inch) pavers in a lawn helps break up the uniform plane. Inset pavers also add drama and firm footing across wet or frosty grass.

FAIR WAY Lawn creates visual relief in a yard; it contrasts and balances with planting areas. Use sweeping swaths of green to connect garden beds, trees, paths, and other features.

ASK THE GARDEN DOCTOR **WHY IS CLOVER GOOD FOR A LAWN?** Clover was once a common part of lawn seed mixes because it adds nitrogen to soil, improving the conditions for turfgrass. White clover grows and spreads easily in poor soil, needs little mowing, and attracts pollinators to the garden.

GREENER LAWNS

An environmentally friendly lawn looks lush and requires minimal upkeep.

Opting for a natural lawn begins by focusing less on perfect turf and more on healthy grass. Then use organic alternatives to synthetic lawn fertilizers, herbicides, and pesticides. Taking these steps will help you keep a natural lawn in top form:

Grow the right turfgrass. Whenever you put down seed or sod, choose a mixture of grasses adapted to your region and the sun/shade conditions in your yard.

Raise the mower's cutting height to 2 to 3 inches. The grass will develop stronger roots and compete better with weeds.

Mulch clippings using a mulching mower and return the grass bits to the lawn. This adds beneficial nutrients and organic matter to the soil and reduces the need for fertilizer.

Enrich the soil with organic fertilizer. Test the soil's pH; amend to reach a rich, slightly acidic soil.

Aerate the lawn annually (see page 99 for details) to encourage deep-rooting grass.

Dig weeds if they appear. A thick healthy lawn crowds out weeds. But when weeds or other problems occur, cure them quickly before much damage is done.

THE RIGHT TURFGRASS FOR A GREAT LAWN

Whether you are installing a new lawn or caring for the one you have, growing the right grass in the right place is an essential step.

Selecting appropriate grasses makes a lawn easier to maintain. How do you select the best grasses for your lawn? Narrow your choices depending on the climate where you live.

Lawns usually contain combinations of grass types, but some feature only one type of grass. Knowing which grasses will grow well in your yard helps you determine how to care for the lawn and keep it in good shape. You get to decide if you want to mow, feed, and water minimally—and then relax in your hammock and admire your buffalograss.

Grasses appear similar, but they vary in texture and growth rate. Grasses vary more in terms of resistance to heat, cold, drought, shade, disease, and insects. Some tolerate heavy foot traffic; others won't spread into bare areas. So it is useful to understand their differences.

Each variety of grass has strengths and weaknesses. There is no single best choice. Your grass selection also helps determine the best time to handle specific lawn care tasks. Check with your county extension service for recommended varieties suited to your location.

EASY-CARE GRASS Select turfgrasses suited to the conditions: sun or shade, dry or damp, high traffic or hillside. Less-vigorous grasses require less mowing but recover slower from heavy traffic or play.

TURFGRASS CLIMATE MAP

Cool-season grasses grow best in the cool temperatures of spring and fall and in northern regions.

Warm-season grasses are best adapted to southern regions. They grow well during hot weather and become dormant and brown during cold weather.

Transition grasses, such as tall fescue, can tough it out in regions with hot summers and cold winters.

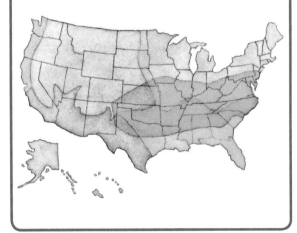

TRIED-AND-TRUE TURFGRASSES

A wide selection of turfgrass varieties offer dependability in different climates and applications. These grasses are often included in seed blends.

COOL-SEASON GRASSES

FINE FESCUE Good for shade, these wispy grass species need little maintenance. In mixes: hard, sheep, and chewings fescues suit dry areas; red fescue suits cooler, wetter areas of transition regions. Zones 4–8.

KENTUCKY BLUEGRASS Popular for its cold hardiness, fine texture, and dark color, bluegrass cannot stand heavy foot traffic or shade. It needs more mowing, watering, and fertilizing than other cool-season varieties. Zones 3–7.

PERENNIAL RYEGRASS This quick-growing, wear-resistant lawn suits transition regions. Ryegrass is fine-textured and dark green with a distinguishing sheen. It has little tolerance for severe winters and drought. Zones 3–7.

TALL FESCUE Tolerant of drought, heat, shade, and pests, this sturdy, coarse grass suits play and utility areas, especially in transition regions. Grow it as a single species, in a blend of tall fescue varieties, or in mixes with bluegrass. Zones 3–7.

WARM-SEASON GRASSES

CENTIPEDEGRASS A coarse slow-grower needing less mowing and maintenance than many grasses, centipedegrass is best for light traffic areas and sandy soil. Zones 7–9.

BERMUDAGRASS Vigorous and quick to recover from wear, it tolerates drought and salt, although it is intolerant of shade and prone to thatch. Zones 7–10.

ST. AUGUSTINEGRASS For a coarse but lush thick lawn, this vigorous, tough grass tolerates some shade and salt but needs lots of upkeep. Zones 8–10.

BUFFALOGRASS This slow-growing native grass with fine blades needs no mowing. Drought and heat tolerant, it grows best in full sun. Zones 3–9.

? ASK THE GARDEN DOCTOR **WHEN SHOULD I PLANT A NEW LAWN?** Plant warm-season grasses between spring and early summer. Plant cool-season grasses in late summer, early fall, or spring. Start with fresh, high-quality seed. Prepackaged mixes are formulated for specific regions.

PLANTING A NEW LAWN

Making a new lawn or replacing an old one is an opportunity to get it off to a good start and ensure that it fulfills the best possibilities.

The best way to cure an ailing lawn is to start over. If your lawn is weak, pale, overgrown with weeds, and less than 50 percent good grass: Replace it. After you've selected an appropriate grass, decide how to plant it. Weigh your options—seed or sod.

Turfgrass seed is economical. The larger the lawn, the bigger the savings. With seed, you'll have more choices of grass varieties and many mixtures formulated for sun or shade. When there are several grass varieties in a single bag, one or more is likely to thrive in your yard. A seeded lawn takes several months to establish before it can withstand any foot traffic. It will also need weeding.

Sod is quicker, easier, and costlier than seed. It transforms bare earth into lush lawn in a day. Sod takes a few weeks to establish, and it prevents erosion on slopes better than seeding. A solid blanket of sod over soil smothers most weed seeds. While fewer types of grass are available as sod, many refined hybrids are grown only that way.

Preparation Counts

The process of preparing soil is the same whether you plant seed or sod. These steps are essential:

First, correct any underlying problems with soil, disease, or pests.

Second, clear the site of old turf and weeds. Old turf can be stripped off and the soil solarized under a tarp or sheet of plastic for one to two months. Or smother the old turf under layers of newspaper or cardboard and compost. That process requires three to six months.

Finally, test and improve the soil according to soil test results.

SEED OR SOD? Seed offers more choices of grass varieties. Fewer types of grass are available as sod, but many refined hybrids are grown only that way.

PREPARING SOIL FOR A NEW LAWN

❶ RAKE Improve soil by spreading a 2-inch layer of compost and tilling it into the top 4–6 inches of soil. Rake to remove stones, roots, and other debris. Use the rake to level the area or to change the grade and improve drainage.

❷ FERTILIZE Consult your soil test results and apply the correct amount of fertilizer and organic matter. Or use a special starter fertilizer according to directions. A drop spreader distributes fertilizer evenly.

❸ RAKE AND ROLL Rake the area again to grade it and mix the fertilizer and any amendments into the top inches of soil. Then use a lawn roller (available from rental centers) to firm the planting bed.

TEST GARDEN TIP

PLANTING PREPARATIONS Figure out how much seed you will need for the square footage of a new lawn by multiplying the width and length of the area. One pound of bluegrass seed covers 500 to 600 square feet. One pound of other turfgrass varieties typically covers 300 to 350 square feet.

1 PRODUCT GUIDELINES See the instructions on the seed package for details about application and postplanting care.

2 BROADCAST SEEDS Sow by hand in a small area. Or use a broadcast spreader to sow seeds uniformly. Sow half the seeds as you walk in one direction. Spread the other half walking crosswise.

3 SEED/SOIL CONTACT Lightly rake (or use a stiff broom to sweep) the soil and settle the seeds into the soil's surface. Avoid burying the seeds.

4 RENT A ROLLER Use a lawn roller to roll over the soil lightly, ensuring contact between seeds and soil. This step helps seeds germinate properly.

5 WATER THOROUGHLY Cover the seeded area with burlap. Sprinkle the area lightly to moisten the burlap and the top inch of soil. After that, sprinkle each day to keep the germinating area damp.

6 AS GRASS GROWS Apply more water less frequently to encourage grass roots to reach deep into soil. Mow the new lawn when it reaches 3½ inches tall.

SODDING A NEW LAWN

For an instant lawn that stays attractive long after you've installed it, follow these steps.

You can sod a lawn almost anytime during the growing season, but it's best to avoid planting during very hot weather and having to water more afterwards.

About a week before planting, call a local sod grower or nursery and order the amount of sod you'll need. Determine the square footage of the area, then have the grower or nursery calculate the number of rolls you need. Buy an extra 5 or 10 percent to ensure that you'll have enough. Most sod suppliers deliver for a small fee—just tell them when and where.

 **ASK THE GARDEN DOCTOR** **HOW LONG MUST I WAIT BEFORE WALKING ON MY NEW LAWN?** It takes up to two years for a new lawn to become fully established with roots that can handle just about anything. Until then, your new grass will be fragile. Give it a little TLC. Avoid heavy traffic for the first season. Water deeply and infrequently, depending on the weather, to help the new turfgrass develop deep, strong roots.

 **TEST GARDEN TIP**

SOD-LAYING PREPARATIONS First prepare the planting bed, improving the soil to encourage root growth. Sprinkle the soil to moisten it. Then sprinkle the soil side of each sod roll as you unroll it.

1 FRESH SOD Plan to lay the sod the day it is delivered. If necessary, stack the sod in the shade for up to 24 hours, sprinkling it once or twice to keep it damp.

2 FIRST ROWS The easiest way to lay sod is to start with a straight edge—along a walk or driveway, for example.

3 BUTT ENDS After you lay the first roll, lay another, butting the ends to complete one strip of lawn. Lay subsequent rolls, butting end and side seams. Stagger the ends. Cut pieces to fit, if need be.

4 ROLL After the sod is laid, roll over it with a lawn roller half-filled with water to ensure good contact between roots and soil.

5 WATER Immediately water the sod thoroughly. If it takes more than an hour or two to sod a large lawn, divide the area into sections and water each section when you complete it.

6 SPRINKLE Set up an oscillating sprinkler and use it to water the sod daily for about two weeks after laying it. Avoid walking on the new sod for 14 days until roots begin growing and establishing.

MAINTAINING LAWN

Consistent care becomes a seasonal ritual and saves extra work by preventing problems.

There's no need for obsessive obedience to a lawn maintenance schedule. Newer turfgrass varieties demand less attention, and more communities restrict watering. If you make lawn care an enjoyable routine rather than a burden, and provide the necessary basics, you'll be rewarded with a healthy lawn. The thicker and healthier the lawn, the better it's able to thrive with minimal care.

What Your Lawn Needs

A lawn needs mowing regularly. Each turfgrass species has an ideal mowing height. The taller you keep the lawn, the stronger it is and the better able it is to survive times of stress such as drought.

A lawn needs some fertilization just to get by. Feeding at least once or twice a year—early spring and early fall—promotes the basic health of turf.

Watering a lawn is not necessary in many regions. If dry weather persists, you can allow the lawn to go dormant (a sleep mode of sorts).

Deal with weeds, pests, and diseases as necessary. Beyond these basics, tend to your lawn according to your personal preferences and resources.

BENEFITS OF MOWING

Regular mowing helps turfgrass grow well.

The way turfgrass grows is what enables it to form a lawn. Unlike other plants, grass grows from its base. Mowing improves a lawn's appearance and promotes the soft turf that's a pleasure to walk and play on.

Turfgrass benefits from regular mowing. By mowing weekly and cutting off no more than one-third of the green growth, you encourage the grass to develop new thick growth. Taller grass is more vigorous and disease-resistant than closely cropped grass. Taller grass shades out weeds.

When you mow and let the clippings fall onto the ground, they decompose and add nitrogen and organic matter to the soil. If you a mow with a mulching blade, the clippings will be reduced to tiny pieces that break down quickly.

Mowing Timesavers

Use the largest lawn mower practical for the size of your lawn. Mowing an acre of lawn with a 24-inch-wide mower saves about an hour over mowing with an 18-inch mower.

Minimize mowing around trees. Reduce wasted time by mulching under trees.

Eliminate corners. Design your lawn with gently curving sides and no sharp turns. If your lawn has corners, round off the corners on your first mowing pass, leaving them unmown until you've finished the rest of the lawn.

If you use a trimmer, trim the edges of the lawn before mowing for greater efficiency.

Tune up your mower and sharpen its blade annually so the equipment starts easily and works dependably every time you mow.

CUT HIGH Set your mower blade at the high end of the height range recommended for your grass.

FREE FOOD Clippings left on the lawn add nitrogen and organic matter to the soil and reduce the need for fertilizer.

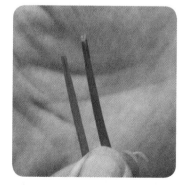

SHARPER EDGE A dull mower blade tears grass tips, leaving them ragged and more susceptible to disease.

HINTS FOR BETTER MOWING

A lawn kept in good shape is easier to maintain than a neglected one that needs restoring.

Mowing is the most important task in maintaining a lawn. Take the two most important steps in mowing: beyond that, details will guide your mowing routine. Keep the lawn within the preferred mowing height, depending on the grass variety, and cut no more than one-third of the blade.

When and how you mow depends on several factors: the type of grass, the season, and the amount of fertilizer and water applied. You'll likely need to mow cool-season grasses more in spring and fall, warm-season grasses more in summer.

Cut with a sharp blade to avoid damaging grass. Sharpen the blade at the beginning of the season and whenever grass looks ragged after mowing.

Avoid cutting wet grass. The cut will be uneven. Wet clumps of clippings clog the mower and mat on the lawn.

Vary your mowing pattern and encourage grass to grow upright and prevent soil from compacting. For safety's sake, mow slopes on a diagonal.

Leave clippings where they fall. This will entail less work for you, more nutrients for the soil. As the clippings decompose, they will not contribute to thatch.

Learn to identify thatch as a tangled mat of dead grass stems, roots, and debris—not clippings—that builds up faster than it decomposes. Read more about it on page 99.

Remove excess clippings from the lawn and spread them on the garden or compost pile.

HOW MUCH MOWER DO YOU NEED?

The answer depends on you as much as the size of your lawn.

Today's choices among lawn mowers reflect modern technology and lifestyles, as well as complex decision-making for consumers. Fortunately, mowers have become more user friendly, with built-in safety and convenience features designed to save time, energy, and the environment.

In addition to lawn size, factor in your physical fitness and free time, as well as site characteristics, such as hills and obstacles.

Narrowing Choices

Performance comes via a wide range of mowers and features. Consider options such as walk-behind or self-propelled; pull cord or electric start; mulching blade, side discharge, or rear bagger; and gas-, electric-, or battery-powered. Self-propelled models do more of the work. Variable speeds adjust to match your pace. A mulching blade reduces clippings to bits.

REEL MOWER On a small, level lawn, it cuts clean and is quiet, nonpolluting, and lightweight, Enjoy the exercise. Look for one with easily adjustable mowing height.

ROTARY / WALK BEHIND First consider the categories of mower types: Electric-, gas-, and battery-powered options all have strengths.

MATCH MOWER TO LAWTN SIZE		
Small lawn	Less than 5,000 square feet	Reel; electric- or battery-powered walk-behind mower
Medium lawn	5,000–10,000 square feet	Gas, walk-behind or self-propelled mower
Large lawn	More than 10,000 square feet	Riding mower or lawn tractor

CORDLESS Rechargeable battery-powered mowers tackle a small yard on a single charge. Battery replacement every few years can be costly.

BAG AND MULCH Most walk-behind mowers give you an option to collect clippings, mulch them, or blow them onto the lawn. The bag attaches to the side or rear of the mower.

RIDING MOWER For large or hilly lawns, riders offer options. Cutting width and horsepower vary. Consider steering and maneuverability as well as comfort features.

LAWN TRACTOR A worthwhile investment for yards measured in acres, a small tractor with a mower attachment offers a wide mowing deck and faster speed.

TRIMMING AND EDGING YOUR LAWN

Neatness counts. If you remember this grade-school adage and apply it to your lawn, you'll see an appreciable difference.

Edging or trimming adds a finishing touch to a lawn's perimeter where grass meets garden or hard surface. Consider it a necessity rather than a luxury. When trimming is a periodic part of your lawn-care routine, it takes only minutes to complete the manicure. Edging a lawn that's gone months without it can take more time than mowing.

Your choice of string trimmer, power edger, or other tool simplifies the task. Electric-, gas-, or battery-powered trimmers offer speed. Try each type before buying to make sure its size suits you. Wear eye and ear protection when operating a power trimmer. Keep your lawn shape simple and avoid planting lawn all the way up to fences and walls for easier edging.

TRIM CORRECTLY Avoid beveling the lawn's edge with a string trimmer. This common mistake scalps the grass, stymieing its growth and inviting weeds.

GARDEN EDGE Set off beds by cutting a neat edge where lawn meets planting bed. Add a decorative strip with stone or brick.

STRING TRIMMER Freehand edging can be tricky. When choosing a nylon-line trimmer or weed whacker, get one with an edging guide.

STEEL-BLADE EDGER Gas- or electric-powered, this option cuts the cleanest edge with its spinning blade.

ASK THE GARDEN DOCTOR **HOW CAN I MINIMIZE POLLUTION FROM GAS-POWERED LAWN EQUIPMENT?** Switch to a reel mower or hand trimmer. Use a no-spill gas can when refueling trimmers, mowers, and other power tools. Millions of gallons of gasoline are spilled annually, according to the Environmental Protection Agency.

FERTILIZING A LAWN

Give turfgrass the nutrients it needs without overdoing it and causing pollution.

Turfgrass fertilizer supplies nitrogen, phosphorus, and potassium in roughly a 3:1:2 ratio—proportionate to the amount a lawn uses. An 18:6:12 fertilizer contains 18 percent nitrogen. Nitrogen is the element most soils lack and the nutrient grass needs most, especially in early spring or early fall when a growth spurt occurs.

Another type of lawn fertilizer contains a higher proportion of potassium. Applied in fall, it is intended to strengthen grass in preparation for winter.

Specialized lawn fertilizers are also available. Weed and feed products contain a broadleaf weed killer for weeds such as dandelion or a preemergent herbicide to prevent crabgrass and other annual weeds from sprouting. Carefully follow product instructions.

New lawn? If you planted in spring, feed your lawn in early fall. If you planted in late summer, wait for early spring before fertilizing.

You'll find lawn fertilizers available in several forms. Water-soluble fertilizers are applied as granules and dissolve easily with rain or irrigation. They're inexpensive, and their effects are short-lived. Controlled-release fertilizers provide nutrients more slowly and uniformly as they decompose.

Organic fertilizers made from plant and/or animal waste also decompose slowly. In addition, organic fertilizer builds organic matter in soil and reduces the chance of overfertilizing. Too much fertilizer burns grass and causes pollution. Use only the amount of fertilizer recommended in product instructions.

DROP SPREADER Dropping fertilizer straight down and in an even path ensures accuracy, especially on small lawns and between planting beds. Carefully overlap wheel tracks for consistent coverage.

BROADCAST SPREADER A spinning disk in the hopper throws fertilizer in a fan-shape swath, which works best for large lawns. For more uniform coverage, cover lawn ends first, then go back and forth lengthwise.

HANDHELD CRANK SPREADER This lightweight implement is an affordable option for small areas and quick applications of small amounts of fertilizer.

REDUCE RUNOFF Sweep errant fertilizer off hard surfaces and into the lawn to help keep chemicals from washing into water supplies, lakes, and streams.

WATERING

When rain is scarce, watering keeps a lawn green. But water is a precious resource, and sensible watering is essential.

It's time to water when you see footprints in the lawn after walking on it or when the grass appears dull green or bluish (depending on the variety). Healthy turf survives eight weeks or more without water; then it goes dormant and turns brown but doesn't die.

Water use and conservation are regulated by law in some places. Unless you have other requirements in your community, use the following tips to help an established lawn stay green while conserving water. Read more about watering in chapter 12.

Grow drought-tolerant grasses if dry periods are common where you live.

Encourage deep rooting by watering deeply (1 inch of water soaks in to 6 inches), watering infrequently (weekly), and mowing high. Taller, healthier plants develop deeper roots. Deeper roots need less supplemental water.

Water early in the morning to minimize evaporation and prevent disease.

Avoid waste by soaking just the lawn instead of rinsing surrounding surfaces where water runs off.

POP GOES THE SPRINKLER Use an in-ground sprinkler system with pop-up heads for efficiency. Otherwise, use a sprinkler that delivers uniform coverage.

LESS IS MORE Most lawns get adequate water from rainfall. But too much rain, like too much watering, can kill turfgrass.

ASK THE GARDEN DOCTOR **WHY IS MY LAWN BROWN IN SPRING WHEN MY NEIGHBOR'S GRASS IS GREEN?**
Your lawn may include warm-season grasses that green up later in the season. Warm soil temperature, not air temperature, prompts grasses such as st. augustinegrass, bermudagrass, and centipidegrass to start growing.

RAKING

Although picking up grass clippings isn't necessary when you mow properly, leaves are another matter. Left on the lawn all winter, leaves will smother the grass. Either rake up leaves or run a mulching mower over them. The mower's blade chops the leaves into small pieces that break down and feed the soil. Or collect the leaves in a mower bag attachment and then compost the bits.

When raking, use a lightweight, flexible type of rake with a light-handed rhythm. Raking too forcefully can damage the lawn.

RAKE IN FALL Clear fallen leaves using a bamboo or plastic rake. The wider the rake head, the more leaves it will collect in one swipe.

RAKE IN SPRING When the lawn is dry, use a spring-tined rake to remove winter debris from the lawn and gently pull out dead grass.

AERATING

If your ground is hard, if it has dry spots where grass won't grow, or if you can't poke a pencil 4 inches into the soil when it's damp: aerate it. The soil under lawn compacts easily under heavy traffic. Clay soils are most prone to compaction. Fine-texture grasses succumb under heavy use more often than coarse-texture grasses.

Aeration opens the soil and allows air to reach the roots of turgrass. Aeration improves drainage, breaks up thatch, stimulates lawn growth, and improves lawn health. Aerate in fall when the lawn is growing actively and will have a chance to recover before winter. You may need to water the lawn the day before aerating to make sure it is damp when the aeration is completed.

CORE AERATION Rent or hire a service that uses a powerful machine to remove plugs from the soil and leave them to decompose. If you like, aerate your lawn and a neighbor's and share the cost. Go over the lawn twice at right angles.

SOIL PLUGS Left after core aeration, the soil in the plugs will break down quickly after mowing—especially if it rains—and return the organic matter to the lawn.

DETHATCHING

As a shallow layer of deteriorating grass blades and roots—not grass clippings—thatch is normal. It acts as a natural mulch around the base of grass plants. It also helps retain soil moisture and keep soil cool.

When thicker than ½ inch, thatch prevents water from reaching roots. What's more, it forms a welcome mat for disease and insect pests.

Aerating resolves most thatch. For extreme cases, dethatching is accomplished with a power rake or vertical mower. This process cuts through the thatch and rips out debris that then must be removed.

DETHATCHING RAKE Comb through cool-season grasses in late summer or early fall, warm-season grasses in late spring or early summer.

POWER APPROACH Dethatch only when necessary because the process is hard on the lawn. Dethatch if the thatch is more than ½ inch thick.

REPAIRING AND REVIVING LAWN

You may be surprised at how easy it is to rejuvenate a weak or worn lawn.

Disease, insects, and drought can damage a lawn. Heavy traffic, seasonal equipment, and winter also take a toll on turf, as do dogs, fertilizer spills, poor soil, and neglect.

Before you take any drastic action to fix a patchy, thin, or weedy lawn, identify the cause of the problem, and then decide how to correct any deficiencies. More often than not, a so-so lawn can be rejuvenated with annual organic fertilizing and fall aerating.

Repair small bare spots in lawn by patching them with fresh sod. Either transplant pieces from one part of the yard to another, or get a roll of sod at a garden center and cut it into replacement-size pieces.

Use a spade to square the edges of the problem area; loosen the soil and remove any weak turf. Fill the opening with fresh turf. Tamp it into place with your foot and water thoroughly.

You can overseed a sparse or weedy lawn, spreading fresh grass seed over the entire area to promote new growth and crowd out weeds. Before overseeding, prepare the lawn by mowing and weeding it. Then scratch and loosen the soil with a garden rake. Sprinkle compost lightly over the lawn and then sow grass seeds. Regular watering proves crucial to establishing new grass.

For small or large patches that need repairing, use seed and follow the steps shown.

① **LOOSEN SOIL** Prepare the planting area by roughing up the soil with a garden rake. If the ground is compacted, loosen it with a garden fork, then level and refine it with the rake.

② **IMPROVE SOIL** Sprinkle compost over the seedbed to amend the soil with organic matter. Rake the compost into the soil.

③ **SOW SEED** Use fresh, high-quality grass seed. Evenly sprinkle the grass seed over the prepared soil. Store unused seed in a cool, dry place. Keep the package tightly sealed.

④ **COVER SEED** Toss a light layer of peat moss over the seeded area to act as a moisture-retentive mulch that won't interfere with seeds germination.

⑤ **WATER WELL** Gently and thoroughly moisten the area. Water every other day to keep the area damp until the grass sprouts.

ASK THE GARDEN DOCTOR

MY LAWN IS MOSTLY WEEDS. SHOULD I START OVER OR CAN I SAVE IT? If more than 50 percent of your lawn is damaged or taken over by weeds, you will need to renovate it. Renovation involves killing all the weeds and remaining grass, and then sowing seed. Repairing the lawn involves seeding over a limited area.

PREVENTING WEEDS

Taking a proactive approach to weeds, pests, and diseases helps prevent them from gaining a foothold in your lawn.

Many lawn problems result from too much or too little fertilizer, too much shade, too much rain or water, and unrelenting sweltering heat. While often beyond your control, a suffering lawn does not automatically require you to douse it with a weed or pest control. Applying too much or too little of a product at the wrong time usually makes problems worse, and it wastes your time and money.

Proper maintenance and good nutrition go a long way to promote a healthy, vigorous lawn that resists weeds, pests, and diseases. Many situations are cosmetic and don't require treatment. When you notice a problem such as weeds, it may be an indicator of poor lawn maintenance. Step back and think through your lawn care routine—something could be missing or even overdone. Look closer and see if the lawn alerts you to other problems.

CHECK FOR PROBLEMS Cut a flap of lawn, using a spade, and roll back the turf to examine beneath it. Look for signs of root damage and grubs (plump white insect larvae that resemble macaroni).

MINIMIZE MOSS Moss thrives where lawn languishes in damp, shady, acidic conditions. Boost the lawn by planting shade-tolerant grass and applying powdered lime.

CORN GLUTEN An organic option to preemergent herbicides, corn gluten meal (a byproduct of milling), helps prevent crabgrass and other broadleaf weeds. Apply it before weed seeds sprout, in early spring when forsythia blooms.

LAWN ALTERNATIVES

If your lawn becomes too much work—too weedy, too weak, too needy—turn to groundcovers for reliable replacements.

No matter how hard you try to nurture a lawn, your yard may have a place where grass grows poorly—under a tree in shade, on a slope, in a high-traffic area. Instead of wasting time and money trying to force grass to grow in unsuitable places, turn to groundcovers, the problem-solving plants.

Easy-care groundcovers can tame a slope, reduce erosion, and elbow out weeds. Their ability to creep and spread makes groundcovers perfect plants for creating pathways that are alive with beautiful textures, colors, and blooms. Most creeping plants stand up to and provide lush carpets for outdoor rooms.

Pick Your Plants

Groundcovers include a vast array of plants, from low creepers to taller mounding options and even sprawling shrubs. The plants spread and sprawl by different means, whether creeping underground via roots and stems or by rooting branches and stems aboveground. Others grow in clumps, spreading wider each year.

Take advantage of the weedy nature of some plants and put them to work as groundcovers. But beware of introducing aggressive plants into your yard unless you take precautions. Install edging between groundcovers and lawn.

'TINY RUBIES' This variety of dianthus (Zones 4–9) forms a pretty carpet in full sun with tiny bright pink flowers and blue-green foliage.

BLUE STAR CREEPER *Isotoma fluviatilis* makes a soft, resilient lawn alternative and grows just about anywhere in Zones 5–9, even in clay soil.

ASK THE GARDEN DOCTOR **WHAT SHOULD I PLANT UNDER A TREE INSTEAD OF GRASS?** If grass grows poorly under a tree, first consider pruning a few of the tree's lower branches or thinning out the canopy to allow in more light. Replace the grass with a shade-tolerant groundcover, such as vinca or pachysandra.

PLANTS THAT KICK GRASS

The trick in using groundcovers successfully comes in selecting suitable plants for your garden. Native perennial groundcovers are good candidates. Nurseries and garden centers usually offer a range of groundcovers suited to the region—see what they recommend.

BUGLEWEED *(AJUGA)* This perennial features purplish-green, bronze, or variegated foliage and flowering spikes in spring; sun to light shade in Zones 3–9.

DICHONDRA *(D. MICRANTHA)* Bright green or silver foliage works well in lawns instead of turfgrass in Zones 9–11. Mow, weed, feed, and water it regularly.

SPOTTED DEAD NETTLE *(LAMIUM)* This perennial sports variegated aromatic leaves on 6-inch stems; blooms in white, pink, or lavender. It likes shade in Zones 4–8.

GOLDEN PEARLWORT *(SAGINA SUBULATA* 'AUREA') Also known as Scotch moss, the perennial looks like moss and forms a chartreuse carpet in sun to light shade; Zones 4–7.

THYME *(THYMUS)* Various forms, from creeping to bushing, as well as different colors, textures, and fragrances grow in Zones 4–9.

STONECROP *(SEDUM)* Perennial succulents range from ground-level creepers to 4-inch-tall varieties for Zones 4–9. The plants need full sun and excellent drainage.

CREEPING SPEEDWELL *(VERONICA REPENS)* The 3-inch plant flowers in white to lavender in spring. Drought tolerant, it thrives in sun and heat; Zones 4–9. It can take foot traffic.

PATHWAYS WITH GROUNDCOVERS

Plant groundcovers in spring or early fall, giving them plenty of time to develop new roots and begin growing before you tramp on them.

Creeping plants are among the many groundcovers to which gardeners turn for filling space between stepping-stones, pavers, or other pathway materials.

You'll find creeping forms of many plants such as herbs. You get a bonus by planting creeping herbs in paths: They release their wonderful fragrances when stepped on. Tuck a plant into a bare pocket and notice how it fills the area within a year or two.

When you want to economize on plants, split large plants into smaller pieces and be patient while they spread. Use the same approach if you're planting a larger area and want the plants to cover more ground. Spacing depends on the size of plants you start with and their potential size at maturity.

If you want quick coverage, start with larger plants or flats of seedlings and plant them closer together.

AFTER In less than one season, a flagstone path is well on its way to becoming a lovely tapestry with creeping mints, pennyroyal, thyme, Irish moss, and bugleweed.

❶ BEFORE Grass and weeds fill in earnestly between the stones of a pathway. Dig up the unwanted plants.

❷ AMEND SOIL Prepare for planting by replacing old, poor soil with fresh topsoil and organic amendments.

❸ ADD PLANTS Nestle new plants into place, giving them room to spread. (Pluck out any weeds if they pop up.)

❹ WATER WELL Water transplants carefully. Mulch between them to preserve soil moisture and prevent weeds.

ASK THE GARDEN DOCTOR

WHEN IS THE BEST TIME TO PLANT A PATHWAY? Plant in spring in order to give plants plenty of time to begin rooting and growing before summer heat arrives. Water new plantings weekly if rain doesn't provide adequate moisture for them to become established.

TRADING LAWN FOR GARDEN

When mowing becomes a tedious chore, replace the grass with undemanding perennials.

Mingling assorted groundcovers and other spreading plants transforms a site into a diverse display of leaf color and form as well as flowers—something grass cannot do. Plants with different heights create a more artistic effect than a monoculture of grass.

All Kinds of Good Groundcovers

When you keep in mind that not all groundcovers are creeping or mat-forming plants, you'll see a multitude of plant possibilities in a new light. Perennials that spread readily without becoming obnoxiously weedy provide effective groundcovers. Use this list to help you identify good candidates for covering ground.

- Tolerate a range of soil types.
- Are easy to remove if they spread too far.
- Have interesting shapes, textures, and colors.
- Need little pruning, mowing, or grooming.

CHAPTER 6

GROWING FLOWERS AND FOLIAGE

Annual and perennial plants add beauty and other delightful effects to a garden as their textures, colors, and fragrances intermingle.

THE BASICS

Using basic techniques, you can plan and plant a beautiful, healthy garden and enjoy it too—trading minimum fuss for maximum satisfaction.

Flowers are what attract many to gardening. But blooms are fleeting, sometimes lasting only a day. Foliage carries the garden when there are few if any flowers. Gardens that include flowering and foliage plants put on a continually changing show, from emerging sprouts to buds, blooms, and seedheads. The interplay of plant heights, bloom times, and textures is part of a bigger picture.

Proven Performers

If trees, shrubs, and vines are the garden's hard-working stage crew, then perennials star while annuals fill the chorus line. Where a complete array of plants works together, rave reviews typically result.

Selected for overlapping bloom times, flowering plants can perform in waves from early spring through summer's hottest days and fall's coolest ones, until frost closes the show. Often chosen for their longevity, perennials unfurl new foliage and flowers each year, sometimes spreading into impressive colonies. Although annuals last for only one growing season, they're tapped for their endurance and sustained color from spring into fall.

Most perennials bloom only for a few weeks. Gardens planted only with perennials may experience lulls in flowering as the seasons change. But gardens that include colorful foliage and annuals boast a longer-lasting display.

Garden Dreams

Before you buy a plant or dig a hole, determine your goals for a flowering garden. Your rationale may involve problem-solving, such as transforming an area where grass won't grow, disguising an eyesore, or dressing a damp area with pretty plants. You may want to improve a view or attract more hummingbirds to the yard.

Half the fun is dreaming. But having a purpose saves time, money, and effort. Also, think about your personal preferences for the aesthetic attributes of plants. You may like the wild prairie look of massed perennials growing among ornamental grasses, or the serene effect of a white-flower, silver-foliage garden.

Grow what appeals to you, realizing that preferences change. Trees grow and create more shade. Plants die and give you an opportunity to try new ones.

COTTAGE GARDEN Flowering and foliage plants work magic in the garden, transforming an ordinary yard into a charming one.

TEST GARDEN TIP

TRIAL COMBOS Use a large container to try plant combinations you'd like to see in your garden, such as annuals and perennials with a small shrub, for a season. If the combo works, transplant it into the garden in early fall and replace the annuals next year.

FLOWER GARDEN SECRETS

Follow these guidelines to successful flower gardening. Enjoy the process, knowing that even the accidents of nature are sometimes gardening's greatest gifts.

■ **Know what you want.** Focus on your garden's purpose: Dress up the foundation. Attract butterflies. Grow flowers for cutting.

■ **Start small.** Gardening takes time, so be realistic about what you can manage. Work in stages over several years.

■ **Choose tough plants.** Select plants with long-season appeal, as well as tolerance to drought, pests, and diseases.

■ **Match plants to place.** Work with your site and choose plants adapted to the light, soil, and climate.

■ **Begin with good soil.** Great flowers grow in great soil. Organic material improves most soil.

GARDENING WITH ANNUALS

For sheer flower power, annuals excel. If you choose them for inexpensive, nearly instant color, you'll learn to love them for so much more.

Annuals live for the moment. They are genetically programmed to complete their life cycle—from seed to mature plant to seed again—within one year. By concentrating their energy into intense performance, these fast-growing and free-flowering plants can make your garden come alive with their colors.

Whether you choose annuals for their flowers or foliage, they come in almost any color, form, and size. No matter your growing conditions, there are annuals just right for your garden.

Annuals are among the most versatile of gardening tools. Use them to fulfill creative gardening goals.

Paint: Create bold swaths with mass plantings or make rich patterns with contrasting plants. Growing annuals allows you to change your mind and your garden's color scheme every growing season.

Weave: Tuck annuals among perennials to extend bloom times, bridge the seasons, refresh displays, and keep the color growing strong.

Experiment: Find your favorites among the newest improved varieties or old-fashioned beauties. Turn to some for their sweet scents and others for their cutting qualities.

Although some are sensitive to heat or chill, plenty of other annuals can keep up the growathon from frost to frost. Some annuals (cleome, bachelor's button, larkspur, and others) are such successful self-seeders, they act like perennials and return year after year. Others really are perennials, but their tropical origin and tender nature means they must be grown as annuals in temperate and colder climates.

Annuals are most budget friendly when you plant them from seeds. Flats or cell packs of seedlings from greenhouses and garden centers are also economical.

COMING RIGHT UP A flat of annual seedlings such as verbena gives you an economical way to add long-lasting color to the garden.

WHAT'S THE DIFFERENCE BETWEEN COOL- AND WARM-SEASON ANNUALS? Cool-season annuals (pansy, stock, twinspur) usually do best in cool soils during fall and spring. Where winters are mild, they can be planted in fall for early-spring blooms. Warm-season annuals (marigold, impatiens, angelonia) grow and flower best in warm months when there is no threat of frost.

EASIEST ANNUALS

The choice of annuals is so vast and versatile, you'll find a delightful variety to brighten any spot in your garden. Annuals will grow and bloom for any gardener. With their wide range of colors and heights, they allow great freedom in garden design and adapt to various planting times.

BEGONIA, WAX (*BEGONIA × SEMPERFLORENS*) This bedding plant forms 12-inch mounds with nonstop blooms in a range of conditions, from sun to shade.

COSMOS (*COSMOS*) These old-fashioned favorites, 18 to 48 inches tall, provide daisylike flowers for fresh arrangements. Sow seeds in warm garden soil.

GERANIUM (*PELARGONIUM × HORTORUM*) Easy and vigorous, these popular plants bloom abundantly in sun or light shade. Some varieties have showy or fragrant leaves.

IMPATIENS (*IMPATIENS*) The lush, mounded plants, in a range of heights and flower types, brighten shade with continuous color. Choose New Guinea types for sunny spots.

MARIGOLD (*TAGETES*) A dazzling array of types and forms from 6 to 30 inches tall for bedding, edging, cutting, pots, and kitchen gardens. Most marigolds have a pungent scent.

PANSY (*VIOLA*) Chilly weather brings out the best in charming pansies and their viola cousins. Choose from various faces and colors. Plant them in early fall or spring.

PETUNIA (*PETUNIA*) Dependable all-season bloomers, these hybrids offer amazing variations of flower color, pattern, and form on bushy or trailing plants.

SAGE, ANNUAL (*SALVIA*) Blue sage (*S. farinacea*) and scarlet sage (*S. splendens*) form ribbons of constant color in beds. The plants love sun, heat, and well-drained soil.

VINCA (*CATHARANTHUS ROSEUS*) For beds, borders, or baskets, this nonstop bloomer with glossy foliage is undaunted by heat and drought, and doesn't need deadheading.

ZINNIA (*ZINNIA*) Grow zinnias for their flowers, in an array of bright colors and sizes. They attract butterflies and hummingbirds, and make long-lasting bouquets.

PLANTING ANNUALS

When you grow annuals, every planting season is an opportunity for a new look and color scheme in your garden.

Many annuals are so simple to start from seeds that a child can do it. Planting annuals from seeds means you can start the gardening season indoors weeks before the trees have leafed out. You can line up a few pots on a sunny windowsill or sprout an entire garden from seed. Growing plants from seed saves money and does wonders for self-confidence.

Most plants bloom within 50 to 70 days after planting. Check the "days to maturity" on seed packets, then count backward on your calendar, starting with the last average frost date in your region, to determine the best time for seed sowing. If you live in a frost-free area, plant seeds in late winter or early spring. When seedlings have strong root systems that fill out their packs or pots, they're ready for transplanting.

Bedding plants—seedlings—are sold in multi-cell packs, multi-pack flats, and larger containers. These days, more gardeners choose to start with popular annuals in 4- or 6-inch pots for their instant-garden appeal. Bedding plants are ready for transplanting, like any seedlings, into prepared soil after frost threat has passed. Plant seedlings at the same level as they were growing in their nursery pots.

Water seedlings a day or two before transplanting because cells packs and small pots dry out quickly. If possible, plant on a cool, cloudy day because harsh sun, heat, or wind stresses seedlings. Otherwise, planting late on a sunny day allows the tender plants to acclimate overnight. Always water plants as soon as they're transplanted.

SOWING SEEDS

SOW DIRECTLY Calendula and some other annuals can be sown in warm, cultivated garden soil after frost danger has passed.

PROTECT SEEDLINGS Lay twigs over a seedbed to protect germinating seeds from hungry birds. Once the seedlings have two sets of leaves, remove the twigs.

POTTING UP SEEDLINGS

SEEDLING TO CELL When seedlings have developed at least two sets of mature leaves, pull them gently apart and plant each in its own cell of potting mix.

CELL TO POT When a seedling's root system fills a cell, move it into a pot to grow on. Transplant each seedling into a 3- or 4-inch pot and you'll have bigger, stronger (garden-ready) plants within a few weeks.

? ASK THE GARDEN DOCTOR **WHICH ANNUAL FLOWERS ARE EASIEST TO START FROM SEED?** Plants recommended for first-time seed starters include calendula, celosia, cosmos, marigold, pansy, sunflower, and zinnia. Varieties of these annuals can be sown directly in the garden.

GARDEN READY Most annuals are ready for transplanting six to eight weeks after they're sown from seeds. Transplants begin rooting and growing in the garden within a couple of weeks.

PLANTING ANNUALS IN A NEW BED

If your goal is to have masses of color in a hurry with minimal cost, rely on bedding plants for one dazzling summer-long show.

Bedding plants get their name from Victorian gardeners, who filled tidy beds with compact, colorful annuals in patterned rows. This still-popular approach to planting transforms a new bed into a carpet of color within weeks. Space plants closer together than recommended for faster effects and farther apart for economy.

A long list of annual all-stars, from ageratum to zinnia, stand up and spread their colors under the hottest sun. Most gardeners are limited to growing the varieties that local garden centers offer, but greenhouses often have a more varied selection. Every new gardening season brings a crop of new varieties with outstanding vigor, nonstop blooms, and fun new colors that combine easily.

Help bedding plants continue their show by shearing them by one third their size in mid- to late summer. Fertilize the plants and watch them bloom with renewed vigor.

① REMOVE PACKS Squeeze and release a seedling's root ball from a cell pack or pot. Set each seedling in place, spacing them as directed on the plant tag.

② PLACE PLANTS Equal spacing between plants and rows creates a uniform look. Use a trowel to make planting holes slightly larger than the plants' root balls.

③ PROMPT ROOTING Pinch off any flowers to prompt rooting. Sacrificing those blooms makes a difference in the new plantings' success.

④ WATER WELL Water each plant thoroughly after planting, using a transplant or starter solution (dilute plant food) to help plants overcome stress.

PLANTING ANNUALS IN AN ESTABLISHED BED

Mature beds benefit from added pops of annual color.

Makeover established beds by culling plants that are no longer welcome and replacing them with annuals. The newcomers will soon bloom and spread.

You can leave areas open in beds and fill them with annuals each year. Or tuck annuals in between perennials in maturing planting areas where the display will be enhanced by the temporary color. Dig carefully to avoid injuring the perennials' roots. Generously incorporate soil amendments before planting. Plant young annuals in groups of three or five to create massed effects.

AFTER A simple planting scheme uses orange-hued annuals—impatiens, coleus, and acalypha—to create warmth amid hostas and phlox.

BEFORE An ordinary-looking shade garden needs more color to relieves monotony. If you have a bed such as this, plan to cull existing plants and amend open ground with compost and rotted manure.

GROWING ANNUALS

Keep annuals flourishing throughout summer by giving them regular basic care. Help your annuals succeed with weekly deadheading and deep watering, and monthly feeding and weeding. Too-rich soil or too much water can promote lush foliage at the expense of flowers and result in weak roots or flopping plants. Usually only the tallest and most top-heavy plants need staking. Although annuals are generally trouble free, monitor your plants for signs of pests or diseases.

KEEP IT UP The slender, upright stems of lisianthus stand straight when given grow-through stakes.

MAKE IT FUN Try something new. Regular pinching turns common coleus into a fabulous tree-form standard.

TEST GARDEN TIP

GARDEN UNIFIER Choose one variety of foliage and plant it throughout your beds and containers to unify the entire garden. Raise or purchase multiples of the plant, depending on the size of your garden, and use them liberally. Chartreuse foliage works as a bright neutral, for instance.

BEDDING PLANTS
These annuals and tender perennials are among the most popular and easy-to-find plants. They won't survive frost but will turn your garden into a showcase for a long-blooming season.

GARDENING WITH PERENNIALS

Where there's a garden, there will be work and there will be pleasure. The trick is having a lovely garden where you can do the kind of gardening you enjoy most.

Just because perennials come back each year does not mean they are care free. But if you aim to keep your garden design simple and avoid prima donna plants, you can have a beautiful garden as well as plenty of time to sit back and enjoy it.

The Growing Garden

Plants change as they age, and their needs change too. A garden in infancy is filled with small, cute plants with lots of space between them. It may be hard to visualize a mature 'Sum and Substance' hosta reaching 7 feet across.

In an adolescent garden, plants may be lazy (overly floppy), moody (refusing to bloom), or obstinate (refusing to grow at all). In middle age, plants begin to mature; the garden fills in and looks spectacular. Eventually, plants lose their youthful good looks and no longer bloom well. The time comes for replacement, division, or other changes.

Perennial Challenges

Although perennials can be used to great advantage in any garden, they present challenges too. There are countless species of perennials and many plant-specific care techniques. The changing nature of a perennial garden requires ample space for plants to reach their potential. Some perennials can wreak havoc, spreading aggressively. All of these challenges are outweighed by perennials' beauty, longevity, and adaptability.

COLOR Start with a single-color scheme. Add hues to build one color family. Change it up with an accent color or neutral white.

TEXTURE Plants' touchable surfaces reflect or absorb light, creating textural effects. Leaf and flower shapes and sizes also play into this quality.

FORM Juxtapose plant shapes and sizes to give a garden variety, rhythm, balance, and scale. Repetition creates cohesiveness.

FOCAL POINT Choose a plant or an object (birdbath, arbor, planter) that draws the eye to rest. It must stand out, while the garden exists in relationship to it.

ASK THE GARDEN DOCTOR · **HOW CAN I SIMPLIFY THE DESIGN OF A PERENNIAL GARDEN?** When you're ready with a garden plan, start with a few long-lived plants, then find companions that complement, contrast, and flower in other time frames. Be sure to include perennials with striking foliage and small shrubs too. Your garden as a whole will ultimately be greater than each added part.

RELIABLE FLOWERING PERENNIALS

When you're planning a perennial garden, it's natural to focus on flowers for creating a colorful display throughout the growing season. Form the backbone of your garden with enduring bloomers such as these. Hardy plants with survivor instincts (tolerating drought, disease, and pests) should also top your plant list for an undemanding garden.

CATMINT (NEPETA)
Tolerating heat, drought, wind, and foot traffic, catmint grows easily in Zones 4-10 and boasts mounds of fragrant foliage and lasting flowers.

CONEFLOWER (ECHINACEA)
Tough and fuss-free in Zones 3–10, coneflowers beckon butterflies, bees, and birds with their blooms summer through fall.

COREOPSIS (COREOPSIS)
Easy growing and long blooming, the plants tolerate heat and drought but flop over in rich, wet soil in Zones 4-10. Deadhead to encourage flowers.

DAYLILY (HEMEROCALLIS)
The robust plants can cope with nearly any growing condition, but they're susceptible to hungry deer, rabbits, and slugs. Zones 3-11.

IRIS (IRIS)
Iris grow from bulbs or rhizomes. They include bearded and beardless groups in the spring-summer bloom season. Many are hardy in Zones 3-8.

PHLOX (PHLOX)
Various species bloom lavishly in nearly every season in Zones 2–9. Plant mildew-resistant varieties of tall garden phlox.

PENSTEMON (PENSTEMON)
The flowers attract hummingbirds. Plant it in drifts, with crowns planted just above soil level, for a strong flower show in Zones 2-10.

SAGE (SALVIA)
Valued for its long bloom season from spring to fall, this tough plant tolerates heat, drought, and humidity in Zones 4-10.

SPIKE SPEEDWELL (VERONICA)
Easy to grow for long-season color from summer until frost, it's a natural choice for cottage or wildlife gardens in Zones 4-10.

YARROW (ACHILLEA)
This hardy North American native has ferny foliage that deer and rabbits resist eating. It's fast growing and drought tolerant for Zones 2-10.

PLANTING PERENNIALS

Planting is easy, but attention to detail makes the difference between plants that thrive and those that merely survive.

Because perennials grow in the same spot for years, it's essential to prepare the soil. Work in loads of organic amendments and make it well draining.

Start perennials from seeds, bare roots, or plants. Or start from divisions or cuttings gleaned from friends or neighbors. Planting requirements vary for each plant, but a few general parameters apply to all.

The best times to plant are when soil and weather conditions favor strong root growth. Spring and early fall planting give plants time to establish roots before summer or winter arrive.

Dig planting holes twice as wide as the plants' root balls. Loosen the sides and bottom of the planting hole to help roots spread. Set the crowns of most plants at soil level. If planted too deep, the plant can rot.

Avoid planting in static rows, placing plants in triangles or staggering them for more pleasing results. Leave enough space between plants for root growth, air circulation, and mature growth. Plants set too close together will compete for water and nutrients, eventually crowd one another, and require transplanting or division.

PLANTING A BARE-ROOT PERENNIAL

Dormant perennials sold without soil have bare roots and need to be planted as early as possible in spring. If the bare roots you purchase have become mushy or dried out, ask the vendor for a replacement. If it's too early in the season to dig in the garden, plant bare roots in pots and keep the soil barely moist. This example shows a bleeding heart (perennial) planting.

❶ **PREPARE TO PLANT** Dig a planting hole and amend the soil. Form a mound at the bottom of the planting hole.

❷ **PLACE THE BARE ROOT** When set on the mound, the bare root should be at the right depth, with the growing tips or crown at soil level.

❸ **SATURATE SOIL** Fill in the planting hole and mark the spot with a plant label. Water thoroughly, then apply a layer of mulch.

ASK THE GARDEN DOCTOR **CAN I MOVE A PLANT TO ANOTHER PART OF THE GARDEN WHEN IT IS FLOWERING?** If you decide that a plant should be planted in another spot, dig it up and transplant it after it has finished blooming. This is less stressful for the plant. Mark a spot in the garden where you want to relocate it, then transplant at an optimal time: late summer or early spring.

SPECIAL SITUATIONS

Some plants have special planting needs.

Perennials with taproots (butterfly weed, columbine, cushion spurge, Oriental poppy) that grow straight down from the crown typically resent transplanting. Take extra care to plant them deeply without damaging or disturbing their roots.

Other plants fare best when provided with especially well-draining conditions from the start. Plants such as lavender and spring-flowering bulbs originated in rocky, fast-draining places; they benefit from a gravelly planting place.

Planting can be stressful for any plant, so handle each one with care and avoid cutting or tearing roots.

MARK THE SPOT Labeling new plantings helps you remember plants' names as well as those which may need extra water.

NURSERY PLANTS Small, young perennial seedlings benefit from nurserying, or growing in bigger pots for a season.

WELL-DRAINING SOIL Grit and gravel help improve clay soil and make it possible to plant lavender, bulbs, and other plants that need well-draining soil.

IMPROVING DRAINAGE Poor drainage can kill plants. Add handfuls of drainage-improving mix to a planting hole or more to a larger planting area.

PERENNIAL PROGRESS Nurtured throughout spring in a nursery pot until it reaches garden-ready size, a foxglove transplant can be moved into the garden where it will bloom in summer.

PLANTING A NEW PERENNIAL BED

A first-year perennial garden appears spare when planted with young nursery plants in 4-inch pots. To achieve a mature look sooner, start with some more fully developed plants in larger nursery pots, include a few shrubs, and fill bare spots with annuals.

By the second year, the perennial garden will be well on its way to maturity and annuals will be needed only minimally for spots of added color. The bed design, based on a color scheme of purple, pink, and chartreuse, remains unified with or without annuals.

1 PLACE PLANTS Following your planting plan, set the plants (still in their nursery pots) in place. Adjust the spacing, giving each plant the room it needs to mature.

2 DIG HOLE Match the digging tool to the job: trowel for small holes, spade or shovel for large ones. Dig the hole only as deep as the root ball and twice as wide.

3 LOOSEN ROOTS Remove the nursery pot. If the roots have filled the pot and appear tangled, gently squeeze them to loosen the mass before planting.

4 ALMOST DONE Place the plant at the appropriate planting depth: at ground level for most perennials. Backfill the planting hole, making the soil even with the surrounding bed.

5 DRINKS FOR ALL Water deeply after planting. New plants need about 1 inch of water weekly to root and establish. Spread a 2-inch layer of mulch between plants.

6 TWO MONTHS LATER The annuals reach their peak; perennials and shrubs have become well established. Remove and compost the annuals at the season's end.

STAKING PERENNIALS

Stake tall or floppy plants to keep them upright and prevent damage from plants falling over. Many of the best supports do their job invisibly; others add a decorative touch.

Preventive staking entails planning and placing a support in early spring before the plant has grown enough to need it. Some plants have inherently thin or weak stems or heavy blooms, which invariably need support to remain upright (aster, goldenrod, showy sedum).

Once in place, many supports disappear among foliage and act unobtrusively. Small branches and twigs saved from pruning trees and shrubs provide natural stakes. Choose sturdy supports designed to endure weather without rusting or rotting, such as bamboo stakes or hoops made of powder-coated, heavy-gauge wire.

STURDY STEMS Grow sturdy plants next to those with weaker stems or heavy flowers that tend to flop. The plants will lean on each other for support.

GROW THROUGH
Stems of clump-forming plants such as peony grow up and through the flat, open support. The support must be installed early in the growing season.

SINGLE STAKE A green bamboo stake, when loosely tied, supports the tall, slender stems of delphinium. A bauble, small overturned pot, or other stake topper eliminates an eye-poking hazard.

UNWIELDY PLANTS Staking a very large or tall plant (such as martagon lily) can be a challenge. Even if your staking looks odd or is done late, it will still work.

LOOP STAKE Similar to a tomato cage, a hoop helps yarrow and other clumping plants, even if a plant has already flopped over. In time, the plant will regain its upright stature.

ASK THE GARDEN DOCTOR

HOW CAN I AVOID THE HAZARD THAT COMES WITH A SHARP STAKE? The tops of some stakes pose a threat of poking a gardener's eye when one bends over in the garden. Hidden in foliage, slender and green stakes prove especially difficult to see before it's too late. Eliminate the hazard by topping a stake with a visible object.

GROWING FOLIAGE PLANTS

Most gardeners are smitten first with flowers, but over time, an appreciation for foliage plants deepens and often grows into a lasting passion. It's no wonder.

Leaves weave tapestries of shapes, textures, and hues in ways that flowers cannot. Colorful flowers grab attention, but they come and go. Foliage creates long-lasting beauty in sun or shade and needs no deadheading—more glory with less work.

Foliage creates balance among the bloomers. It also works independently. Foliage-only combinations prove entirely harmonious and satisfying. Even better, foliage is dependable on an ongoing basis, bringing its strengths to the garden from spring through fall.

Foliage patterns enable you to contrast leaf sizes—from the tiniest of groundcovers to the massive lobes of tropicals—and overall plant forms.

FOLIAGE FOR SHADE This scheme includes hostas, ferns, and browallia along with sedge, goatsbeard, and dead nettle.

Foliage challenges you to see how it illuminates shady spaces. Choose leaves with silver, bronze, or another metallic hue to reflect light and act as surprising unifiers when repeated in the garden. Explore the gamut of greens, from chartreuse to blue-green, plus purple, orange, and other leaf colors.

ALL-STARS FOR SHADE

In the universe of foliage plant possibilities, these three shine with stellar proportions in shade.

CORAL BELLS The genus *Heuchera* includes a kaleidoscope of leafy colors, forms, and tinted patterns. Plant in sun to part shade.

FERN Hardy ferns grow 1 to 4 feet tall and thrive in varying shade, especially if given enriched, well-drained, damp soil. Hardiness varies by species.

HOSTA Prized for their array of leaf colors, sizes, and textures, hostas flaunt flowers too. Use these versatile shade plants as accents or en masse.

? ASK THE GARDEN DOCTOR **WHICH FLOWERS GO WELL TOGETHER?** If you're unsure about trying a new plant combination, gather a leaf from each of the prospects and get a clearer picture of how they will work together. At the nursery or garden center, group potted plants in a shopping cart to see whether they create a satisfying effect.

FUSS-FREE FOLIAGE

The leafy portion of plants plays a larger role in gardens than many realize. On the other hand, hostas, ornamental grasses, and other foliage families are the stuff of many plant collectors' dreams. Whether you're well acquainted with their finer qualities or not, these are a few favorites from the leafy realm.

BUGLEWEED (AJUGA) Quick-growing varieties create a dense mat. Flower spikes form on low-growing leaves in part sun to shade; Zones 3–11.

CALADIUM (CALADIUM) The color-splashed foliage brings drama to shade throughout summer. These tropicals grown from tubers must spend cold winters indoors.

CANNA (CANNA) These easy-to-grow tropical bloomers have large paddle-shape leaves and reach 4 to 10 feet tall. Dig and store the rhizomes indoors over winter. Zones 7–10.

DEAD NETTLE (LAMIUM) Cultivated for its chartreuse or silver-variegated leaves with season-long color, this ground-covering perennial also blossoms in spring. Zones 3–9.

COLEUS (SOLENOSTEMON SCUTELLARIOIDES) Once limited to sun-averse varieties, this genus of extroverted tropical plants includes hybrids adapted to sun and shade.

DUSTY MILLER (SENECIO CINERARIA) A compact, bushy annual with silver leaves, it reaches 8 to 16 inches tall. There are several varieties with different leaf forms.

MAIDEN GRASS (MISCANTHUS) Among the splendid ornamental grasses, this genus includes many pretty sprays from 4 to 6 feet tall with dramatic autumn plumes. Zones 4–9.

ORNAMENTAL KALE (BRASSICA OLERACEA) This colorful annual perks up plantings when temperatures tumble. It prefers sun to part shade and moist soil.

DRACAENA (DRACAENA) Also known as corn plant or spike, this tropical has narrow arching leaves and varying forms. Some varieties have stripes.

GROWING SPRING-FLOWERING BULBS

Plant hardy bulbs in fall to enjoy their beauty in spring. The keys to success: Choose planting areas with well-draining soil that will receive plenty of sun in spring.

Hardy bulbs stay in the ground over winter and bloom in spring. Tulips and daffodils are the hands-down favorites, but many lesser-known delights await fall planting. You can plant up until the ground freezes but it's better to give bulbs a chance to begin rooting by planting in fall after the soil has cooled to 40 to 50°F.

Naturalizing Bulbs

Many bulbs will multiply and prosper for years—naturalize—if planted well. Plant drifts of a dozen or more bulbs under deciduous trees, in lawns, or in rock gardens. Planting bulbs in loose groups randomly placed, rather than in soldier-straight lines, creates a natural effect.

Here are a few other tips to help you plant bulbs and ensure their success:

Choose bulbs suited to your region's climate.

Improve the soil's drainage by covering the bottom of the planting hole with gravel or sand.

Place a 2-inch tulip bulb at least 6 inches deep—pointy end up. The planting depth should be three times the bulb's height.

Plant bulbs to bloom in natural-looking clusters. Position groups of seven or more bulbs randomly in planting holes with their points up.

Remove spent flowers but allow foliage to ripen, turn yellow and brown, and wither before mowing or cutting it. The leaves provide food for the bulbs—and next year's flowers.

DIG HOLES Use a shovel or spade to dig planting holes big enough to hold a handful of bulbs.

PLANTING DEPTH Plant bulbs three times as deep as their height. Shown: Species tulip bulbs planted 3 inches deep.

SPRINKLE GRAVEL Protect bulbs from hungry critters, especially if squirrels, chipmunks, and burrowing rodents are a problem in your region.

PROTECT BULBS Another method of protecting bulbs from furry munchers: Enclose bulbs in hardware cloth or chicken wire.

COVER BULBS Mark the planting area with a golf tee to avoid digging there.

ASK THE GARDEN DOCTOR **WHY DON'T MY TULIPS AND DAFFODILS COME BACK EVERY SPRING?** Some hardy bulbs return each spring. Many varieties of daffodils, scilla, and species tulips naturalize (multiply and spread) on their own. Hybrid tulips, hyacinths, and others bloom for a year or two and then do not return again because the nutrients in the bulbs are depleted, causing the bulbs to decline in vigor.

FAVORITE HARDY BULBS

Among the easiest types of garden plants to grow, bulbs perform their amazing magic with minimal attention. Bulbs planted in clusters and en masse make the biggest impression, so be generous when you plant. If you must store bulbs before fall planting time arrives, keep them temporarily in a cool, dry, dark place such as the basement.

ALLIUM *(ALLIUM)*
Long-lasting ornamental onions vary from low-growing star shapes to hip-high giant asterisks. Some are hardier than others.

CROCUS *(CROCUS)*
Signaling the end of winter, these bright and early bloomers rise 4 to 6 inches tall and shine year after year. Plant fall-blooming crocuses too.

DAFFODIL *(NARCISSUS)*
Countless variations trumpet spring with early- to late-season blooms: short or tall, bright or pastel, sweet scented or subtle, and more.

FRITILLARIA *(FRITILLARIA)*
Species differ in size, color, and overall form, but all have bell-shape flowers. Each brings dramatic character to the garden.

TULIP *(TULIPA)* So many types, so little time to tiptoe through the early-, mid-, and late-season varieties. Hardy species tulips return for years most reliably and even naturalize.

GRAPE HYACINTH *(MUSCARI)*
Blue, purple, or white grapelike flowers on 6-inch stems grow easily. Plant dozens of them to form exquisite drifts. They make good cut flowers.

HYACINTH *(HYACINTHUS ORIENTALIS)*
Few flowers can match the perfume of these stocky 6- to 10-inch bloom stalks. A range of colors combine beautifully with other spring bloomers.

GROWING SUMMER-FLOWERING BULBS

Grace your garden with some of summer's most glorious flowers and lavish foliage.

Most summer-flowering bulbs are tender by nature and cannot survive cold winters without protection. Still, these exceptional plants are well worth growing.

In warm-climate zones, summer bulbs perform as perennials. At season's end in frosty areas, you can dig and save summer bulbs indoors over winter—or not. Grow them as annuals, if you prefer. Or grow them in pots and winter the pots indoors.

However you grow them, summer bulbs are especially easy and rewarding. Plant once the weather is dependably warm, then wait for vibrant colors, bold textures, and sweet scents to develop. Summer heat encourages their performance. If summer is short in your area, start bulbs in a pot to get a head start on the growing season, then transplant into warm garden soil in late spring.

To protect summer bulbs from frost, gently dig and lift them with a garden fork or small shovel. Shake or brush off excess soil. Snip the remaining stems to 4 inches or so. Rinse the bulbs and let them air-dry for a few days. Pack the bulbs into a box of damp peat moss and store it away from heat and cold until spring.

IN POTS In spring, plant lily bulbs in gallon pots and keep the soil damp. When plants develop and emerge from the soil, transplant them into the garden.

IN THE GROUND In fall or spring, plant lily bulbs. When they bloom, fertilize the plants to encourage their return next year.

TYPES OF LILIES

Dazzling trumpetlike lily flowers are the backbone of a summer garden. Their heights range from 12 inches to 6 feet. Select varieties for a parade of blooms from June to September in well-drained fertile soil and full sun: Asiatic hybrids (June and July), Martagon (June and July), Oriental hybrids (July and August), and Trumpet (July and August).

ELEPHANT'S EAR: tuber **LILY:** bulb **CALLA LILY:** rhizome **CANNA:** rhizome **DAHLIA:** tuber

ASK THE GARDEN DOCTOR

WHEN IS THE BEST TIME TO PLANT LILIES? Plant hardy lily bulbs in early fall (the preferred season) or spring, in well-drained fertile soil and full sun. When plants emerge, spread mulch among them to help retain soil moisture.

SUPER SUMMER BULBS

Summer bulbs grow from tubers, rhizomes, or tuberous roots as well as bulbs. Use the tropical look of the plants to your advantage, making a garden rendition of a favorite tropical vacation spot, complete with fragrant tuberoses, lush tuberous begonias, and nodding elephant ears. Try different summer bulbs to find your favorites.

CANNA (CANNA) Reaching 3 to 6 feet or more, this showy tropical has torchlike blooms and large sculpted leaves; colors depend on the variety. Cannas are hardy to Zone 7.

CALADIUM (CALADIUM) Grown for its flamboyant foliage, caladium grow to 30 inches tall. Some varieties require shade; other tolerate a few hours of sun daily. They're hardy in Zones 9 and higher.

CALLA LILY (ZANTEDESCHIA) Colorful leaves (not flowers) unroll in white, yellow, hues of pink, and more. Grow in sun to light shade. The rhizomes are hardy to Zone 8.

DAHLIA (DAHLIA) For drama in bold colors, choose from a range of bloom types and plant heights. Some need support. The tubers do best in rich, sandy loam. They're hardy to Zone 8.

ELEPHANT'S EAR (ALOCASIA, COLOCASIA, AND XANTHOSOMA) The massive leaves dance on 3- to 6-foot stems in part sun or shade and create a tropical vibe. It's excellent in a pot or a water garden.

PINEAPPLE LILY (EUCOMIS) If you want to dazzle your friends, grow this South African native in a pot and enjoy its long-lasting pineapple-like blooms. Grow it in full to part sun; in gardens in Zones 7–10.

GROWING A SHADE GARDEN

A well-planted shaded garden can be just as appealing as a sun-drenched one. Low-light conditions suit a range of beautiful plants, from annuals and perennials to shrubs and small trees.

A wide selection of wonderful plants can join the standard hostas and impatiens in a shade garden. Some of the most outstanding plants include those with bright or textural foliage (fern, coleus, lungwort) or colorful flowers (columbine, foxglove, astilbe). Plants respond to differing light levels, so observe seasonal light patterns, then choose and situate plants according to the amount and quality of light they'll receive.

Shade is a broad term with nuances. Light or dappled shade comes through lattice or an open-canopied tree for four to eight hours a day. Heavy shade is found under a dense-foliage tree or on the north side of a house, wall, or fence. Plants receive less than four hours of light a day in full shade.

Areas of shade may be particularly damp or dry, depending on the soil and prevalence of nearby trees. The type of shade also guides plant selection, as some may prefer one situation and won't tolerate the other.

Some trees (walnut, butternut) produce a natural substance—juglone—that discourages plants from growing under them. Plants that are sensitive to juglone can be damaged or killed by it.

COOL SHADE Instead of planting under a tree, plant nearby. Then pull a couple of chairs into the shade and enjoy the view from there.

SEDGE (CAREX) Similar to ornamental grasses, sedges prefer moist, shaded areas. Try variegated and chartreuse types in Zones 5–9.

LUNGWORT (PULMONARIA) Plants have silver- or white-streaked or spotted foliage and spring blooms. Grow in damp soil; Zones 4–8.

ASTILBE (ASTILBE) This summer bloomer has feathery flowers and rugged foliage. Plants reach 2 to 4 feet tall in part to full shade; Zones 4–8.

GROWING A NATIVE-PLANT GARDEN

Plants native to a geographic area or type of habitat are tough, colorful, and self-sufficient. They attract and sustain butterflies, birds, and bees.

Natives include the wildflowers flourishing along mountain streams, shrubs basking in the dappled light at the edge of a woodland, tall perennial flowers, and grasses deeply rooted in prairie soil. All of these and many more natives can adapt gracefully to similar conditions in a cultivated place.

Once established, native plants thrive without pampering. But before you plant, understand the processes that take place in the native setting. Then choose plants or seed mixtures that target the land, factoring in moisture levels, sunlight patterns, and the degree and direction of slope. Focus on adaptable plants before considering colors and aesthetics.

A large plot is not necessary. Simply adding native plants to your garden helps nature happen no matter where you live. With natives, the garden evolves and works for the location. The curbside strip of prairie plants shown is one of the many native plant schemes possible.

BUTTERFLY BUFFET This garden includes food plants for caterpillars and butterflies with pollen- and nectar-rich flowers (bee balm, queen anne's lace, joe-pye weed).

SWITCH GRASS *(PANICUM VIRGATUM)* This dynamic ornamental grass adds movement and seasonal change to a garden. Grow it in Zones 4–9.

GOLDENROD *(SOLIDAGO)* Contrary to common belief, the long-lasting summer flowers do not trigger hay fever. It's a sturdy plant for Zones 3–9.

BUTTERFLY WEED *(ASCLEPIAS TUBEROSA)* This native perennial needs heat to prosper and flower in Zones 4–9.

GROWING A DRY GARDEN

Drought-tolerant plants thrive in hot, dry conditions. They keep a garden looking fresh, colorful, and even lush where rain is rare and water is conserved.

Choosing appropriate plants for a dry garden is the first step in growing success. Many water-wise plants grown today originally hailed from the Mediterranean or arid West. It's not by chance that some plants flourish as the temperature rises and the soil dries out. Drought-tolerant plants may have deep taproots, water-storing roots or leaves, or woolly or silvery leaves. All of these adaptations help the plants maximize available water and minimize moisture loss.

New plants need regular watering until they're established. Water as needed to sustain plants during the first year. Water during dry spells after that. A 2-inch layer of compost or other organic mulch slows evaporation and also helps moderate soil temperatures. Avoid overwatering, which can encourage lush foliage and shallow roots.

Fertilizer is unnecessary in a dry garden. It promotes leafy growth and makes plants more vulnerable in tough conditions.

COLOR RICH Drought-tolerant perennials weave a tapestry of colors and textures in this rocky, sunbaked bed along a driveway. The plant roster includes helianthemum, sedum, salvia, lavender, and artemisia.

STONECROP (SEDUM)
With succulent foliage, discreet flowers, and all-season good looks, numerous varieties of the groundcover grow easily in Zones 3–9.

LAVENDER (LAVANDULA)
The clump-forming plants grow in a 2-foot mound of gray foliage; Zones 5–10. Shear plants after blooming to prompt new growth.

BLANKET FLOWER (GAILLARDIA)
The loosely upright or sprawling plants reach 2 feet tall in Zones 3–9. Colorful flowers bloom into fall. Deadhead for neatness.

GROWING A RAIN GARDEN

Typically made in shallow depressions of the landscape, rain gardens are designed to catch storm runoff from roofs, driveways, patios, and other hard surfaces.

As more and more land is paved for roads, parking lots, housing developments, and buildings, big rains cause increasing problems, from boggy soil and wet basements to flooding, erosion, and water pollution. Rain gardens can help.

Where there is a rain garden, the water seeps naturally into the ground instead of running into the street and on into local rivers or lakes. A rain garden prevents pollution by filtering runoff, decreases flooding, refreshes groundwater supplies, and increases habitat for wildlife. Ideal for sunny, low areas where water gathers naturally, rain gardens can be formed as a shallow low point off to one side of the yard or at the base of a slope—but not near your home's foundation.

The best plants for a rain garden are native perennials that thrive in soggy soil but can ride out dry spells too, because rain gardens are dry most of the time. Most plants do not tolerate extremes of moisture or poorly aerated soil.

SOAKING RAIN Compared with a conventional lawn, a rain garden allows about 30 percent more water to soak into the ground. This garden harbors native prairie plants and runoff from a nearby downspout.

BEE BALM *(MONARDA DIDYMA)*
A tough perennial for sun to part shade in Zones 3–9, it blooms in summer and spreads. Choose a powdery mildew-resistant variety.

BLACK-EYED SUSAN *(RUDBECKIA)*
Grow this 2- to 4-foot-tall perennial in full sun and well-draining average soil; Zones 3–9. Choose a hardy species such as *R. fulgida.*

IRIS, BLUE FLAG *(IRIS VERSICOLOR)*
Native to lakeshores and bogs, this 1- to 2-foot-tall perennial prefers full sun to part shade in Zones 3–9. It flowers in spring.

GATHERING YOUR GARDEN FLOWERS

Fresh bouquets bring instant cheer indoors for all to enjoy. Gathering a bunch of blooms from your garden can be as simple as it looks.

No training is necessary to pick posies and plunk them into vases. Snip what you like. Flowers are inherently beautiful. You don't need a plan for arranging them. Let the plant materials and your eye create casual displays.

Few gardeners have the luxury of a cutting garden devoted solely to growing blossoms for display. But you might be surprised how much potential material lives in your yard, from flowers to foliage, berries, branch tips, and seedheads. When adding plants to your garden, also consider their cutting potential.

Gathering bouquets from your garden has other benefits. Cutting flowers stimulates most annuals and many perennials to produce more blooms. If you cut short branches from flowering shrubs (forsythia, lilac, hydrangea), you won't need to prune them as much later. Also, wandering around the yard with a bucket of water and pruners in hand gives you a chance to visit plants closely and check for progress or potential problems.

Conditioning Stems

Gather flowers during early morning or evening to ensure their peak moisture content. Cut stems using clean, sharp pruners or a knife. Immediately plunge the cut stems into a bucket of cool water. Bring the bucket indoors and let the flowers stand for at least one hour to take up water—this is called conditioning—before arranging them in a vase of fresh water. Conditioning helps flowers last longer.

Mix and match flowers as you like. Keep it super simple by gathering a single-plant bouquet (try zinnias only) or one color and its hues (try yellows only). Foliage adds a lush finishing touch. Use colorful or fragrant leaves, such as hosta, coleus, or scented geranium for special effects.

SPRING FLOWERS Possibilities include daffodil, peony, bleeding heart, columbine, and sweet pea for your first-of-the-season cuttings.

SUMMER FLOWERS Grow zinnia, tansy, delphinium, foxglove, poppy, nicotiana, geranium, and lisianthus for bright displays.

FALL FLOWERS Choose from snapdragon, coneflower, salvia, dahlia, cosmos, and ornamental grasses for autumn bouquets.

ASK THE GARDEN DOCTOR **HOW CAN I MAKE CUT FLOWERS LAST LONGER?** Sprinkle floral preservative powder into the vase water before you add the flowers. Keep the water fresh by changing it every other day and adding preservative powder again. When you change the water, lift the flowers from the vase and give them a fresh cut, slicing off the bottom inch of their stems.

KEEPING FLOWERS FRESH

Once you have gathered flowers from the garden, give your bouquets staying power. Follow these simple steps to help flowers last longer.

START CLEAN Before placing stems in a vase, remove any lower leaves that might rot underwater.

SNIP OFTEN At each water change, snip up to 1 inch off the bottom of each stem. Cutting at an angle lets the flower take up more water.

MULTIPLE BOUQUETS Use your fresh flowers to make several small bouquets instead of one large display. Set them around the house or share them with friends.

WHAT TO DO AFTER PLANTS BLOOM

Removing spent flowers encourages many plants to rebloom and makes your garden appear neater, among other benefits.

Most annuals increase flowering after deadheading. Perennials that bloom on leaf-bearing stems also keep producing flowers when deadheaded. Cutting back some perennials, such as catmint, blanket flower, and geranium, promotes a second flush of flowers and a denser habit later in summer.

Snap off flowers with succulent stems that break easily, or use pruners to cut withered stalks at their base. Remove only faded flowers, leaving buds to produce the next wave of blooms.

Some plants don't need deadheading. Attractive seedheads of ornamental grasses and other perennials can be left over winter to add interest to the garden. Also leave seedheads to develop if you want to collect seeds or let the plants self-sow.

THE SHOW GOES ON *Salvia splendens* is one of the many annuals that benefit from deadheading. After deadheading, it reblooms within a couple of weeks.

1 TIME FOR TRIMMING When blooms fade, turn brown, wither, or otherwise appear unattractive, it's time to trim them off.

2 PINCH OR CUT Sever the stem at its base, using a thumbnail or pruner to make a clean cut and avoid tearing the stem.

3 NEXT UP Removing blooms signals new buds to develop. It also stimulates more profuse blooming.

? ASK THE GARDEN DOCTOR **WHY BOTHER DEADHEADING ANNUALS THAT BLOOM REPEATEDLY ON THEIR OWN?**
Deadheading promotes more-continuous blooms among annuals and some perennials. In particular, it prevents the plants from producing seeds and extends their bloom cycle. If you don't deadhead annuals, they will most likely complete their life cycle sooner.

TEST GARDEN TIP

SELF-CLEANING PLANTS Sterile plants that do not produce seed will bloom continuously without deadheading. More of these self-cleaning plants are being bred, including varieties of calibrachoa, petunia, lobelia, and bidens.

FLOWERS' FINISH Cut the stems of spent daffodils and other flowering bulbs. Leave the foliage to wither naturally and help feed next year's flowers.

PINCH AN INCH Remove the tips of some plants (heliopsis, chrysanthemum, bee balm) in spring and early summer to maximize branching later.

PROLIFIC SEEDHEADS The flowers of some plants (garlic chives, columbine) develop seedheads and sow themselves with abandon unless you cut off the seedheads.

SOFT STEMS Pinch or snip a stem near ground level after the flower fades to promote new growth (pansy and other annuals, penstemon, veronica).

TOUGH STALKS Use sharp pruners to cut a stem just above a leaf or set of leaves or at the base of the flower stem (lily, peony, phlox).

MULTIPLE STEMS Shear the tops of plants with lots of small flowers (coreopsis, dianthus, shasta daisy) just above foliage level.

FALL CLEANUP

Help your flowering and foliage plants survive winter's ravages and get a good start in spring using these tips.

As autumn's golden light begins to slant through the garden, perennial growth slows, leaves turn color, and seedpods form. Before cold weather sets in, clean the garden and tuck in plants for their winter's sleep.

Early fall offers an ideal planting opportunity. Root growth excels during autumn, with cooler temperatures, sunny days, and dependable rain. In mild climates, almost any type of perennial can be planted successfully. In cold climates, plant hardy perennials, such as bee balm, penstemon, peony, veronica, and yarrow. Come spring, the new plants will have established root systems and be ready to take off into their first full growing season.

 Rake leaves out of beds, chop them, and mulch beds with the bits.

GET A MOVE ON Start cutting stems of perennials and annuals that have browned. Discard any parts from diseased plants to prevent spreading disease.

GOODBYE, ANNUALS
Remove spent annuals when they're withered, browned, or killed by frost, and compost the remains. Tuck in cold-tolerant pansies or kale as replacements.

PERENNIAL CARE Cut back perennials whose form will not persist through the winter. Leave seedheads for winter interest or sustenance for birds.

RECYCLE GERANIUMS
Before frost, lift well-watered geraniums, shake off soil, and cut back tops by one-third. Store each plant in a paper bag indoors over the winter.

SAVE SUMMER BULBS
Tender bulbs, such as dahlia and calla lily, must be dug and stored indoors over winter. Gently remove soil and nestle bulbs into a box of damp vermiculite.

 **ASK THE GARDEN DOCTOR**   **DO I NEED TO CLEAN UP FALLEN LEAVES BEFORE WINTER?** Left on beds or lawn, leaves mat down over winter. They can smother plants and prevent adequate moisture from reaching roots. Rake up leaves and add them to the compost pile. By spring, the transformation will be complete: You'll have a free soil amendment.

SPRING: PREPARING FOR A NEW SEASON

As winter wears on, spring can't come early enough for many gardeners. But if you live in a cold climate, resist the urge to remove protective winter covers too early in the season. Wait until any chance of freezing weather has passed. Avoid stepping on wet soil; wait until it dries before digging.

REMOVE COVERS Clear away excess fallen leaves when perennials have emerged and begun leafing out. Compost the debris.

CLEAR CUT Remove spent portions of herbaceous perennials that were left over winter. Some plants remain mostly green over winter and need only tidying.

CUT DOWN Herbaceous perennials such as peonies that die to the ground in winter will reemerge in spring and signal cleanup time. Cut and clear away spent plants.

CUT BACK Woody perennials such as Russian sage need trimming only to remove browned stems and leaves. Wait until midspring when new growth shows before cutting.

CHECK FOR LIFE Woody perennials and late-season plants leaf out later than others. Avoid cutting them down because they appear dead. Nick the bark near the ground and look for green—it's alive.

TIDY GRASSES Left to stand over winter, ornamental grasses add interest to a garden. Before new growth begins in spring, cut them to an inch above ground level, using grass shears or hedge trimmers.

BUSY SEASONS Accomplish garden chores the easy way—bit by bit—during the busiest times of spring and fall. Avoid the urge to get it all done at once. Instead of pushing to finish, simply enjoy the process.

CHAPTER 7

GROWING TREES AND SHRUBS

Enhance the beauty and value of your home's landscape with some of the most varied and easy-care plants of all.

CHOOSING YOUR IDEAL TREES

Understanding trees' potential will help you make good plant and site selections—as well as some of the best landscape investments possible.

Trees establish the framework of your home's landscape and create a personal skyline. They team with shrubs to add beauty through the seasons with foliage, flower, and form. Trees make living areas outdoors and indoors more comfortable. They provide privacy and shelter, shade and wind protection. As homes for birds and other wildlife—as well as rope swings—trees are valuable.

Trees work together and individually to make unique yards that also blend into neighborhoods and towns. Rooting communities with their continuity, trees mark the seasons and bring people together to plant and make memories.

Planting for Posterity

Because most yards have room for only a few long-lived trees, it pays to make the most of existing ones and choose new trees carefully. Some trees don't grow fast enough for impatient gardeners. Yet fast-growing varieties (silver maple, poplar, sycamore, arborvitae) involve trade-offs that include weak wood, loads of litter, pest problems, and less longevity.

A large tree is the only garden investment you can make that will increase in size, value, and usefulness as long as you live—and then some. Once chosen and planted, trees become a living legacy and an essential part of the environment. They need occasional care over the years to be their best.

Matching Trees to Your Yard

Select trees through a process of informed elimination. Ideal trees look good in all seasons and suit the conditions of soil, light, and climate in your garden. Decide what's important to you: Consider the season and color of bloom, bark, branching habit, berries, wildlife appeal, and seasonal foliage color.

Make a list of prospective trees and research each variety to ensure its suitability. Measure the tree's prospective site, ensuring that the tree will have adequate growing room, to avoid planting a problem. Visit a nursery and compare your yard's conditions with the plant label descriptions. Choose trees that can reach maturity within these parameters. Note the potential amount of sun, the wind direction and intensity, seasonal temperature extremes, and precipitation at the planting site. Also evaluate varieties in terms of their ease of maintenance.

SPECIAL TALENTS Consider prospective trees' unique qualities. The weeping willow is a fast-growing shade tree that thrives in wet sites.

WHEN BUYING A TREE, HOW DO I KNOW WHICH ONE IS THE BEST OF THE BUNCH?
Purchase a tree that is healthy, with a substantial root ball and a vigorous well-formed crown. The best value is usually a tree with a 2-inch-diameter trunk that can be transported and planted by one or two people with shovels.

TREE SHAPES INFLUENCE USES

Trees have many shapes and sizes, each useful for certain situations.

Choose trees that appeal to you aesthetically. Select varieties with growth habits that will fit into your landscape and serve it throughout their lives. Trees are available in various forms—columnar, weeping, dwarf, and multistemmed. Planting a variety of tree shapes helps create contrast and interest in a yard. The most common rounded trees contrast nicely with oval and vase shape ones.

MAKE ROOM FOR TREES Large (50 feet or taller) trees should be planted no closer to a house than 35 feet. Plant medium trees (30 to 50 feet tall) at least 20 feet from a house or outbuilding, small trees (10 to 30 feet tall) at least 10 feet away.

COLUMNAR Columnar trees serve formal garden designs and group well to form green walls.

GLOBE Rounded trees need space to reach their ideal shape as formal specimens or in a formal row.

OPEN HEAD IRREGULAR Open, irregular trees grow up and out asymmetrically and blend well with other trees.

FASTIGIATE Oval trees work effectively in even rows or informal clusters.

WEEPING Weeping trees create living sculptures, commanding attention, especially next to water.

VASE Vase-shape trees open to the sky, forming a high, wide canopy.

BROAD CONE Broad cone or pyramidal trees lift the eye skyward with their commanding presence.

HORIZONTAL SPREADING Spreading trees provide wide-reaching shade and accentuate the horizontal lines of a house.

PLANTING A SHADE TREE

Determine your planting strategy before you choose a tree. Site your tree to cast shade where and when you want it.

Both deciduous trees (which lose their leaves each fall) and evergreens (which keep their leaves) provide shade. Many of the same trees planted for shade can be planted for privacy to block unwanted views, muffle noise, and screen intense light or wind.

A deciduous tree with a large canopy provides maximum summer shade and winter sun. For best shading, plant trees on the east, southwest, west, or northwest sides of a building or area to be shaded.

When planting near shade trees, keep in mind that shade patterns change through the day and through the seasons. Noon shade falls underneath a tree. West-facing areas are shaded in the morning; east-facing ones in the afternoon. In North America, summer sun is more directly overhead than in winter.

Planting Success

Trees and shrubs are sold in different forms. Young trees that are dug with bare roots should be planted while they're dormant. Some young trees are grown in a container for a year or two.

Other trees are dug with a soil ball around the roots and potted or wrapped with burlap. A balled-and-burlapped tree costs a bit more but transplants readily. Plant potted or balled-and-burlapped trees in spring or late summer for best results.

Carry plants in a closed vehicle to protect them from wind damage. To avoid damaging the trunks or stems of large plants, lift them by their containers rather than by the trunk. Plant your tree as soon as possible.

GREATEST BENEFIT Trees save the most energy when planted on the east and west sides of a house.

PLAN AHEAD Place a shade tree where it can help you and where you will enjoy it most. Future generations will reap the benefits.

? ASK THE GARDEN DOCTOR **WHAT IS THE BEST PLACE TO PLANT A SHADE TREE?** Trees are nature's air conditioners. If you plant only one tree, remember "west is best" to shade the house during the hottest part of the day. Just three large trees, planted to shade your home, can cut air-conditioning demands by 25 to 40 percent. Shading the air conditioner allows the unit to run 10 percent more efficiently.

TEST GARDEN TIP

TO AMEND OR NOT When backfilling the planting hole for a tree or shrub, amend the soil with no more than a few shovelfuls of compost. Instead of stamping on the soil, water deeply to eliminate air pockets.

1 PLANTING TIME Plant trees in early spring or fall. Give them time to establish and grow new roots before extreme weather (of summer or winter) sets in.

2 REMOVE TIES Prepare the planting hole by digging it twice as wide and the same depth as the root ball. Remove and discard any twine or wire binding on a balled-and-burlapped tree.

3 REMOVE WRAPS Lift the tree by its root ball and set it in the hole. Remove extraneous burlap. Fabric buried below the soil surface deteriorates eventually. Backfill around the root ball.

4 RIGHT DEPTH Plant the tree at the same depth as it was at the nursery. Mound soil at the planting hole's perimeter. Spread a 2-inch layer of mulch over the basin.

5 WATER NOW Keep mulch away from the tree trunk. Water deeply at planting time. Water weekly as needed throughout the growing season if rainfall is less than 1 inch per week.

6 ENJOY A young tree such as this *Magnolia* 'Yellow Butterflies' typically needs neither fertilizing nor pruning its first few seasons. It will begin blooming within a couple of years.

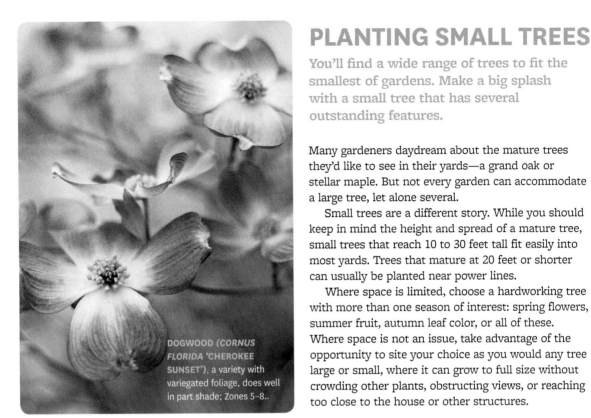

DOGWOOD *(CORNUS FLORIDA 'CHEROKEE SUNSET')*, a variety with variegated foliage, does well in part shade; Zones 5–8..

PLANTING SMALL TREES

You'll find a wide range of trees to fit the smallest of gardens. Make a big splash with a small tree that has several outstanding features.

Many gardeners daydream about the mature trees they'd like to see in their yards—a grand oak or stellar maple. But not every garden can accommodate a large tree, let alone several.

Small trees are a different story. While you should keep in mind the height and spread of a mature tree, small trees that reach 10 to 30 feet tall fit easily into most yards. Trees that mature at 20 feet or shorter can usually be planted near power lines.

Where space is limited, choose a hardworking tree with more than one season of interest: spring flowers, summer fruit, autumn leaf color, or all of these. Where space is not an issue, take advantage of the opportunity to site your choice as you would any tree large or small, where it can grow to full size without crowding other plants, obstructing views, or reaching too close to the house or other structures.

CRAPE MYRTLE *(LAGERSTROEMIA INDICA)* has brilliant blooms in Zones 7–9. Newer varieties have improved cold hardiness.

JAPANESE MAPLE *(ACER PALMATUM)* features a size and shape for most yards and offers outstanding fall color in Zones 5–9.

EASTERN REDBUD *(CERCIS CANADENSIS)*, an excellent front yard tree, has heart-shape leaves. It's hardy to Zone 5.

SERVICEBERRY *(AMELANCHIER)* a single- or multistem tree, has spring blooms, sweet berries, and fall color in Zones 4–9.

ASK THE GARDEN DOCTOR **WHAT ARE SOME GOOD TREES AND SHRUBS FOR A SMALL YARD?** Look for dwarf or compact varieties of trees and shrubs that will suit the size of your yard and your region's climate. As another option, trim a mature medium or large shrub into a tree form by removing the lower branches to reveal the trunk.

TEST GARDEN TIP

SMALL IS BEAUTIFUL Smaller trees typically have less-extensive root systems and compete less aggressively for soil nutrients and moisture. They also produce less litter, which means less maintenance work for you.

CRABAPPLE (*MALUS*)
Multiple species and hundreds of cultivars command attention with their flowery branches in the spring. A range of sizes, shapes, and bloom colors suit Zones 3-9.

SHADE TREES FOR ALL SEASONS

Selecting a shade tree for your home landscape is one of the most challenging and enjoyable tasks you will face in making your little corner of the world a better place. Start by drawing up a list of the features you desire in your yard: fall color, shade for the patio or deck, or backbone for a wildlife garden. Consider your options from there. Then make your commitment to a better future with a shade tree.

BEECH, EUROPEAN (*FAGUS SYLVATICA*) Magnificent and graceful, varieties of this 50- to 60-foot tree grow slowly and live long in moist, well-drained, acid soil.

ELM, AMERICAN (*ULMUS AMERICANA*) This once-common urban tree is making a comeback with disease-resistant varieties for Zones 2–9. It tolerates pollution.

HORNBEAM, AMERICAN (*CARPINUS CAROLINIANA*) The eastern native reaches 20 to 30 feet. It does well in damp soil; sun or part shade in Zones 3–9.

LOCUST, BLACK (*ROBINIA PSEUDOACACIA*) A fast grower with fragrant spring flowers, this tough tree is suitable for poor soil in Zones 3–8.

GINKGO (*GINKGO BILOBA*) The slow to moderate grower for Zones 4–9 has fan-shape leaves and golden fall foliage. Female trees bear stinky fruit.

LINDEN, LITTLELEAF (*TILIA CORDATA*) This hardy, pyramidal tree reaches 40 to 70 feet tall in Zones 3–7. 'Greenspire' is one variety well adapted to urban conditions.

MAGNOLIA (*MAGNOLIA*) Varieties from small to large provide a spring-flowering ornamental tree. Each is suited to different climates.

MAPLE, RED (*ACER RUBRUM*) One of the most easily grown specimens for Zones 4–9, this 40- to 60-foot-tall tree turns yellow to fiery red in fall.

OAK, WHITE (*QUERCUS ALBA*) A stately presence, from 50 to 60 feet tall, this long-lived native American tree suits spacious sites in Zones 3–8.

PLANTING UNDER A TREE

Have you ever tried to grow grass under a tree and struggled to keep it alive? You're not alone. Planting under a tree can be done with natural-looking results. The tree and select plants growing beneath its canopy can coexist successfully.

Planting under a tree must be done carefully to avoid disturbing or damaging the tree's roots. No matter the size of the tree, most of its roots occupy the top 12 to 18 inches of soil, while several large roots reach deep down to support the tree. Adding more than a 2-inch layer of soil over the tree roots can reduce the exchange of oxygen and carbon dioxide, harming the tree or causing it to die.

Some trees (crabapple, ginkgo, redbud, white oak, willow, and others) tolerate underplanting. Be careful planting under sugar maples, other oaks, magnolias, pines, lindens, larches, hemlocks, and dogwoods.

Choose groundcovers and other perennials that appreciate dry shade for an understory situation. Spring-flowering bulbs work well under trees. A small shrub or tree is appropriate under a high canopy. (If the shade tree has an extremely dense canopy, consider having it thinned to allow more light and rain to get through.)

Start with plants in 3- or 4-inch pots to minimize the digging required for planting holes. Prepare to plant by smothering any existing turf under the tree: Spread newspaper sheets 6 to 10 deep. Top with up to 2 inches of compost. Wait three months for the paper and turf to decompose, or carefully dig through the layers to plant.

Minimize damage to a tree by keeping mulch at least 6 to 12 inches away from the trunk.

Avoid building a planter box around the base of a tree. Piling up soil in a planter can injure the tree.

PLANT CAREFULLY Dig with a trowel and tuck plants into planting holes without disturbing tree roots. Water after planting and weekly as needed.

LEAVE GROWING ROOM Plant sparsely under a tree. When selecting plants, consider their mature size, and give them plenty of room to spread.

ASK THE GARDEN DOCTOR

WHAT CAN I PLANT UNDER A MATURE MAPLE TREE? Few plants can survive the dry, low-light conditions under a dense-canopied tree. Any plantings must also compete with tree roots for moisture and nutrients. Clumps of spring-flowering bulbs and shade-tolerant groundcovers, planted at least several feet away from the trunk, create a naturalistic effect. They emerge and blossom before the tree fully leafs out.

PLANTING AN EVERGREEN TREE

Add year-round color, texture, and interest to your garden with beautiful and bold evergreens.

Evergreens keep color alive and unify your garden throughout the seasons. Needled and broadleaf evergreen trees and shrubs vary in the conditions they prefer and their landscape uses. Needled evergreens are also known as conifers because they produce cones. Broadleaf evergreens hold their leaves over winter and often produce berries.

Many evergreens save you time and effort because they require little pruning. Slower-growing dwarf varieties save space in limited areas.

Evergreen Buyers Guide

Containerized plants (lifted from the ground and transplanted into a nursery pot), as shown on these pages, establish less quickly than container-grown or balled-and-burlapped plants, but they typically take off more readily than bareroot plants.

To spot a healthy evergreen, look for a plant with good color and lush needles or leaves. Brown leaves or bare stems may be a sign of stress and should be passed over for a healthier specimen.

Determine the best site for trees and shrubs by positioning potted nursery plants in the garden and imagining them at their mature size. Play with colors of evergreens, mixing green, yellow, and blue foliage. Contrast a lacy texture against a denser texture or darker color. Many evergreens have a distinctive silhouette and may exhibit a layered growing habit, weeping branches, or twisted growth. Take advantage of the tree's form, using it artfully.

KEEP TAGS Remove the plant tag and keep it in a handy file or garden journal where you can refer to it as needed. Many tags include a good deal of helpful information.

READY ROOTS At planting time, gently loosen the tree's root ball. Squeeze the root ball and tickle the bottom roots to free them.

DEPTH: JUST RIGHT When planting, use your shovel handle to check the correct depth of the hole. The top of the root ball should sit at or just below the soil's surface.

? ASK THE GARDEN DOCTOR **WHAT ARE THE BEST EVERGREENS FOR MY YARD?** Look around your neighborhood and note evergreen varieties that appear to be thriving there. Ask your neighbors to identify their trees if need be. These are some of the trees you can depend on for success. Visit local nurseries, the county extension service, and *bhg.com/gardening* to identify more good options.

TEMPORARY QUARTERS If you purchase a tree or shrub in late summer or early fall and aren't sure where to site it, plant it temporarily. Lift the plant and give it a permanent home in spring. Check potential sites by viewing the potted tree or shrub in place from every direction.

1 **WELCOME HELP** Digging a generous planting hole helps your new tree establish itself. Make the hole twice as wide and the same depth as the nursery pot.

2 **ROOM FOR ROOTS** Use a garden fork to loosen the sides of the planting hole to make it easier for roots to reach out and grow into their new home.

3 **REMOVE POT** Safely loosen a potted tree by laying the container on its side, stepping firmly on the pot, and rolling it back and forth under your foot.

4 **HOLD THE ROOT BALL** Slide the root ball out of the pot. Lift the plant by the root ball and set it in the planting hole. Check the stem to see that it is standing straight.

5 **FILL HOLE** Backfill around the root ball with soil taken from the planting hole. If you amend the soil, blend in a few shovelfuls of compost only before backfilling.

6 **APPLY MULCH** Form a moat around the planting area by heaping soil and mulch around the perimeter. Water your new tree thoroughly.

PROTECTING WOODY PLANTS

In cold climates, help young trees and shrubs survive winter without damage from frigid temperatures, freeze-thaw cycles, and drying winds. One way to prevent evergreens from dehydrating when blasted by winter winds is to spray plants with an antitranspirant. The liquid coats the plant with a protective film. It should be applied in fall, before freezing temperatures occur.

Other ways to protect plants from harsh winter conditions include: Water deeply and monthly in fall and early winter. After late summer, avoid pruning and fertilizing, which stimulate new growth that can be damaged by freezing weather.

On exposed sites, form a protective windscreen around tender evergreens, using stakes and burlap. Leave space between the screen and the plant. Loosely fill with leaves.

STAKING A NEW TREE

Staking is root reinforcement; it keeps a tree from falling over or leaning until its roots are strong enough to anchor it. Most trees do not need staking and are better off without it. You may decide to stake a bare-root tree, tall evergreen, or top-heavy tree for one or two growing seasons, however. On a windy site, stake any new tree to keep it from blowing over. Use two or three strong stakes and loose ties that will allow the tree trunk to sway in any direction. Swaying helps trees develop stronger roots, enabling them to develop faster. Avoid wire, rope, or wire covered with garden hose for staking trees. These materials can damage the trunk.

? ASK THE GARDEN DOCTOR **SHOULD I WRAP THE TRUNK OF A NEW TREE?** Wrapping the lower portion of a young, tender tree trunk using a roll of the crinkly paper made for this purpose can help protect it over the winter from damage due to nibbling rodents. Tree wrap also helps prevent dehydration and sunscald that can occur, especially the first winter after planting. Always remove the wrap in spring.

EVERGREEN TREES FOR ALL SEASONS

Just as deciduous trees and shrubs grow in various shapes dictated by their branching patterns, so do evergreens. The shapes, sizes, colors, and textures of evergreens make them essential ingredients in a balanced and complete garden design. Use evergreens to define the garden's edges, form a backdrop for colorful perennials, and solve landscape challenges. Look for varieties that offer the size, shape, and color you desire.

ARBORVITAE, AMERICAN (THUJA OCCIDENTALIS) An upright, slow grower with a fine texture reaches 20 feet tall in Zones 3–7. It makes an excellent hedge or privacy screen.

FIR, WHITE (ABIES CONCOLOR) This classic conical tree with blue-green needles grows from 30 to 50 feet tall and withstands heat and drought in Zones 4–7.

HEMLOCK, CANADA (TSUGA CANADENSIS) Slow-growing and long-lived, this graceful, pyramidal evergreen thrives in Zones 3–7. The 40- to 70-foot-tall tree has delicate deep green needles.

JUNIPER, COMMON (JUNIPERUS COMMUNIS) Versatile and adaptable trees (and shrubs) for Zones 3–9, they have foliage that ranges from green to blue and gray.

LARCH, COMMON (LARIX DECIDUAS) The moderate to fast grower reaches 75 feet tall in Zones 2–6. It has a lovely pyramidal shape with golden fall color.

PINE, EASTERN WHITE (PINUS STROBUS) This fast-growing tree with fine, soft needles reaches up to 100 feet tall in Zones 3–8. Use it in groves or screens.

SPRUCE, ORIENTAL (PICEA ORIENTALIS) A graceful form and glossy dark green foliage make this a fine 60-foot specimen in a mixed border; Zones 6–8.

YOUR IDEAL SHRUBS

Think of shrubs as garden workhorses. They can handle many jobs quickly and easily. They're budget friendly too.

Shrubs offer creative opportunities for experimenting with their diverse forms. They range from large, broad types that reach 20 feet tall to low-growing, spreading varieties only 6 inches tall. Evergreen or deciduous, flowering, fruiting, fragrant—you'll find options to star in each season, and many offer year-round appeal.

Planting Plans

Shrubs beg to be planted in groups—in mixed borders, foundation plantings, side yards, and even small gardens without room for trees. Shrubs invite mixing and matching; grouping magnifies the effect of a single plant. Best of all, even the newest varieties of shrubs are affordable and widely available, putting them within any gardener's reach.

Most shrubs grow swiftly, blooming and spreading the first season after they're planted. You'll find a wide selection hardy enough to withstand drought, resist disease, and need little upkeep other than occasional feeding and trimming.

Think about shrubs' shapes and sizes as you plan their uses in your garden. Use them in symmetrical patterns to suggest a formal style or in asymmetrical combinations that enhance any setting year after year.

TRIED AND TRUE Old-fashioned shrubs, such as flowering almond (above), lilac, and mock orange, remain dependable, long-lived plants.

UPRIGHT and vase-shape forms can block eyesores, and they work for small spaces.

SPREADING shrubs combine well with other forms. Use their small, medium, or large broad forms for contrast.

PROSTRATE or trailing shrubs grow low and horizontal, covering ground, draping a wall, or accenting a feature.

ROUNDED forms suit spacious sites where they can reach their full stature.

ARCHING shrubs form graceful silhouettes, whether used as expressive specimens or in thick hedges.

DIVERSITY WORKS
A garden that includes a range of flowering and evergreen shrubs achieves colorful, interesting effects year-round. Lilac and azalea team up here with evergreens in distinctive shapes, colors, and sizes.

 **ASK THE GARDEN DOCTOR** **WHICH SHRUBS SHOULD I PLANT NEXT TO THE FOUNDATION OF MY HOUSE?** The key to successful foundation planting is a sense of scale and proportion. Large shrubs often look best with a tall house of two or more stories; smaller shrubs complement a one-story house. Choose shrubs for their mature size. Use them to soften the corners of the house and tie it to the landscape.

PLANTING A SHRUB

Whether you're planting a solitary selection, establishing a privacy screen, or forming a windbreak, plant shrubs with care and then protect your investment.

Although shrubs and trees cost more than other garden plants, their jobs are multipurpose and long-term. If you start with container-grown or balled-and-burlapped shrubs, you'll pay more but the well-developed roots usually establish quickly. The plants will mature within a few years. Bare-root and containerized plants will need more time and care to develop.

Get your shrubs off to a good start, watering them weekly if needed through the first season. After that, they'll grow more independently and need only occasional pruning if they are damaged, misshapen, or overgrown. Mulch shrubs annually to preserve soil moisture, insulate roots from temperature extremes, discourage weeds, and gradually improve soil.

FALL COLOR This mixed border includes a dwarf burning bush along with perennials and ornamental grasses.

❶ CHECK SPACING Measure the planting site and allow room for the shrub to reach full size.

❷ DIG WIDE Dig the planting hole twice as wide and only as deep as the root ball.

❸ REMOVE POT Slide the nursery pot off the root ball. Lift the shrub by the root ball into the planting hole.

❹ FILL HOLE Backfill around the root ball, using leftover soil and sod to form a rim for watering.

❺ MULCH AND WATER Cover the rim with a 2-inch layer of mulch. Keep mulch away from the shrub's trunk.

? ASK THE GARDEN DOCTOR

WHAT CAN I DO TO ENSURE THE SUCCESS OF A NEW TREE OR SHRUB? During the first year after planting, water is the most important factor in new tree and shrub survival. Ample water given occasionally is much better than shallow watering. Let the water trickle from a hose for 10 to 15 minutes on the soil surface beside the tree or shrub.

BARE BUDGET If you want to save money or plant large quantities of shrubs, buy bare-root plants. Soak the dormant roots in a tub of water for several hours before planting.

BLAZING GLORY
Dwarf burning bush (*Euonymus alatus* 'Compactus'), a 6- to 8-foot-tall and wide shrub for Zones 4–9, turns brilliant red in autumn. Before planting in your area, check with the extension service to make sure it is not invasive there.

NEW SHRUB CARE

Provide young plants with basic care and then watch them succeed.

POSTPONED PLANTING If you cannot plant right away, store potted and balled-and-burlapped plants in a cool, shady place away from direct sunlight and wind.

IDEAL TIMING Spring, late summer, and early fall are the best times to plant shrubs. Avoid planting during the hottest part of summer.

WATER ADEQUATELY Water a new shrub deeply after planting; then weekly in the absence of rain throughout the first season.

FEED LATER New shrubs and trees do not require fertilizer their first year in the garden.

CHOOSING SHRUBS FOR ANY GARDEN

By taking advantage of shrubs' versatility, you'll make the best use of them in your garden. Plan for a continuous show and get the most impact from shrubs' forms, colors, and textures.

Many shrubs have multiple strengths with a series of flowers, foliage, berries, and bark from season to season. When you consider shrubs for your garden, tally their seasonal strengths and identify the candidates with the most potential.

From the year's earliest witch hazel and winter daphne to the final hydrangea and rose of sharon, spring- and summer-flowering shrubs set the garden's pace. Beyond the color and fragrance that come with many flowers, compare the shrubs' type of blooms: large blowsy roses, fluffy spirea, dainty sweetspire.

A shrub's flowers may win your heart, but select a plant first for its form (size and shape) and foliage.

Foliage sustains a shrub's appeal from season to season. Investigate the array of varieties with leaves other than standard green: chartreuse, blue-green, gray, and purple, for instance. Then consider shrubs that turn color and create brilliant autumn displays.

Berries that ripen in late summer or fall and last into winter can be a shrub's best feature as they attract and sustain birds. Planting berried shrubs brings life, color, movement, and song to your garden.

As leaves fall, the colorful bark and architectural forms of some shrubs bare of foliage take center stage to command the winter garden.

EASY CARE Evergreen shrubs create a lush year-round display and need little maintenance.

SPRING FLING The garden season begins with the beauty of flowering shrubs such as rhododendrons and their wafting fragrance.

? ASK THE GARDEN DOCTOR **OUR YARD IS SMALL. HOW CAN WE FIT SHRUBS INTO THE SCHEME OF THINGS?** Use shrubs to make a small garden appear larger. Use light, bright broadleaf foliage at the front and darker, small-leaf varieties at the back to create an illusion of space. Choose slow-growing dwarf varieties and use them here and there as focal points.

SHRUBS FOR ALL SEASONS

Shrubs demand less and give much more than most plants. When you choose shrub varieties with drought, disease, and pest resistance and amend the soil regularly, you'll minimize maintenance even more. These shrubs are among the most adaptive for a range of soils and climates.

CYPRESS, GOLDEN SAWARA THREADLEAF *(CHAMAECYPARIS PISIFERA* 'FILIFERA') A slow-growing, mounding evergreen, this is favored as an accent plant for Zones 4–8.

DOGWOOD, RED-OSIER *(CORNUS SERICEA)* Widely favored for its red stems in winter, the mounded shrub is good for hedges or in mixed borders in Zones 2–7.

ELDERBERRY 'BLACK LACE' *(SAMBUCUS NIGRA)* With its dark foliage and contrasting flower clusters, this shrub adds a dramatic accent to a perennial border in Zones 4–7.

EUONYMUS *(E. FORTUNEI* 'EMERALD 'N' GOLD') Use the compact, golden-variegated broadleaf evergreen as an accent or easy-care hedge plant in Zones 5–8.

INKBERRY *(ILEX GLABRA)* From the vast holly family this upright, rounded and slow-growing broadleaf evergreen likes damp soil in Zones 5–9.

JUNIPER, PFITZER *(JUNIPERUS CHINENSIS* 'PFITZERIANA') This spreading shrub reaches 3 to 5 feet tall and 6 to 10 feet wide; tolerates full sun and drought in Zones 4–9.

NINEBARK, PURPLE *(PHYSOCARPUS OPULIFOLIUS)* This arching shrub has multiseason appeal: Flowers, textured foliage, fruit, and colorful stems in Zones 3–8.

SPIREA, VAN HOUTTE *(SPIRAEA ×VANHOUTTEI)* Arching branches of this 6- to 8-foot spring bloomer bear white flower clusters in Zones 3–8. 'Bridalwreath' is ideal for hedges.

VIBURNUM *(VIBURNUM)* Consider this diverse group of shrubs with flowers, fruit, and stunning fall foliage for Zones 3–9. Some are evergreen, others deciduous.

PLANTING A HEDGE

Thoughtfully plan a hedge, then plant it with care for trouble-free results.

A hedge is more than plants set out in a row. Hedges mark property lines, line walkways, improve privacy, and highlight a garden focal point or even become it. A hedgerow provides an ideal habitat for birds.

Best Hedge Plants

Choose long-lived, pest- and disease-resistant plants that suit your climate and garden conditions. Wise plant choices help make a healthy hedge that's easy to maintain. Slow- and moderate-growing plants are best; fast growers mean more frequent upkeep. A tidy, formal hedge needs regular clipping, while a naturalistic design entails only annual trimming.

Your choice of shrubs should also be guided by the style of hedge you want. Formal hedges, with a solid architectural form, neatly frame a yard or rooms within it. Single-plant varieties (lilac, spirea, forsythia) and evergreens (boxwood, arborvitae, holly) suit formal hedge designs. Go for an informal layered effect using a flowering plant variety or different plants of varied heights. Flowering shrubs create magical effects that fences cannot.

Measure the length of the planting area and consider the shrub's mature spread to determine the number of shrubs you will need for your hedge.

BOXWOOD (*Buxus*) forms a classic evergreen hedge, whether clipped or left loose and natural. The height of a boxwood hedge and its hardiness depend on the species selected.

LILAC (*Syringa vulgaris*) suits an informal or naturalistic garden. Lilacs are long-lived, spectacularly fragrant shrubs that can cope with most conditions in Zones 3–7.

HOW TO PLANT A HEDGE

This hedge features two shrubs: red chokeberry (*Aronia arbutifolia* 'Brilliantissima'), 3 foot wide, 6 foot tall, with fruit for birds and nectar for insects; and dwarf inkberry (*Ilex glabra* 'Nordic') a 3-foot-tall and -wide hardy evergreen.

1 **PLOT LINE** Stake and mark the planting area, whether in a straight line or a curved one. Use a measuring tape as a guide.

2 **SPACE PLANTS** Set the potted shrubs in place, allowing room for the plants to reach their mature size. Stagger plants in two rows for a thicker hedge.

3 **MARK HOLES** Use the mature width of the shrub as the spacing between the plants' root balls. Use the pots to mark places for planting holes.

4 **REMOVE POTS** Dig the planting holes. Remove the shrubs from the nursery pots and set them in place. Check the shrubs' spacing. Fill in the planting holes.

5 **WATER WELL** Form a ring of soil around the outer edge of the planting hole to hold water, then water each shrub deeply. Water as needed throughout the first growing season.

6 **ADD MULCH** Spread a 2- to 3-inch layer of shredded wood mulch between the plants. Keep the mulch away from the plants' stems to allow water to reach the roots.

GROWING AZALEAS AND RHODODENDRONS

These spectacular shrubs burst into riotous bloom each year, mostly in the spring. Chances are, you can grow them successfully if you give them what they crave.

The genus *Rhododendron* includes thousands of rhododendrons and azaleas with diverse sizes, flower forms, colors, and garden uses. Rhododendrons, or rhodies, are evergreen shrubs, including large and dwarf varieties, with leathery leaves. Evergreen and deciduous azalea varieties range from 1 to 8 feet tall. Some azaleas are cold hardy to Zone 3; others have heat and sun tolerance and are increasingly popular in hot, arid regions.

Most rhododendrons and azaleas bloom in the spring. Some summer-flowering forms exist and can be used to extend the blooming season. Rhodies take a little work to get started, but they are not at all demanding once established. Light shade or filtered sunlight is best for most rhododendrons. Some varieties can grow well in sun.

The key to success with rhodies and azaleas is acidic, very well-draining soil. Plant them in berms or raised beds filled with this soil mix: 2 parts pine bark mulch, 2 parts topsoil, and 1 part sand. Water plants weekly during summer. Fertilize once annually, after bloom, with a product made for acid-loving plants.

HARDY RHODIE 'HENRY'S RED'
One of the hardiest red-flowering, large-leaf rhododendron cultivars, it's reliable in Zones 5–9. It reaches from 6 to 15 feet tall.

'TRI LIGHTS' AZALEA
One of the very hardy (Zones 3–7) Northern Lights series of deciduous azaleas, this one incorporates three bloom colors and grows to 4 or 5 feet tall.

? ASK THE GARDEN DOCTOR — **WHEN IS THE BEST TIME TO PRUNE AZALEAS AND RHODODENDRONS?** Like other spring-flowering shrubs, prune most rhododendrons and azaleas right after they finish flowering. Just snip off or shear the spent flowers. The same approach holds true for varieties that bloom at other times. For more details about pruning shrubs, turn to Chapter 13, page 266.

 **TEST GARDEN TIP**

PREFERRED PICKS Rhododendrons and azaleas can provide masses of astounding blooms in vivid colors, but select plants with care to avoid clashing hues. Combine different sizes and varieties in a large garden; choose dwarf varieties with handsome foliage for small gardens.

ON AND ON Encore brand azaleas bloom in spring like other azaleas, then again in summer and fall, given 4 to 6 hours of full sun daily.

GROWING HYDRANGEAS

With their strong textures and dramatic blooms, hydrangeas take center stage in the garden where they show off throughout summer and fall.

Hydrangeas include dozens of varieties of deciduous shrubs that vary in size, from small (3 to 5 feet tall and wide) to large (10 to 15 feet). They need at least 4 to 6 hours of direct sun to produce flowers. Dappled afternoon shade is best.

Plant hydrangeas in fertile, well-drained soil. Amend soil with loads of compost and chopped leaves. Hydrangeas may wilt for a short time during hot weather. Overwatering slows flower formation.

Play the Blues

Common wisdom suggests that amending the soil around a hydrangea, making it more or less acidic, can change the bloom color. If you plant a blue or pink bigleaf hydrangea (*H. macrophylla*), acid soil (5.2 to 5.5 pH) brings out blue tones; alkaline soil (pH above 6) prompts pink tones. Applying elemental sulfur or iron sulfate annually can help promote bluer blooms over a season or two. Aluminum sulfate is no longer recommended as a soil acidifier; it can produce aluminum toxicity in soil.

Enjoy your hydrangeas long after the garden season is over by cutting flowers for bouquets. Snip long stems with mature flowers (that feel almost papery), strip off the leaves, and stand the stems in a bucket full of warm water for several hours. Recut the stems at an angle before arranging them in a vase with fresh water.

SOIL ACIDIFIER This packaged product typically contains elemental sulfur. Scratch it into soil beneath hydrangeas in the spring.

FANCY FOLIAGE Variegated hydrangeas, including *H. macrophylla* 'Lemon Wave,' make a big splash with their unusual foliage. This variety has bluish lacecap-type blooms.

CUT AND DRIED Cut hydrangeas for gorgeous bouquets that dry naturally and last for months. For best results, collect the blossoms early in the day, before the dew has dried.

ASK THE GARDEN DOCTOR

CAN A POTTED HYDRANGEA FROM THE FLORIST BE TRANSPLANTED OUTDOORS?
Greenhouse-grown gift hydrangeas do not adapt well to growing in the garden. But you can extend their life in an outdoor container protected from afternoon sun.

**BIGLEAF HYDRANGEA
(H. MACROPHYLLA)**
Includes the hortensia group or mopheads with large, rounded blooms. They do best in Zones 6–10.

HYDRANGEA MACROPHYLLA also includes the lacecap group that has flat blossoms with lacy centers surrounded by a ring of larger petaled flowers.

**SMOOTH-LEAF HYDRANGEA
(H. ARBORESCENS 'ANNABELLE')** is a compact shrub for Zones 3–9 that has massive blooms and does best in full sun.

**PANICLE HYDRANGEA
(H. PANICULATA)** is an easy-growing background plant, especially in gardens of Zones 4–9, with old-fashioned, long-lasting blooms.

**OAKLEAF HYDRANGEA
(H. QUERCIFOLIA)** has large oaklike leaves that turn burgundy and purple in fall. A stately accent in Zones 5–8.

CHOOSING ROSES FOR ANY GARDEN

From the fleeting beauty of a single blossom to the lasting spectacle of a rose-draped arbor, there's a rose for any garden. Choose the best candidates for your place.

Adding roses to your garden entails the same practice of matching plant to site and conditions as any other shrub. The big difference is that there are so many different types and varieties of roses. How is it possible to sort out and explore the vast array of roses and find ideal options for your garden?

Consider the families of roses, from petite miniatures to massive climbers, and decide where you want to plant them. Then make a list of desirable varieties that you read and hear about. Prioritize hardiness for your region's climate and disease resistance. Choose roses on the basis of their size, bloom color, name, introduction date, or whatever qualifications might suit you. Some gardeners choose roses for their history or their fragrance.

If you want the beauty of roses without the work often ascribed to them, you'll find an increasing selection of hardier plants. By growing different varieties, you'll see how easy roses can be. Buy own-root roses, grown from cuttings and cultivated on their own roots (not grafted onto a different rootstock), which are typically hardier and virus-free.

'LENA' SHRUB ROSE An ever-expanding selection of modern roses takes various forms, from neat bushes with a profusion of long-lasting flower clusters, to tall arching and sprawling plants.

ROSE OPTIONS When buying roses, choose from bareroot, potted, or packaged bare root plants. Look for green (not brown) bare roots and plant when they're dormant or just sprouting.

ASK THE GARDEN DOCTOR **WHICH ROSES ARE MOST FRAGRANT?** Many heirloom roses boast exquisite fragrances, from sweet to spicy, fruity, musky, and more. You'll find many other fragrant varieties among David Austin, hydrid tea, and grandiflora roses. The scent of any rose is affected by the climate where you live. Fragrance is enhanced by mild humidity and warmth.

TYPES OF ROSES

Technically, roses are shrubs. But there are diverse families of roses, and varieties within those groups, which offer sizes, colors, shapes, and forms to suit every garden. The family of shrub roses (see page 164) includes some of the toughest, most pleasing ones of all. They're the choicest plants for 4- to 5-foot hedges or 6- to 8-foot screens. Meet some of the other rose families.

FLORIBUNDA This includes hardy 3- to 4-foot shrubs with profuse clustered flowers on short stems. Good for mixed beds and low hedges. Shown: 'Iceberg'.

GRANDIFLORA The shrubs reach 4 to 6 feet tall with abundant clusters of continuous blooms. Vigorous background plants for perennials. Shown: 'Earth Song'.

HYBRID TEA The most widely grown rose type produces a large bloom on a single stem. Upright plants from 3 to 5 feet tall blossom repeatedly. Shown: 'Double Delight'.

MINIATURE These diminutive treasures suit small spaces, pots, and bed edges. Some grow to only 6 inches; climbing varieties reach 8 feet. Shown: 'Caliente'.

OLD GARDEN The antique roses have survived generations with their rugged hardiness. Their flowers have delicate petals and dizzying scents. Shown: 'Harison's Yellow'.

CLIMBERS, RAMBLERS These large shrub roses with sprawling canes reach as tall as 15 feet. Give them strong support, such as a fence, wall, or pillar. Shown: 'New Dawn'.

SPECIES OR WILD These roses are the toughest; upright or low spreading and notoriously thorny. In late season, most have big hips (fruits). Shown: 'Frau Dagmar Hastrup'.

PLANTING ROSES

Proper planting gives your rose a sustainable foundation that helps protect the plant from the inevitable challenges of life in the garden.

The better health a rose has from its start in your garden, the better its chances of thriving. A well-planted, healthy rose is better able to fight off diseases and pests, reach out its roots to find water and food, and produce more leaves to help sustain the plant. Spring and fall are the best times to plant roses.

How Deep to Plant

Follow the steps below when planting any rose, whether bare root, own root, or containerized. The main difference is the depth at which to plant. To check the depth of your rose, lay a shovel handle across the planting hole and add or remove soil to adjust the planting level.

Plant own-root roses with the crown (where the main stem and roots meet) at ground level. In cold climates, set the crown 2 or 3 inches below soil level for extra winter protection.

Some bare-root or containerized plants have a graft union (a swollen knobby part of the stem just above the roots) where a desirable rose was grafted onto the roots of a more vigorous rose to combine the best of two plants. The graft union can be easily damaged by cold, so plant the graft union 1 to 4 inches below the soil level in cold-winter regions. In climates where winter temperatures do not drop regularly below 10 degrees F, the graft can be planted at soil level or an inch above.

1 SOAK ROOTS As soon as you get a bare-root rose, carefully remove it from any packing material. Soak the roots in a bucket of water for several hours.

2 PRUNE LIGHTLY Snip off any damaged branches and roots. Your rose needs as many healthy roots as possible to reestablish itself once planted.

3 DIG A HOLE Make the hole at least twice as wide as the root system. Work in soil amendments, such as compost or peat moss, as you dig.

4 SET ROOTS Gently spread the roots in the bottom of the planting hole. Backfill to eliminate air pockets and keep the plant from settling too low.

5 WATER DEEPLY Finish backfilling the planting hole. Mound and shape a moat of soil around the plant. Fill the moat with water. Let the water soak in; water again.

ASK THE GARDEN DOCTOR **ARE THERE SOME ROSES THAT ARE EASIER TO CARE FOR THAN OTHERS?** Roses with the Earth-Kind designation are tested and recommended for low maintenance, particularly for outstanding performance without the use of chemicals. The Texas A&M University program has inspired research in other states with other landscape plants.

TEST GARDEN TIP

ROSES CONTAINED Almost any rose can be grown in a container. Select a pot that provides plenty of rooting room: a 10- to 15-gallon pot for most roses. Use a larger container for larger roses; a smaller pot for miniatures.

MULCH SEASONALLY
Apply a 2- to 3-inch layer of shredded bark, chopped leaves, or another organic material to prevent weeds and retain soil moisture.

GROWING ROSES

It is easier than you might think to grow healthy, gorgeous roses. Tend to your plants' basic needs, then enjoy fragrant bouquets.

Choose disease-resistant rose varieties. This doesn't mean plants are immune to problems, especially by the end of a long, hot, humid summer. Desirable plants will also have resilience to weather extremes in your region. Get names of good prospects from local rosarians, master gardeners, and cooperative extension agents.

Start right. Plant roses where they'll get at least six hours of full sun daily. Give them enough room to reach their full size, with space around plants for air circulation. Roses need well-drained, slightly acid (pH 6.2 to 6.8) soil.

Sustain roses. Provide 1 inch of water weekly when rain doesn't come, and mulch around plants to conserve soil moisture. Feed roses throughout their bloom season, applying your choice of fertilizer according to package directions. Lay off fertilizer by late summer to help plants be ready for winter.

Prepare plants for winter. In cold regions, protect roses from freeze-thaw cycles and frigid winds. In late fall, heap the plant's base with 12 inches of compost or topsoil. In spring, pull back this amendment gradually and work it into the plant's surrounding soil.

CLEAN CUTS After cutting roses, clean pruners thoroughly using rubbing alcohol or a disinfecting type of household cleaner to help prevent spreading disease among plants.

BOUQUET CAVEAT Not all roses make good cut flowers. Some blooms fall apart when snipped. Try cutting just one flower and floating it in a small bowl.

ASK THE GARDEN DOCTOR **HOW DO I MOVE A ROSE BUSH?** When transplanting a rose bush, dig as generous a root ball as possible. Use your best judgment to balance the length of the root system with the length of the canes. Cut the canes to the length of the roots before replanting. Then give the plant time to reestablish, keeping it well watered throughout the process.

PREVENT PROBLEMS Before applying winter protection to roses, spray the base of each plant with a lime-sulfur dormant oil to eliminate insects that might try to overwinter there.

KEEPING ROSES HEALTHY

Replace a fear of growing roses with the confidence that comes with success. Take a preventive approach to rose health care.

■ **Replace** a plant that regularly develops problems with diseases or pests.

■ **Remove** diseased leaves from plants and the ground under them. Dispose of diseased plant material, rather than composting it. Disinfect pruners after cutting roses.

■ **Watch** for Japanese beetles, aphids, and spider mites; treat them accordingly.

■ **Revitalize** plants with a handful of alfalfa pellets (available from a feed store or organic garden supplier) scratched into the soil.

■ **Cutting** flowers stimulates new bud growth. Refrain from cutting as summer ends to help plants prepare for their winter rest.

HARDY STOCK Start with hardy roses that have disease resistance. 'Prairie Princess' is a shrub rose reliable in Zones 3–9 that shakes off insects and disease.

CHAPTER 8

GROWING VINES AND CLIMBERS

The most acrobatic of all plants add beauty and other delightful effects to a garden with their diverse textures, colors, and fragrances.

BENEFITS OF VINES AND CLIMBERS

Take your garden to impressive heights with versatile vines. Plant them in strategic places, give them a couple of seasons to establish roots, then stand back as vines perform their acrobatic climbing prowess.

Vines and climbers grow where other plants cannot: scrambling up a wall, arching over an arbor, or sprawling along a fence. With the wide range of vining and climbing plants available, you can have blooms from spring to frost on annuals (changeable each year) or long-lived perennials (bigger and better each year).

Beautiful vines are among the garden's most impressive superheroes. Vigorous ones can scale tall buildings, reaching up to 20 feet in a single season. Although vines seemingly defy gravity, they do need support to keep up their vertical growth. If left to sprawl horizontally, many vines become excellent groundcovers.

Put Vines to Work

Planting the right vine in the right place allows you to take advantage of its talents. Where garden space is tight, the only way to go is up. Let vines climb as fast as they can and spread their bold beauty. Depending on your choice of plants, flowering vines can add color or fragrance at nose level or the cooling cover of foliage overhead. Use vines as a soft drape for a wall, pergola, or other structure. Transform a chain-link fence or lattice panels into a green screen by planting a vine at the base of a fence post.

As you consider adding a vine to your garden, picture its mature height and spread in addition to the strength of its potential support. Mailboxes and lampposts can handle only small climbers such as smaller clematis. Match a larger structure with heavier sprawlers such as fall-blooming clematis. Allow a rose or small-leaf flowering vine to climb a tree or large shrub for a pretty effect.

TEAM VINES Extend the bloom season by combining vines and climbers. A clematis thrives at the base of a golden honeysuckle because it likes to have shaded roots.

TEST GARDEN TIP

ANNUAL TRYOUTS If you aren't sure where to plant a perennial vine, audition an annual vine in its place. Select a plant with similar light needs. For the price of a seed packet, you can plant a vine and see how it fits into your garden.

HOW VINES CLIMB

If you understand how a vine grows, you can plant it in an appropriate place and help it fulfill its function.

CLIMBING TENDRILS Dainty-yet-strong corkscrewlike tendrils reach out and wrap around narrow lattice, chain link, string, shrubs, and such. (Clematis, passion flower, sweet pea)

ROOTLIKE HOLDFASTS Tiny aerial rootlets along the vine's stems attach to vertical surfaces, such as a masonry wall or tree trunk, without support. (English ivy, trumpet creeper, wintercreeper euonymus)

ADHESIVE DISCS The tiny suction cups attach to a surface, enabling the vine to cling to it. (Virginia creeper, Boston ivy)

TWINING STEMS The vine wraps its entire stem around a support. Once started, it becomes self-sufficient. (Honeysuckle, morning glory, wisteria)

UP A TREE Planted nearby, this hardy 'William Baffin' climbing rose leans on a tree for permanent support and adds dimension to the summer garden.

TYPES OF VINES

The sky's the limit when you incorporate vines into your garden. Choose from annuals or perennials—or both—to get the effects you desire.

You'll find an array of vines with individual strengths and rewarding ways to grow them. First, consider the broad categories.

Annual vines live only for one growing season, but their quick growth provides instant color that can be changed easily each year. Although many annual vines put on a show in record time, they'll be felled by frost or the season's eventual end.

Easy-care perennials live on, adding character year after year. Once planted, most vines fend for themselves, needing only occasional trimming. Climbing plants tend to be tough, seldom fussy about soil, and resistant to most diseases. Many are drought-tolerant and produce week after week of bloom.

Trimming is Good

If you trim spent flowers from annual vines, you'll promote new blooms. Some perennials, such as trumpet creeper and wisteria, can grow quickly out of control unless disciplined by regular pruning.

Flowering perennials should be trimmed right after blooming to give next year's flowers maximum time to develop. If your vine has fruiting potential, stand back and wait as flowers give way to berries.

LOOKING UP
Climbing rose and royal trumpet vine (just beginning to bloom) shelter a sunny sitting area. Strong wire trellising helps keep both plants upright.

? ASK THE GARDEN DOCTOR **HOW LONG DOES IT TAKE FOR A PERENNIAL VINE TO START BLOOMING?** Many perennial vines and climbers take two or three years to become established and commence flowering. In the meantime, complement them with annual vines that will bloom in their stead.

EASY-GROWING ANNUAL VINES

Colorful flowers, an undemanding nature, and a remarkable capacity for fast growth make an annual vine an asset in a garden. Most annuals grow easily from seeds; some can be sown directly in warm garden soil. Annual vines weigh less than woody perennials and require less support. Pruning is usually unnecessary. Fertilize in spring and early summer to promote fast growth.

BLACK-EYED SUSAN VINE *(THUNBERGIA ALATA)* Grow this 6- to 8-foot twiner from seed and enjoy the bright color blooms from midsummer on. It's an excellent container plant.

CARDINAL CLIMBER *(IPOMOEA ×MULTIFIDA)* The 10- to 15-foot twining vine with delicate foliage and scarlet flowers lures hummingbirds. It needs well-draining soil.

CANDY CORN VINE *(MANETTIA INFLATA)* This unusual 6-foot-tall bloomer is also known as firecracker plant. Easy to grow in a pot, it attracts hummingbirds and butterflies.

HYACINTH BEAN VINE *(DOLICHOS LABLAB)* Growing rapidly to 15 to 30 feet, this showy twiner has purple flowers, foliage, and seedpods. Contrast it with silvery blue plants.

MANDEVILLA *(MANDEVILLA ×AMABILIS)* A tropical treat for Zones 10 and 11, it grows elsewhere in containers. Show off the summerlong blooms on a patio or sunny porch.

MORNING GLORY *(IPOMOEA TRICOLOR)* Blooming in a range of colors, this sun-loving twiner grows up to 10 feet tall. The flowers open in the morning and close by afternoon.

SCARLET RUNNER BEAN *(PHASEOLUS COCCINEUS)* This 15-foot twiner, with bright red flowers and large edible beans, needs ample support, sun, and moisture.

SWEET PEA *(LATHYRUS ODORATA)* Known for its fragrant, colorful flowers, the 6-foot vine climbs via tendrils and make a fantastic hedge or screen, especially in cool climates.

SWEET POTATO VINE *(IPOMOEA BATATAS)* The colorful foliage of this 4- to 6-foot trailing vine is an asset in container gardens. Train the vines to a trellis using soft ties.

PERENNIAL VINES

As well-established fixtures in your garden from year to year, perennial vines add color, texture, and fragrance to the setting. Pair a perennial vine with a strong structure that can support the plant for many years. Some perennial vines take a year or two to settle in and take off. Prune plants every year to remove deadwood and manage them.

BITTERSWEET, AMERICAN (*CELASTRUS SCANDENS*) The woody twiner fruits in fall when a male and female vine are planted. Avoid invasive Oriental bittersweet.

HONEYSUCKLE (*LONICERA*) These twining, deciduous, or evergreen vines with fragrant flowers attract hummingbirds and butterflies. They can become invasive.

HOP, COMMON (*HUMULUS LUPULUS*) In Zones 5–8, this vigorous twiner grows 10 to 15 feet in a season. Ornamental 'Aureus' has showy chartreuse foliage.

HYDRANGEA, CLIMBING (*HYDRANGEA ANOMALA PETIOLARIS*) Clinging by rootlets, it prefers some shade and reaches 30 to 50 feet in Zones 4–8.

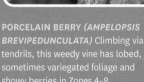

JASMINE (*JASMINUM*) Different types add their enchanting fragrance to a garden with their white flowers in summer. Hardiness varies. Grow it in a pot in cold climates.

PORCELAIN BERRY (*AMPELOPSIS BREVIPEDUNCULATA*) Climbing via tendrils, this weedy vine has lobed, sometimes variegated foliage and showy berries in Zones 4–8.

TRUMPET CREEPER (*CAMPSIS RADICANS*) This fast-growing twiner with showy flowers attracts hummingbirds in Zones 4–9. Prune yearly to control it.

BOUGAINVILLEA
This subtropical vine's sprawling stems grow up to 20 feet a year in Zones 9 and 10. Spectacularly colorful leaflike bracts surround the flowers and persist for weeks.

FAST GROWERS Research a vine before planting it. Assertive vines can overgrow a site and crowd out other plants. Think twice before adding an invasive vine to your garden. Invasive vines include: Chinese privet, English ivy, Japanese honeysuckle, Oriental bittersweet, trumpet creeper, and silver fleece vine.

COMBINING VINES WITH STRUCTURES

Put vines to work, pairing them with sturdy supports. Match a support to the weight and strength of the vine you're growing. Twiners such as honeysuckle or trumpet creeper may please you at the outset on a wooden trellis, but they will soon advance from tender shoots to very strong cords and then to wrist-size woody stems, with enough weight to crush anything but the strongest iron posts or similar structure.

BETTER FENCES Cucumber, one of many climbing edibles, teams beautifully with vintage iron fencing.

OVER AND ABOVE Arches and arbors, small or large, form simple frames such as this one for malabar spinach in a container garden.

QUICK PRIVACY Sturdy, lightweight bamboo makes a long-lasting trellis for Virginia creeper or another fast grower.

DISGUISE AN EYESORE A cloak of sweet autumn clematis turns an old shed into an attractive storage area.

UPWARDLY MOBILE Plant a vine such as clematis at the foot of an obelisk or other upright structure, giving it support from the onset.

POLE JUMPERS A trumpet creeper hides an unsightly pole, but the vine must be cut back annually to keep it in check.

SUPPORT SYSTEM
A pergola proves capable of holding up a vigorous and heavy wisteria. In the process, a shaded outdoor room takes shape.

ASK THE GARDEN DOCTOR

HOW DO I TRAIN A VINE TO CLIMB A SUPPORT? Install the structure first, then plant the vine at least 6 to 12 inches away from the strong support. Secure the plant to the support using soft ties, or gently twine it around the structure. Periodically, twine the vine some more, leading it in the direction you want it to grow.

GROWING CLEMATIS

Few flowering vines compare with the flower power of clematis. Variable and versatile, these vines give you options for riveting displays from spring into autumn.

Clematis offer a wide range of flower colors and shapes as well as various plant forms. These woody or herbaceous vines include vining forms that wend up to 10 to 20 feet among larger plants or form a colorful garden backdrop on fences and walls. Shrubby forms sprawl into 2- to 4-foot mounds.

Clematis need support, whether grow-through stakes for shrubby varieties, or netting, a light trellis, or chain-link fencing for larger climbers. You can plant them to grow through shrubs, such as lilac or other spring-bloomers. Or pair a clematis with another vine that has a different bloom season.

Give clematis a sunny location. Dappled shade during the hottest part of the summer is beneficial. Many gardeners recommend shading clematis roots with another plant, mulch, or the vine itself.

Plant clematis deeper than other climbers, burying the stems 2 inches deep in enriched soil. Dig a handful of superphosphate and scoops of peat moss into the planting hole. Scratch slow-release fertilizer into the soil each spring. Clematis benefit from consistent, deep watering between rains, as well as generous mulching.

Key to Success

Prune clematis to 18 to 24 inches in the early spring of their first year in the garden, no matter the type. After that, pruning depends on the type of clematis and is essential to the healthy life of a plant. Root and top growth should occur proportionately to ensure the plant's vitality as it develops over the years. If pruned regularly, clematis can live for decades.

WHICH CLEMATIS IS WHICH?

EARLY-FLOWERING These bloom in spring on previous summer's shoots. They need little or no pruning, just deadheading. Shown: *C. montana*

LARGE-FLOWERING HYBRIDS These bloom from spring into summer, summer into fall, or both. The plants fare best when protected from wind. Shown: 'Crystal Fountain'

LATE-FLOWERING The small- and large-flowering varieties include some of the most vigorous ones. They produce flowers on new growth. Prune in spring. Shown: *C. ternifolia or* sweet autumn

ASK THE GARDEN DOCTOR **MY CLEMATIS PRODUCES VERY FEW FLOWERS. WHAT'S THE PROBLEM?** Several factors could be affecting the plant: It may be receiving inadequate light—full to part sun is best. The soil may need a dose of phosphorus to boost flowering. Apply a slow-release fertilizer with a higher middle number (15-30-15) each spring to promote strong flower bud growth. You may be pruning at the wrong time of year and snipping off flower buds by mistake.

GROWING WISTERIA

Among the most beautiful of flowering vines, wisteria is known for its strong, vigorous growth and occasional stubbornness about blooming. Discover how to overcome the challenges that come with wisteria.

Like a living waterfall, Japanese wisteria (*Wisteria floribunda*) and Chinese wisteria (*W. sinensis*) produce dramatic 12-inch cascades of fragrant flowers in spring. Numerous cultivars offer violet-blue, white, or pink flowers. Growing in full sun, the plants are typically hardy in Zones 5 to 9, but some newer selections prove hardier.

The woody twiner develops a heavy, twisted trunk and artful character over time. Plan for your wisteria's long, healthy life by giving it a substantial support such as a heavy-duty pergola or an iron arch.

Wisterias require regular pruning to keep them within boundaries. Prune right after flowering, removing long shoots to shape the plant. Flowers develop on spurs or short side shoots off the main stem. Prune back to spurs with two or three buds to promote flower development. Prune in summer too, cutting current green growth—not older, brown stems—to spurs with buds. For more details, see Chapter 13, page 266.

What, No Blooms?

Resolve this common complaint about wisteria by using these tips:

- Start with a plant of blooming age. Seedlings can take up to 10 years to begin flowering.
- Plant in full sun.
- Avoid using nitrogen fertilizer, which promotes leafy growth at the expense of blooms. This vigorous plant can do without fertilizer.

IDEAL CONDITIONS Give your wisteria full sun, well-drained soil, adequate water during drought, and annual pruning to promote the best blooms.

WHITE-FLOWERING WISTERIA This variety has a stronger fragrance than the purple and blue varieties, and it adds a dramatic element to a moon garden that is especially enjoyable in the evening.

GROWING CLIMBING ROSES

If you're searching for a place to add a rose to your garden, look up! Give climbers the support they need to reach their potential. Then guide them to grow up and over a structure for maximum effect.

Climbing roses help you take your garden to greater heights. Generally, a climber is a rose with long, vigorous canes. Any rose that grows longer than 6 feet will need support to remain upright. True climbing roses have canes that reach up to 20 feet. Within this category of roses, there are also ramblers that bear clustered flowers on flexible canes and trailing roses that are well adapted to growing on walls, banks, or the ground. You'll find climbing forms of many rose types, from miniatures to hybrid teas and shrub roses. You might even find a climbing form of your favorite rose variety.

Structures add the style of a long-lasting architectural feature to the garden. Embellish an arbor, trellis, or pergola with a climbing rose to create a marvelous focal point. Guide a rose along fence rails or rooflines, or over an entry, porch, or window. Choose fragrant climbers for optimal effects.

Climbers need good air circulation to stay healthy. When you use a trellis, space it at least 18 inches from any solid surface. Although most rose canes have thorns, those won't cling to the support the way a vine would. Use a loose, flexible tie that will withstand weather. Secure canes periodically during the growing season. Training a rose requires patience (and tough gloves) to bend the canes and gently guide them to fit a structure.

Early each spring, prune deadwood and the oldest canes. See Chapter 13, page 266 for more information about pruning roses.

FULL SUN Grow climbers on the sunny side of a structure for best results. The more sun a rose receives, the happier and healthier it will be.

SCENTS APPEAL When selecting a rose for an arbor, choose a fragrant one so you can enjoy the scent whenever you walk under the structure.

SECURE CANES Use a soft or flexible material to lash climbing rose canes to their support. Avoid twist ties with wire centers or hard plastic material that can cut into canes.

ASK THE GARDEN DOCTOR **WHAT KIND OF SUPPORT IS NECESSARY FOR A CLIMBING ROSE?** A strong arbor or pergola works well. Plant the rose next to an upright support. Multiple climbing roses trained vertically up a wall or fence can be planted as close as 3 feet apart to create a cover. Climbers trained horizontally on a fence should be planted 8 to 10 feet apart.

HOW TO PLANT A CLIMBING ROSE

By pairing a climbing rose with a sturdy support, you'll form an ideal marriage. At first, you'll need to encourage the relationship between rose and structure. The rose will take off within a few months and it will take only a few years to attain a rose-covered structure.

1 **AMPLE HOLE** Prepare the planting hole 6 to 12 inches away from the plant support. Make the hole twice as wide and as deep as the potted rose's root ball.

2 **REMOVE POT** Set the root ball in the planting hole. Tip the plant back slightly toward the support. Mix a couple of shovelfuls of compost into the backfill. Fill in the planting hole.

3 **SOIL LEVEL** Situate the plant's crown (where the stems and roots meet) at ground level in a warm climate, or 2 inches below ground level in a cold climate, to protect the crown.

4 **WATER DEEPLY** Mound soil around the perimeter of the planting hole to hold water. Water weekly between rains throughout the first summer.

5 **ADD MULCH** Spread a 2-inch layer of mulch over the planting area. Keep the mulch away from the base of the plant. The mulch will help conserve soil moisture.

6 **TIE LOOSELY** Use a soft or flexible material to lash your new climbing rose to its support, coaxing the canes to hug the upright. In the second or third season, add or adjust ties as needed.

CHAPTER 9

GROWING EDIBLES

Cultivate a luscious landscape that will provide you with fresh vegetables, herbs, and fruits all season.

BETTER BEDS Where soil quality and drainage are poor, opt for raised beds and fill them with ideal soil.

GETTING STARTED

Site your edible garden right, and you'll reap the rewards of fresh, homegrown food throughout the season.

When you grow vegetables, herbs, and fruits, you'll get all kinds of benefits in addition to delectable produce. You'll experience the simplest of pleasures, biting into a luscious vine-ripened tomato, just-picked from the garden and still sun-warmed. Knowing that you grew it creates special satisfaction. Raising healthful food with superlative flavor also plays into a goal of self-sufficiency. You'll gain peace of mind that you are growing and eating food that has not been treated with pesticides or herbicides. Besides, you can think of an edible garden as a convenient personal produce section.

Site Requirements

Before you buy plants and start turning soil, consider where your edible plants will grow best. Whether you plan a utilitarian plot of vegetables or a few pots on a patio, meeting basic requirements ensures the plants will thrive and provide you with bountiful harvests.

Most edibles need full sun. A little late-afternoon shade can be helpful. Crops planted near shrubs and trees may get too much shade, and their roots will have to compete for water and nutrients.

The plants also need well-draining soil. Few crops thrive if the plants' roots are too often wet. In poorly draining soil, plants cannot absorb nutrients easily, and roots may rot.

You can easily incorporate a range of edibles into a new or established garden. Plan ahead when adding trees, shrubs, or perennials, such as apples, blueberries, and strawberries, to your yard, and allow room for mature plants. Also keep plants within easy reach of the kitchen and a water spigot. Add fencing, motion sensors, or lighting to discourage wildlife.

 **ASK THE GARDEN DOCTOR** **ARE THERE EDIBLE PLANTS THAT CAN BE GROWN IN SHADE?** Although most edibles need full sun, some will perform well in partial shade, with 3 to 6 hours of sun daily. Alliums (chives, garlic chives, onions); berries (blackberry, currant, gooseberry, strawberry); greens (arugula, cabbage, kale, lettuce, spinach, swiss chard *shown);* herbs (mint, parsley); and legumes (bush beans, peas, shell beans) can be successfully grown in partial shade.

PLANNING YOUR GARDEN

A good plan is like a road map—a helpful tool on your gardening journey. Make a plan for your growing season and you'll give your garden an organized head start.

Before you tuck that first seed into the ground, come up with a planting plan, whether general or specific. You may already have in mind some favorite plant varieties that you'd like to include, but first make sure you understand your region's climate and the length of your growing season. Using each season efficiently will improve the quality of your garden's produce and extend its growing season.

Match crops to the appropriate season. Vegetables include cool- and warm-season crops. No matter where you live, you can grow both kinds. The trick is timely successive planting. Plant cool-season crops early in the year, follow them with warm-season crops during the summer growing season, then replant cool-season crops for fall harvest. If you live in a warm climate, you can enjoy homegrown food year 'round.

WARM-SEASON CROPS Some popular vegetables, such as tomatoes, peppers, and eggplants, are subtropical plants. They perform best during the height of summer, when days and nights are warm. They're killed by frost and don't germinate or perform well when temperatures fall below 50°F. Sustain warm-season crops into fall by protecting them with cold frames, row covers, or other season-extending devices.

COOL-SEASON CROPS Many leafy vegetables, such as Swiss chard, lettuce, and kale, thrive in cool temperatures between 40 and 75°F. Typically, cool-season crops can be planted two to four weeks before the last spring frost. They will stop producing when summer's heat kicks in. In regions where nights remain cool, make small successive sowings throughout summer. In hotter regions, plant heat-tolerant varieties as early as possible in spring and then replant them for a fall harvest.

GROWING VEGETABLES

From earth to table, nothing tastes as fresh as homegrown vegetables. Decide what you like to eat, then get growing.

When it comes to weighing which vegetables to plant in your garden, the choice is obvious: Grow what you like to eat. A lot of vegetables are fun to grow, but if you cannot use all of your crops, share them with neighbors, friends, or the local food pantry.

Your garden's size might place some limitations on your plant choices. Sprawling vines such as pumpkins and cantaloupe might need more room than an entire small garden can provide. For limited spaces and containers, select varieties developed for their compact form and confined growth habits. Dwarf, patio, petite, and mini plants often yield full-size produce.

Plants or Seeds?

Most gardeners grow only a few plants of each kind of vegetable and merely buy a four- or six-pack of plants at their local garden center. The price of that pack might be only a little more than the cost of a seed packet, and it saves the effort of growing the plants from seed.

Nonetheless, sowing seeds remains a key part of vegetable gardening for practical reasons. First, rapidly germinating vegetables, such as turnips, radishes, squash, corn, and beans, are generally easier to grow from seed planted directly in the garden. Second, seed companies offer far more varieties than you'll find for sale as seedlings, giving you more options. Besides, it's just plain fun to watch seeds germinate and grow.

When planting seeds, follow the packet instructions regarding planting time, depth, and spacing. It's typical to plant more seeds than you need, then begin thinning (plucking out) excess seedlings after they develop several leaves.

FRESH FAVORITES Whether you start from seeds or seedlings, vegetable gardens begin paying their dividends quickly with fresh produce within a few weeks.

ASK THE GARDEN DOCTOR | **WHICH VEGETABLES SHOULD I START INDOORS FROM SEEDS?** One way to decide which plants you'll raise from seeds is the number of days required for plants to reach maturity. If the growing season is short where you live, start long-season plants from seed, including Brussels sprouts, eggplant, melon, pumpkin, tomatillo, and some tomatoes.

ORNAMENTAL EDIBLES

Combine vegetables, flowers, and herbs for a garden that's a feast for the palate and the eyes.

Many gardeners relegate vegetables to one section of the yard and flowers to another. But the most striking gardens are often those that mix edible and ornamental plants to create beautiful and bountiful results in any size space. This works even better when you include varieties of edible plants that offer more ornamental qualities than standard types.

From Functional to Fabulous

Most vegetables thrive with the same care you give to flowering plants. But when you plan and plant your garden, select edible plants for aesthetic as well as practical reasons. Select varieties for their size, form, color, and texture. Mingle purple-leaf basil and feathery dill with glossy broccoli and your favorite flowers. Choose from a paint box of colorful lettuces, chard, peppers, and eggplant. When tucked into beds, they'll only add to the display.

Think outside the box when working ornamentals into your garden design. Take advantage of the range of plants from ground-covering herbs to towering Jerusalem artichokes. Plant climbing beans and vining tomatoes on handsome supports as eye-catching vertical elements. Grow edible flowers such as pansies to add color to your fresh greens. Enhance a perennial bed with the dramatic large leaves and buxom forms of rhubarb and summer squash.

PURPLE PASSION Mix flowers and vegetables for a more ornamental bed. Here, kohlrabi (a cousin to cabbage) and petunias (edible) in different shades of purple celebrate a favorite color.

HAPPY TOGETHER Edible plants create a beautiful garden full of colorful, textural treats. This plot includes tomato, sunflower, potato, calendula, purple basil, and signet marigold.

PLANTING AND TRANSPLANTING

Soil, seeds, water, and time produce delightfully delicious results in an edible garden. Whether you start with seeds or plants, you'll discover advantages with both.

Plants can be grown from seeds or seedlings started indoors or planted directly in the garden. Starting with seeds, you can raise plants indoors weeks before garden season usually gets rolling (around the last average frost date). Or you can wait until then, and plant directly in the garden.

Besides giving you a leg up on the growing season, starting vegetables and herbs from seed has other practical advantages. Seeds offer a wider selection than plants at less cost. They are a practical way to grow a large number of plants for you to enjoy or share with friends and family. Some seeds are best sown directly in the soil; others need to be planted indoors for transplanting into the garden later.

Some seeds are tricky and time-consuming either to start indoors or to sow directly in the garden. Buy these vegetables and herbs as transplants at your local garden center or place an order with a plant company to have them shipped to your doorstep at planting time. When shopping for transplants, look for sturdy, short plants that have a strong stem and healthy foliage.

Planting a Raised Bed

You can plant a variety of edibles and access them easily from all sides of a small-but-efficient raised bed. Use stakes and string to divide the bed into a grid, and plant each section with something different. See page 76 for information on how to make a raised bed.

① PLANT IN SECTIONS
Plant seed potatoes in one section. Dig planting holes about 4 inches deep and 6 inches apart.

② PLANT BEAN SEEDS
Plant seeds 1 inch deep and 2 inches apart in staggered rows. When seedlings have at least three large leaves, thin them to about 4- to 6-inch spacing.

③ PLANT LEEKS Space seedlings about 3 inches apart. As they grow, harvest every other leek, leaving more space for the remaining plants.

④ PLANT CABBAGE Give seedlings plenty of growing room, spacing them 24 inches apart. Plant small-headed varieties 12 to 18 inches apart.

⑤ ADD MARIGOLDS
Surround the perimeter of the bed with marigolds to deter insect pests and add summer-long color. See the mature garden *opposite*.

? ASK THE GARDEN DOCTOR **WHAT ARE COMPANION PLANTS?** Experienced gardeners and research studies will tell you that some plants specifically benefit others when planted in proximity. Known as companion planting, this practice uses marigolds and onions, for instance, to discourage pests.

 **TEST GARDEN TIP**

LAYER OF PROTECTION Mulch a raised bed to deter weeds and conserve soil moisture. Elevated beds dry out more quickly than ground-level gardens. Also, soil covered with dark organic mulch, such as compost or shredded leaves, will keep cooler than bare soil exposed to light—a boon to cool-season crops.

RAISED BED OPTIONS
This 3x6-foot bed was made with a kit, but you can build yours using cedar, pressure-treated, composite, or recycled-content lumber. Lumber treated with preservatives and other chemicals may leach toxins into the soil,

PLANTING TECHNIQUES

The way you plant is as important as the varieties you choose. There are numerous ways to make the most of your available gardening space.

Traditional rows are easy to cultivate, manage, and harvest. Gardeners have long planted vegetables in rows because deciding where to plant each crop influences how your garden grows overall.

For example, plant tall crops, such as corn and pole beans, on the north side of the garden to keep them from shadowing shorter crops, or on the south side if you want to cast intermittent shade on shorter, heat-sensitive crops.

Spacing between seeds and rows depends on what you are planting. As a general rule, follow the guidelines on the seed packet for the best results. Large plants, such as squash and eggplant, need rows at least 3 feet apart and should be spaced 30 inches apart in the row. Smaller plants, such as onions and radishes, can tolerate rows 8 to 9 inches apart and can be planted 2 to 4 inches apart.

Wide-row planting makes efficient use of space, instead of giving it up to paths between narrow rows of plants. It allows you to plot the planting space in a densely planted grid, and works well for greens, radishes, carrots, and beets.

Succession planting allows you to plant two crops more efficiently in the same space, pairing a short-season crop that comes and goes before the longer-season crop develops and needs more growing room. For example, plant seeds of spinach and beets at once. By the time the spinach crop is done and gone, the beets will have begun to fill in the voids.

SPRING GREENS Spokes of lettuces include "cut-and-come-again" varieties. Once cut, they continue to grow and provide more harvests.

PLANT MARKERS Transform thrift-store silverware into plant markers that help you remember what you planted and where.

PERMANENT INK Write on the handle, then plunge your long-lasting marker into the soil for a charming effect.

ASK THE GARDEN DOCTOR **CAN I GROW MY TOMATOES IN THE SAME SPOT AS LAST YEAR?** Vegetables from the same families are often susceptible to the same pest and disease problems. Avoid planting closely related vegetables in the same spot for at least 3 years to minimize problems. Rotate plants in the same family—tomato (pepper, potato, eggplant), cabbage (broccoli, cauliflower, kohlrabi, kale, collards), and squash (cucumber, melon, pumpkin)—to different locations.

TEST GARDEN TIP

GO VERTICAL Be creative and make use of often-underutilized space: Just grow up. Save precious ground in a small garden by using trellises, stakes, and fencing to train vining crops such as pole beans, tomatoes, melons, and cucumbers.

BETTER TRANSPLANTS Soaking the roots of seedlings in a liquid starter solution stimulates root growth, so the plant can take off as soon as it is planted.

SPACE SAVERS Harvest more from a small garden by combining crops in the same area. For example, fast-growing radishes come and go, making room for a slower-growing crop of broccoli.

PLANTING PARTNERS Smaller plants can be grown in the spaces between other plants. Bushy, low-growing parsley fills in among caged tomato plants.

PLEASING POTS Some edibles, such as sweet potato vine, grow well in containers. This a good option for small spaces and urban gardeners. Water potted edibles consistently.

PLANTING GRIDS As this raised bed layout demonstrates, any given plot will hold more plants when arranged in a grid pattern rather than rows. Tuck one or more plants into each square, depending on their size.

HEAPING HILLS Some plants, such as summer squash and cucumber, prefer to be planted in hills because the soil drains especially well. Mulch to keep the heaped soil from drying out.

GROWING TOMATOES

The must-have summer crop is not difficult to grow. Use this planting advice to spur your success.

Which type of tomato and which varieties will you grow? It depends on the amount of space you have and how you plan to use the fruit: fresh for salads and eating out of hand, in cooking, or preserving for later use. Stagger your crop with early and late varieties. Opt for disease-resistant varieties.

Determinate tomatoes: Ideal for containers, these varieties grow into bushy plants that need little more than a stake for support. The uniform, limited crop develops in a condensed period of weeks, often early. Taller, heavier plants benefit when supported by a stout stake.

Indeterminate tomatoes: The continually vining plants produce an unlimited stream of flowers and fruit throughout the season until frost. Keep indeterminate tomatoes upright by surrounding them with heavy-duty wire cages, or use your favorite tomato support system.

When buying seedlings, choose healthy plants that show no signs of flowering or yellowing leaves. At planting time, use red mulch, a plastic sheeting that benefits tomato plants by warming soil, suppressing weeds, conserving water, and improving fruiting.

Keep plants healthy by allowing ample room between them for air circulation. Water regularly at the base of plants to avoid wetting leaves, and feed with liquid plant food. Spread a 4-inch layer of organic mulch between plants.

① PREPARE SHEETS Cut the plastic mulch into a 2-to 3-foot square for each plant. Cut an X opening large enough for your hand and tomato seedling to fit through.

② PINCH BRANCHES Remove a seedling's lowest leaves. Then bury the stem to the lowest remaining branch to encourage more-vigorous root growth.

③ PLANT THE TOMATO Small bush varieties should be planted 2 feet apart. Larger varieties, especially sprawling plants, need at least 3 to 4 feet of growing room.

④ FEED THE SEEDLINGS Give tomato plants a big gulp of good nutrition with a serving of fish emulsion.

⑤ SET THE CAGE Set the plant support in place. If you try to stake a plant later when it is larger, you might damage tender stalks.

ASK THE GARDEN DOCTOR **WHY ARE MY TOMATOES CRACKING AND SPLITTING?** Cracking can be caused by wide fluctuations in temperature and moisture. Watering deeply each week and mulching help prevent cracking. Rapidly growing fruit is also susceptible to cracking. Avoid using excess fertilizer.

TOMATO GROWING TECHNIQUES

You'll need to stake, cage, or trellis some tomato plants. Indeterminate vining plants grow lush and rangy, requiring you to tie them to stakes or support them with heavy-duty wire cages. Alternative supports such as bamboo trellises also work. Coax plants to grow within a support; prune them occasionally if need be.

TOMATO CAGE Heavy fruits are enough to topple a tomato plant under its weight. Give plants ample support by setting a tomato cage in place as soon as you plant.

FENCING VINES A vining cherry tomato plant climbs a fence with a little help. A cage supports the base of the plant while garden twine secures extended branches in their ascent.

CHOICE VARIETY 'Maskotka', a tumbling-type cherry tomato, grows happily in a large bowl-shape pot or basket. The plants spill over the sides and need no additional support.

HARVESTING TOMATOES

Tomatoes reach their peak of juicy, tangy flavor when their color develops fully, but you can also pick fruit as soon as it shows a hint of color.

Ordinarily, when you pick ripe tomatoes, you keep them at room temperature out of direct sunlight until you're ready to eat them. Avoid chilling tomatoes in the refrigerator, where the cool temperature breaks down their flavor and texture.

By the time the end of the garden season rolls around, you'll want to grab the crop while you can. Before the first frost takes the last of those precious tomatoes, harvest green fruit and use it as is or save it for later—you'll enjoy fresh tomatoes long after you've put your garden to bed.

READ ALL ABOUT IT Wrap green tomatoes in newspaper and allow them to ripen in a cool place such as a basement. Check the tomatoes periodically and use the fully colored fruits.

AT SEASON'S END Set not-quite-ready tomatoes on a windowsill to finish ripening. At this stage, flavor will continue to develop in the fruit.

ALL-STAR VEGGIES

Here's a taste of some of the most popular vegetable crops. All are widely adapted and easy to grow. But don't stop here. Explore a world full of wonderful varieties whose flavors, colors, and tolerance to growing conditions vary widely. Find the veggies best suited to your taste and garden.

ASPARAGUS Long-lived asparagus sends up spears for weeks each spring. Work composted manure into the soil between plants annually.

BEAN, GREEN Bush beans grow knee high; pole beans vine up to 6 feet with a sturdy trellis. Consider dried and shelling bean varieties too.

BEET Valued for their sweet roots and earthy-tasting greens, beets grow easily from seed. Choose from red, yellow, white, and striped varieties.

BROCCOLI Easy to grow and packed with nutrients, this cool-weather crop will bolt and go to seed when hot weather arrives.

CABBAGE Harvest the leafy heads in spring or fall. The root stub left behind may produce more tiny heads. Protect plants from cabbage butterflies.

CARROT This crunchy, nutritious, and sweet root grows especially well in cool weather. Grow it in sandy, damp soil and raised beds.

CUCUMBER Productive plants grow easily in rows, beds, containers, or hills. Limit the quantity of plantings unless you plan to make pickles.

EGGPLANT Start seeds early; plant seedlings after the last frost date. Eggplant grows best during periods of high heat and humidity.

GREENS Rich in colors and nutrients, leafy Swiss chard, collards, kale, and other frost-tolerant crops grow easily and beautifully.

LETTUCE Leafy varieties, in hues from chartreuse to purple, grow easily. Sow seeds in early spring and fall; stagger plantings for a continual harvest.

MELON Heat-loving melons hide under rambling, leafy vines. The plants need ample space, nutrients, and water to grow and produce well.

ONION, LEEK, AND GARLIC The members of the onion family grow in any garden. Plant in full sun and in soil high in organic matter.

PEA Shell, snow, and snap peas are among the spring garden's treasures. They all thrive in full sun to part shade and well-drained soil.

PEPPER Harvest sweet or hot peppers when they're green or let the fruit ripen to full flavor and color, whether red, yellow, orange, or purple.

POTATO Plant in early spring, starting with seed potatoes from a garden center or mail order source. They're easy to grow in a roomy container.

TOMATO Tomatoes thrive on heat, grow in almost any soil, bear abundantly, and need a long season in which to mature.

SQUASH Summer squashes (zucchini, yellow, scallop) produce generously. Winter varieties include acorn, butternut, and spaghetti.

PLANT SUPPORTS

Some vegetables are born to climb. If you have plants with places to go, be sure to provide a strong support system.

There are several advantages to supporting and training edibles to grow upright and away from soil.

When supported, vining plants such as pole bean, tomato, Malabar spinach, and sweet potato vine take up less space in a bed. Using vertical space opens up more opportunities for you to tuck in another crop of your favorite companion plants. Some plants demand support, especially those that bear heavy fruit (melon, cucumber, squash).

Stems and leaves will get better air circulation when they grow upright. Moisture from rain or overhead watering dries off more quickly. Their fruits receive more sunshine so they ripen sooner and more evenly. Plus, just being off the ground means the fruit is less likely to suffer disease or injury by soil-dwelling insects, which means a better harvest.

Some plants naturally intertwine around supports, while others need a little lesson in how to do it themselves. To train your climbing plants, use soft twist ties or garden twine to tie the plant to the support. You might need to do this several times before the plant commits to its support system.

LATTICE PANELS Wood panels support cucumbers and other heavy-bearing vines. Heavy-duty steel rebar anchors the panels and secures them.

JUTE TRELLIS It's easy to make your own trellis. Construct a sturdy frame and add eye hooks to the inside of the supports. Tie lengths of jute onto the hooks in a grid pattern.

CREATIVE STAKE The repurposed handle of a croquet mallet upholds a knee-high pepper plant loaded with fruit. The stake also adds color to the garden.

ASK THE GARDEN DOCTOR **DO I NEED TO STAKE VEGETABLES GROWING IN CONTAINERS?** It depends on the plant. Any tall plant without strong stems benefits from staking. Many tomatoes, some peppers, and eggplant need help to remain upright. You'll find a variety of small ready-made trellises that suit container gardens.

 **TEST GARDEN TIP**

STRATEGIC POSITION Orient trellis panels on a north-south axis to avoid having the vines growing on them throw undesirable shade onto lower-growing plants nearby.

STEEL FENCING Inexpensive lengths of steel fencing are available at farm supply stores. Set them in the ground using metal stakes. Lash them together and let vining vegetables such as cucumbers take off with strong support.

ARTFUL SUPPORT A stout obelisk provides ornamental support for a climber such as a lunchbox-type watermelon. The structure should be well anchored.

HARVESTING VEGETABLES

When your vegetables reach peak flavor, it's time to pick a peck. Harvest time in the garden means you'll have the freshest flavors at the table.

Because different vegetables mature at different rates, the trick is to pick each crop at its prime. Most crops reach their peak flavor when they're young and tender. As vegetables and fruits pass maturity, they can become fibrous, tough, or rotten.

FAMILY TIME Harvest time provides sweet rewards for backyard gardeners, in fruits as well as special moments.

It's up to you to learn when a fruit or vegetable has reached its optimum harvest time. This might mean picking asparagus and tomatoes daily, and eggplant and lettuce every few days. Harvest ripening peas and pole beans every couple of days to promote ongoing production over the season.

Eat or store freshly picked produce promptly. If you allow vegetables to sit on a counter for days, they lose moisture and vitamin content. The sugars in some crops such as corn or peas begin turning to starch unless the produce is refrigerated swiftly. To prevent vegetables from continued ripening, put them in a plastic bag in a refrigerator or cool, dark cellar.

Carry a basket during garden strolls and you'll be equipped to bring in a load of ready produce.

GOOD PICKINGS Place harvested vegetables in a flat-bottomed trug or in a shallow bowl, so veggies aren't crushed under the weight of the harvest.

 **ASK THE GARDEN DOCTOR** **DOES IT MATTER WHAT TIME OF DAY I HARVEST PRODUCE FROM THE GARDEN?** The time of day when you pick the garden's bounty is important. For most fruits and vegetables, early morning is best for harvesting because that's when produce contains maximum sugars. Pick produce right after the dew dries.

HARVEST TIPS

No magical date on the calendar signifies that harvest time is here. Depending on what you plant and when, you may be harvesting vegetables for several weeks—or even months. Keep these tips in mind to get the most from your crops.

LETTUCE Pinch or snip the plants' outer leaves or an entire head. Leafy cut-and-come-again varieties will grow back if you leave an inch or so of plant when cutting.

RADISH Pull the mature roots as soon as they're big enough to enjoy. Radishes left in the ground too long can crack, become woody, and develop an unpleasantly hot flavor.

GARLIC Plant in the fall and harvest the following summer when at least half the leaves have begun to yellow. Cure bulbs by hanging them in a warm, airy, shaded place for several weeks.

CARROT Bigger is not always better. Harvesting these vegetables while they are small means capturing a sweeter flavor; larger carrots often taste bitter and may be woody.

BROCCOLI When the head is fully developed and the flowers are tightly budded, use a knife to cut the stem about halfway down it. The stalk will continue to produce side shoots.

SWEET POTATO Root crops such as sweet potatoes can be harvested any time they are ready. But gather them before a heavy frost or freeze occurs that can damage the crop.

CHERRY TOMATO These wee fruits, along with grape- and currant-type tomatoes, are ready to pick and eat when fully colored. Snip the entire cluster, if you like.

EXTENDING THE SEASON

Stretch your growing season—in early spring and late fall—with these ideas for protecting plants from cold weather.

Most vegetable gardeners agree: The warm sun of late spring and early summer arrives too late and frost comes too early. While most vegetables require high temperatures and plenty of sun to grow, ripen, and produce, the growing season doesn't need to be limited by first and last frost dates.

The most effective way to extend the season is to protect seedling or maturing crops from frost. This usually entails some kind of covering. There are several ways to warm the soil around plants, from inexpensive products you can buy to freebies that you pull from the recycling bin. One of the most popular options is the cold frame, a bottomless box with a hinged clear plastic or glass lid.

In the spring, a cold frame allows the gardener to get an earlier start on the gardening season, nurturing seedlings in the protected environment. Whether you start seedlings yourself or purchase them from a greenhouse, a cold frame provides a good temporary home until planting time arrives.

In the fall, quick-maturing vegetables, such as lettuce and greens, may be planted in cold frames from mid- to late summer for fall harvests. A cold frame can be set in the garden to shelter leeks, beets, and cabbages, allowing them to survive well into winter. For added protection in the harshest climates, gardeners insulate cold frames with bales of hay around the perimeter.

COLD FRAME Make a shelter for seedlings by hinging an old window sash to a wooden frame. Ventilate the box on sunny days by propping open the lid.

MILK JUG Cut out the bottom of a plastic jug and use it as a protective cloche, similar to a mini greenhouse, for young plants. Wiggle the cut end of the jug into the soil.

WATER WALL Water-filled tubes in the Wall-o'-Water give off energy that warms the air and ground around your plant, giving it an earlier start.

FABRIC COVER Drape low plants with lightweight garden fabric to insulate plants from frost. Use rocks here and there to keep the fabric from blowing away.

ASK THE GARDEN DOCTOR
DO I NEED TO PROTECT PLANTS FROM EXTREME SUMMER HEAT? Although temperature concerns often focus on season extension and protecting plants from cold, modifying temperatures in hot climates can also be beneficial. Create a shade screen to keep soil cooler and protect plants from sunscald and drying winds. Shade can extend the season for cool-weather crops, slowing them from bolting and developing bitter flavor during hot weather.

TEST GARDEN TIP

REGULATE THE TEMPERATURE Remove coverings on warm or sunny days to keep from baking your plants. Most coverings are effective only at temperatures above 20 degrees F. Tender plants may need protection from wind and hail, in addition to potentially damaging temperatures.

ROW COVER Most garden fabrics are lightweight enough to drape directly over a crop. Pulled over wire supports, the fabric forms a tunnel and holds warmth.

GROWING HERBS

Herbs reward with their distinct scents and fresh flavors, whether you grow them in garden beds or containers, outdoors or indoors.

Most herbs grow as happily in containers as they do in garden beds. Work with the space you have and design a formal or informal scheme, an entire landscape, a plot outside the kitchen door, or a handy indoor windowsill garden.

Most herbs are as ornamental in the garden as they are useful after harvest. Those with flowers, such as chives, rosemary, and lavender, are attractive in their own right. Others have handsome foliage that pairs well with other plants in the garden. For instance, purple-leaf basil contrasts nicely with leaf lettuce, and the wispy foliage of dill or fennel makes a soft background for sun-loving flowers such as roses.

Herbs are no more difficult to grow than vegetables or flowers. They are hardy and rarely succumb to diseases and pests. Most herbs need little more than fertile soil with good drainage and regular weeding. Frequent harvesting keeps plants growing as lushly and productively as possible throughout the growing season.

Getting Started

Herbs that grow easily from seed include basil, cilantro, and dill. Some start better as seedlings, including rosemary, French tarragon, and bay.

If you want just a couple of plants of each herb, start with seedlings in the spring. When buying herbs, check the botanical name to be sure you get the plant you want. Smell an herb and take a nibble to learn about its flavor and intensity.

PRETTY EDIBLES Combine herbs with other edibles or flowers. This bed features potatoes, tricolor sage, purple basil, and signet marigolds.

SENSORY GARDEN A potted garden holds trailing nasturtium 'Gleam Yellow', French thyme, tricolor sage, and curly parsley—pleasing to the nose, eyes, and palate.

ASK THE GARDEN DOCTOR **IS IT TRUE THAT HERBS TOLERATE POOR SOIL?** Many herbs are tough plants that can withstand various conditions. But they will grow more vigorously if planted in good-quality, well-draining soil, loaded with organic amendments. Go light on fertilizer, which encourages soft, cold-sensitive growth that has less fragrance and flavor.

EASY HERBS

Here's a taste of some of the most popular herbs. Most are exceptionally productive, contributing fresh flavor to your favorite foods from spring through fall. All are widely adapted and easy to grow. But keep looking. The world is full of wonderful varieties with unlimited flavors, colors, and tolerance to growing conditions.

BASIL *(OCIMUM BASILICUM)* Pinch plant tips often to encourage branching and prevent flowers from forming. Harvest and use leaves fresh throughout the summer.

CHIVES *(ALLIUM SCHOENOPRASUM)* This perennial grows to 15 inches, with slender foliage and fluffy blooms. Harvest both and use them fresh or frozen for their delicate onion flavor.

DILL *(ANETHUM GRAVEOLENS)* Sow dill seeds directly in warm garden soil, planting every three weeks from spring until midsummer for a continuous supply of aromatic foliage.

LAVENDER *(LAVANDULA)* There are many varieties of this wonderfully fragrant herb. Add gravel to planting holes to give plants the well-draining conditions essential to their growth.

OREGANO *(ORIGANUM VULGARE)* The signature flavor in Italian cooking, this herb thrives in full sun and well-drained soil. It grows up to 2 feet tall. Use the leaves fresh or dried.

PARSLEY *(PETROSELINUM CRISPUM)* For a steady supply of leaves, sow seeds in spring and midsummer. Curly-leaf parsley makes a frilly edging for garden beds.

ROSEMARY *(ROSMARINUS OFFICINALIS)* A tender perennial, rosemary grows into to a 2- to 4-foot-tall shrub. Snip side branches to encourage bushy growth.

SAGE *(SALVIA OFFICINALIS)* Earthy and pungent, this woody evergreen perennial grows to 2½ feet. Harvest the leaves as needed and replace the plant after five years.

THYME *(THYMUS)* Perennials, available in many varieties, need room to spread. Low-growing selections work well as garden edging or fillers between stepping-stones.

SUCCESS WITH HERBS

Because of their beauty and wide range of sizes, shapes, colors, and textures, herbs offer a nearly limitless palette for the landscape.

Pay careful attention to the range of an herb's hardiness, its light and moisture requirements, and your region's last frost dates. All of these factors influence which herbs can grow successfully in your climate and where and how you raise them.

Most herbs will thrive with at least six hours of full sun daily. Many perennial plants, including thyme, rosemary, lavender, and sage, are native to the Mediterranean. They grow best in full sun and very well-drained, slightly alkaline soil.

Herbs don't need their own garden. Tuck them among vegetables and flowers for beautiful effects. Fit in a few basil plants among the tomatoes; replace spring pansies with cilantro. For a second crop of fast-growing annual herbs such as chervil and dill,

plant seeds in midsummer to allow time for them to mature before the end of the growing season.

To get the most benefit and pleasure from growing herbs, make them a part of your everyday life, rather than something saved only for special occasions. In the kitchen, popular uses for herbs include making delicious pesto, flavored spreadable cheese, piquant salad dressings, and much more. Use them as aromatic garnishes for drinks and surprising additions to desserts.

Beyond their edible appeal, you can also use aromatic herbs around the house in fragrant bouquets and soothing body-care preparations. Growing herbs can lead you into a fascinating realm as you discover different ways to use your plants.

SUNNY SIDE Herbs flourish in full sun. Integrate them into a kitchen garden, mixed border, or flower bed. They adapt well to almost any spacious container, from a window box to patio pots.

MOVE INDOORS Near the end of the growing season, transplant a few herbs, such as parsley and rosemary, into pots and then move them indoors, to a sunny windowsill for the winter.

DENSE GROWTH Before herbs blossom, pinch off any buds. When harvesting herbs, stand fresh-cut stems in a glass of cool water and keep them handy for several days on the kitchen counter.

? ASK THE GARDEN DOCTOR **HOW DO I HARVEST FRESH HERBS FOR COOKING?** Strip fresh leaves off a stem by sliding your thumb and forefinger from stem top to bottom. Snip off larger leaves such as those of parsley that don't strip off readily; chop them just before adding to a dish.

HARVESTING HERBS

Snip and savor fresh herbs as often as possible. Near the end of the season, harvest plants and freeze or dry the leaves for extended use throughout the winter.

The more frequently you snip your favorite culinary herbs, the more densely they'll grow and continue producing. Cut stems from plants early in the day, after the dew has dried but before the sun bakes the plants' essential oils (the essence of their flavors and fragrances). Harvest no more than one-third of the stem's length, and the plant will continue to produce throughout the season.

FRESH BASIL Harvest basil leaves as needed and pinch off any flowers that begin to form. Try different varieties of basil and experiment with their flavors, from spicy to lemony.

NEAT AND TIDY Compact spicy globe basil forms a neat, 8- to 12-inch edging plant. Shear plants often to maintain their low, mounding shape. The tiny leaves hold big flavor.

GOURMET FLOWERS Give fennel a place in the garden for its feathery foliage and its licoricelike aroma. Gather the flowers and use their pollen in cooking.

PRETTY RISTRAS String spicy chiles, garlic, and sage for a decorative addition to the kitchen. Hang the ristra in a place away from light and heat to protect the herbs' flavors.

DELICIOUS DILL To keep dill producing tasty leaves, snip flowers as soon as they form. Cut the mature seedheads, dry them in a paper bag, and store the seeds in a jar.

STORING HERBS Once herbs are fully dried, the whole leaves can be stripped from the stems and stored in opaque containers away from light and heat.

GROWING BLUEBERRIES

Add these sweet treats to your landscape. The perennial plants will produce tasty fruit for weeks during the summer.

The shrubs offer year-round beauty: spring blooms, summer fruit, a showy fall display, and winter bark. Use the 4- to 6-foot-tall woody plants as a hedge. Or select from lower-growing dwarf varieties (2 to 3 feet tall) for colorful additions to foundation plantings and mixed borders.

Blueberries grow best in full sun and acidic, moist soil. Growing them may require adjusting the soil pH to around 5, but it is well worth it. Work peat moss into the soil at planting time. Amend the soil with decayed pine bark in fall; mulch with pine needles in spring. Scratch in fertilizer or soil acidifier, being careful not to damage blueberries' shallow roots.

The delicious berries have supreme nutrition. Birds love the berries too. Unless you're willing to share the crop, protect the bushes by draping them with garden netting.

BLUEBERRY GOODNESS This shrub loves full sun and well-drained acidic soil. To lower the pH of garden soil that is not acidic enough, mix the soil 50/50 with sphagnum peat moss before planting. Plant two varieties of blueberry to achieve fruiting from the plants cross-pollinating each other.

GROWING STRAWBERRIES

There's a strawberry variety to suit every region and any garden.

Although the 6-inch-tall plants prefer full sun and loose, well-drained loam or sandy loam, they will grow well with less sun and in containers.

Choose varieties suited to your region. Check with your county extension service to find out which varieites are recommended. June-bearing plants produce fruit in early- to midsummer and grow by sending out runners and spreading. Everbearing varieties fruit from early summer into fall. Day-neutral varieties produce fruit their first year in the garden.

Plant strawberries in early spring where winters are mild. Use the plants as a groundcover or garden edging, if you like. Work loads of compost and composted manure into planting areas before adding plants.

PATIO PILLOW Strawberries send out runners, which helps them spread. If you want to contain your berries, plant them in a "patio pillow," or a large compost bag. Cut holes in the top of the bag to plant the strawberries.

CONTAIN THE CROP Confine your strawberry plants to a raised bed or large container and allow them to grow and spread freely. Lay a 2- to 4-inch layer of organic mulch to help keep the berries clean and ready to eat.

GROWING BRAMBLES

These plants are vigorous and can become unruly, but when maintained, they are satisfyingly productive.

Closely related, raspberries and blackberries are known as brambles and get their name from their prickly canes. They grow easily as shrubby plants, producing lots of delicious fruit. Brambles thrive in full sun and enriched well-drained soil. If a well-draining site is not possible, plant canes in a raised bed. Amend the soil yearly with compost and rotted manure. Mulch to prevent weeds and preserve soil moisture. For best fruit production, size, and flavor, water plants well—1 to 2 inches of water per week—especially as the fruits are developing.

Raspberries

Raspberries are one of the most worthwhile home-garden crops. The fresh-picked fruit is a superb on-the-spot garden snack and a bargain compared to store-bought berries. Various fruit colors (red, yellow, purple, black) and ripening times make it easy to enjoy a long harvest of raspberries with a diversity of pretty fruits. Red and yellow varieties grow one or two crops per year on stiff canes; purple and black varieties grow one crop on trailing vines that need to be trellised. They're either summer fruiting or everbearing, from summer into fall.

Blackberries

Blackberries are either upright, stiff-caned plants or trailing. They can be thorny or thornless. They produce fruit on 2-year-old canes. Trailing varieties include marionberry, boysenberry, dewberry, and loganberry.

Blackberries and raspberries are prone to disease. Buy only disease-resistant varieties and those hardy in your region.

GOLDEN OR YELLOW RASPBERRIES With sweeter and juicier fruit than red berries, they produce crops in late summer and early fall.

BRAMBLES OF BERRIES Raspberries (red, black, purple, and yellow) have different plant forms. Red raspberries spread by underground runners. Purple and black varieties grow on upright canes or trailing vines that require trellising.

ASK THE GARDEN DOCTOR   **CAN I GROW STRAWBERRIES IN A POT?** Yes. Make it a spacious container or else the soil will dry out too quickly and the plants will not thrive. Plant them in a hanging basket to keep the berries out of reach of chipmunks and other hungry critters.

GROWING TREE AND VINE FRUITS

Fruiting trees pay double dividends—sprays of spring blooms and harvests of juicy, delicious eating.

Fruit trees are available in a range of sizes that grow almost anywhere as long as they have full sun and well-draining soil. Standard-size fruit trees grow from 20 to 40 feet tall. Semidwarf varieties reach 10 to 15 feet. Dwarf trees grow up to 8 to 10 feet tall. Vining fruits such as grapes reach 20 feet and need strong support.

Dwarf varieties and training methods allow you to grow several fruit trees in a small yard and still have plenty of space available for vegetables or flowers. Dwarf varieties are ideal for a container garden. They will need extra protection in a cold climate.

Use fruit trees to create shade, accent a border, frame a yard, or form a hedge. Apple, cherry, pear, and plum trees are as ornamental as they are productive, with spring blossoms and summer fruits. These fruits require cross-pollination to make fruit, meaning you must plant two trees of different varieties within 100 feet of each other.

Modern varieties have better disease resistance and tolerance of special soil and climate conditions, which means better results for home gardeners. Your success will be determined mostly by taking these steps: Choose varieties appropriate to your climate and site. Manage disease and pests. Water plants deeply and regularly the first year to encourage strong root growth. After their first year, prune fruit trees and vines annually to promote healthy plants.

GRAPES GALORE Plant grapes in full sun and deep sandy loam. Choose a south- or east-facing slope with good air circulation to promote healthy vines. Support them with a fence, pergola, or trellising.

CHERRIES JUBILEE Whether you prefer sweet or sour cherries, a cherry tree provides a beautiful addition to the home landscape. Its flowers are a harbinger of spring.

ASK THE GARDEN DOCTOR **WHICH FRUITS CAN I GROW IN MY YARD?** Depending on the climate where you live, in addition to berries you might grow these tree fruits: apricot, pawpaw, peach, pear, plum, or quince. You can also grow nuts, including almond, chestnut, filbert, or pecan; or subtropical fruits, such as avocado, citrus, and kiwi.

APPLE A DAY
Homegrown apples may not have the picture-perfect looks of their supermarket cousins, but they boast freshness and excellent flavor. Start with disease- and insect-resistant varieties and site trees where they'll get plenty of sun, air, and water.

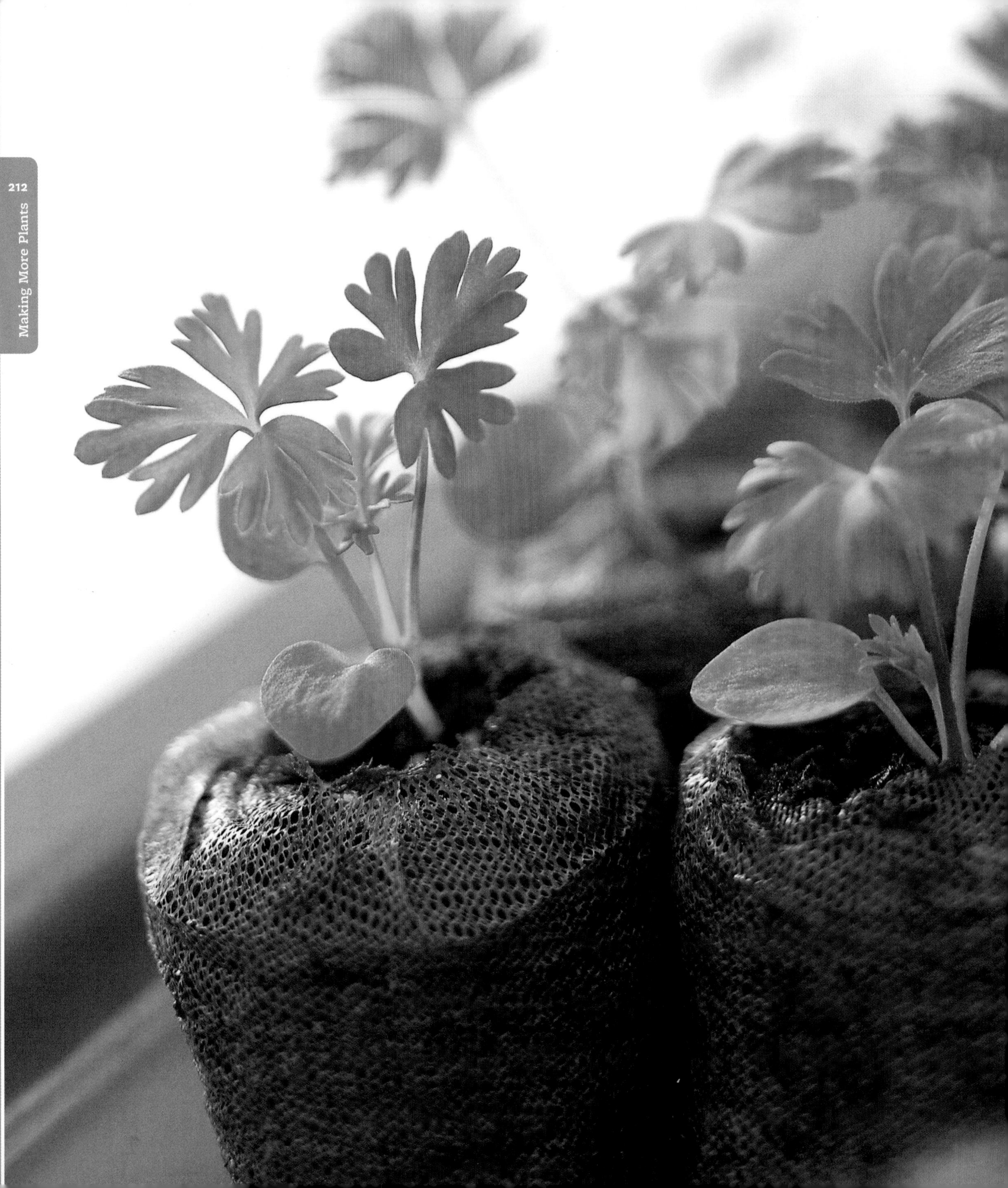

CHAPTER 10

MAKING MORE PLANTS

Great expectations and nurturing new life are part of the fun of gardening.
Somehow, there's always a need for more plants.

STARTING PLANTS FROM SEEDS

The techniques and materials involved in starting seeds are few, but the rewards for gardeners are great.

Starting plants from seeds has practical benefits: saving money, getting a head start on the growing season, and selecting from varieties more diverse than those available at your local garden center. There are also the seemingly magical benefits: the joy and wonder that come with watching a wee seed sprout into a living plant. You will be so proud!

Knowing that your garden plants can be grown from seeds or seedlings (transplants), plan ahead. Start vegetables, herbs, and flowers from seeds indoors when the outdoor world remains wintery, or sow them directly in the garden in spring when conditions allow.

When purchasing seeds, check packets for freshness dates and choose the best varieties for your garden and climate. It's easy to get carried away and purchase too many seed packets. What's more, a packet of seeds includes dozens— even hundreds—of potential plants, most likely more than you will need for this year's garden. Buy only what you need and have room to raise, then save leftover seeds for next year or share them with friends and neighbors.

COUNT THE DAYS
Use your calendar and details on the seed packet to figure out when to plant. Count back from the last average frost date or usual outdoor planting time.

SOW LARGE SEEDS
Use the eraser-end of a pencil or your finger to poke the seeds into the planting medium, spacing them evenly.

GLORIOUS SEEDLINGS
You can grow new and heirloom varieties from seeds that you won't likely find at a garden center.

READ PACKETS
The back of a seed packet contains all the planting details needed: seed spacing, depth, number of days until maturity, and much more.

SOW TINY SEEDS
Pick up seeds one at a time and plant them using the dampened tip of a pencil or chopstick.

ASK THE GARDEN DOCTOR **HOW CAN I ENCOURAGE MY CHILDREN'S INTEREST IN GARDENING?** One of the greatest joys of gardening comes from poking seeds into soil and then watching them sprout and grow. Let kids start with a quick-growing crop or flower that they will enjoy most (green bean, radish, pumpkin; sunflower, zinnia, marigold). Watch the amazement blossom!

SEED SOURCES Reliable sources for packaged seeds include mail order catalogs, local garden centers and nurseries, and online purveyors. Try different sources for specialty seeds. Get to know a seed company by starting with a few of its seed varieties. Keep records of seed purchases and germination success.

PLANTS THAT GROW EASILY FROM SEEDS

Although most seeds take six to eight weeks to reach transplantable size, other seedlings require less (four weeks) or more time (12 to 14 weeks) to develop. If you start seeds too early, you'll have to keep the seedlings indoors until the weather permits transplanting into the garden. If kept in the confines of nursery containers for too long, seedlings can become spindly and weak.

Many plants grow well indoors when planted from seeds. Try these:

Ageratum	Cleome	Nicotiana
Alyssum	Cosmos	Pepper
Basil	Cucumber	Petunia
Broccoli	Eggplant	Snapdragon
Cabbage	Leek	Statice
Calendula	Lettuce	Stock
Cauliflower	Marigold	Tomato
Chard	Morning glory	Tomatillo
Celosia	Moss rose	Verbena

GERMINATING SEEDS

To sprout seeds, you need only a few supplies. Then become acquainted with seeds' basic needs and forge ahead.

Germination is a seed's process of sprouting from a dormant plant embryo and growing into a wee plant. A seed stores the plant's initial food supply within its protective coating. What a seed needs from the gardener is conducive conditions (moisture, temperature, air, and light).

It is possible to start a few seeds on a very warm and sunny windowsill. Better yet, set up a nursery on a shelf or a tabletop where you can be messy with soil and water, and there is access to electricity. Basic materials for a nursery include containers, growing medium, fluorescent light, heat mat, and timer. A basic inexpensive setup of equipment lasts for many years.

Containers: Start with clean containers that allow excess moisture to drain away. Plastic trays are sold in kits with planting packs and covers. Packs vary in size and number of cells for transplant-size seedlings. Some gardeners reuse plastic nursery containers, including flats, packs, and pots of various sizes. Others repurpose household containers, from yogurt cups to greengrocer packaging. Wash containers and disinfect them with a weak bleach solution before filling with soilless medium.

Growing medium: Seedlings root quickly and stay healthier when grown in a sterile, fine-textured seed-starting mix rather than soil. Commercial seed-starting mix, available from garden suppliers and nurseries, usually includes peat moss, perlite, and vermiculite. Premoisten the medium by sprinkling it with warm water, then fill containers with damp mix. Different forms of ready-made peat pellets are also available that only need premoistening.

HOMEMADE POTS Make biodegradable pots using newspaper. Or use cardboard tubes cut to make 3- or 4-inch-deep pots.

THE RIGHT LIGHT Some seeds need light for germination, others do not. After germination, light is essential for all seedlings.

PEAT PELLETS Place a peat pellet in each cell of a pack. Add warm water to hydrate the pellets, filling the cell with soilless medium.

FILL CELLS Place cell packs on a watertight tray and fill them with soilless seed-starting medium.

ASK THE GARDEN DOCTOR

I PLANTED SEEDS BUT THEY DIDN'T SPROUT. WHAT HAPPENED? Seeds require the right conditions to germinate. All seeds need moisture to sprout and must not dry out, but they shouldn't sit in saturated soil either. Unearth the seeds and see if they rotted. A plastic cover over the germination tray helps keep seed-starting medium damp but not too wet. Some seeds sprout in a few days, others require weeks. Refer to the seed packet for germination information.

SPECIAL SEED-STARTING TECHNIQUES

Treat your seeds right and ensure their germination success. Check the seed packet for special instructions.

Some seeds need special treatment, such as presoaking or nicking their coats, to prompt germination. Avoid overdoing it. Soak seeds for a few hours or overnight—soaking them longer can harm them. When scarifying hard seedcoats (right), scratch them lightly and avoid breaking through them. Other seeds require chilling in a cold, moist environment for 8 to 12 weeks before they are planted—a process called stratification. Stratify seeds by wrapping them in a damp paper towel or mixing them in moist sand, and then chilling them in the refrigerator. Allow extra time to start pansy, phlox, primrose, and others.

SOAK SEEDS Some seeds (nasturtium, beet, spinach) germinate more readily if they are soaked in water overnight before planting.

SCARIFY SEEDS Morning glory and other hard-coat seeds need to be scuffed (scarified) to help germination. Rub seeds between pieces of sandpaper before planting.

ESSENTIALS FOR SEED GERMINATION

Seeds vary in the amount of light and heat they need to germinate. Check the seeds daily and keep the medium damp.

Whether you start seeds in a basement, utility room, or elsewhere, you just need a convenient, level area where you can place trays and hang a fluorescent light. Seeds usually need a soil temperature of 75–85 degrees F for germination. A waterproof heat mat provides vital warmth. Some seeds need light for germination; others need little if any light. If you have windows with bright, direct light most of the day, take advantage of them. Otherwise, use artificial light.

MOISTURE After sowing and initial sprinkling, water seed-starting trays from the bottom to keep the mix damp, not wet.

HEAT Gentle bottom heat encourages early sprouting of seeds. Place your seed flats on a heat mat or pad.

LIGHT If your seeds need light to germinate, place trays within 3 or 4 inches of a fluorescent light.

STARTING SEEDS INDOORS

Getting a jump-start on the season means you'll have seedlings ready to transplant as soon as the weather permits.

Starting plants indoors lets you give them ideal conditions and ensures their maturity, especially where the growing season is short. Most seedlings will be ready for transplanting in the garden within six to eight weeks. Move seedlings outdoors when they are big enough to survive the elements.

If problems occur in the process of starting seeds, use the opportunity to learn more.

If your seedlings become leggy: Long, spindly stems and lots of space between leaves are usually the result of too little light, overly warm conditions, or overcrowding.

If the leaves of your seedlings curl up: This is likely due to overfertilizing. Until they're ready for the garden, most seedlings don't need fertilizer.

If mold begins growing on the surface of the seed-starting medium: The medium is too wet. Allow it to dry a bit before watering again. Transplant the seedlings into fresh mix, if you prefer.

GARDEN READY A flat full of seedlings started indoors is ready to be moved outdoors and into the garden.

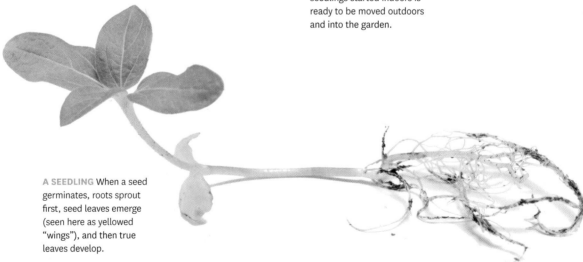

A SEEDLING When a seed germinates, roots sprout first, seed leaves emerge (seen here as yellowed "wings"), and then true leaves develop.

 **ASK THE GARDEN DOCTOR**   **WHAT IS "DAMPING OFF"?** This fungal condition causes seedlings to suddenly wilt and die for no apparent reason. To prevent damping off, use a sterile soilless medium, avoid sowing seeds thickly, and water from the bottom. In addition, avoid overwatering, and thin seedlings at the first sign of crowding. If your seedlings have already wilted, it's time to start over with fresh sterile mix and a clean container.

TEST GARDEN TIP

STRONGER SEEDLINGS When seedlings have developed their first set of true leaves, try this: Gently brush your hand back and forth over the tops of the seedlings daily for a few seconds to help encourage stocky stems. The action mimics wind, which helps outdoor plants grow sturdier.

1 MOISTEN MIX Prepare potting mix by premoistening it in a pan or pail, adding warm water and blending thoroughly.

2 FILL CELLS Fill packs or pots with the moistened mix to ¼ inch from the top. Firm the mix slightly but do not pack it.

3 SOW SEEDS Poke one or two large seeds into a cell. Sprinkle a few smaller seeds from the seed packet into a cell. Cover with vermiculite.

4 LABEL PLANTINGS Always label newly planted seeds to avoid any confusion. Write each plant name on a crafts stick and tuck it into the edge of the cell.

5 ADD WATER After planting, keep the soilless mix damp. After seeds germinate, water from the bottom of the container to avoid damping off.

6 COVER SEEDS Use a tray lid or sheet of plastic to hold in humidity until germination occurs. Once sprouts appear, remove the plastic.

STARTING SEEDS OUTDOORS

Direct-sowing seeds in the garden is nature's way, and it's also the best way to plant certain types of seeds.

Planting seeds directly in the garden saves time compared to sowing them indoors and then transplanting seedlings into the garden or into larger containers to grow on. But some plants don't transplant easily. For instance, it is best to sow nasturtiums, carrots, and others directly. Other plants grow so easily from seed that you will want to simply plant radishes, squash, and others in garden soil too.

Take time to prepare a seedbed. Remove remaining debris from last year's garden, as well as large clods, stones, and sticks. Use a shovel, spade, or garden fork to cultivate the top 6 to 8 inches of soil, working in 2 inches of compost to improve soil fertility and drainage. Use a garden rake to break up crusty soil and clods.

Mark planting rows with a string if you like. Plant seeds in rows, wide rows, or blocks, following packet directions. Scatter fine and medium-size seeds, such as carrot and basil, onto the soil's surface. Mix very fine seeds, such as thyme, with sand and sprinkle the mix evenly. Either cover seeds with soil or seed-starting mix to help maintain moist surroundings and prompt seeds to sprout. Label plantings, writing the plant name on a tag using an indelible marker or pencil. Keep seed packets for future reference.

A FEW SUPPLIES A handy tote keeps supplies—string, stakes, plant markers, hand tools—ready for seed-planting time.

PRETTY ROWS Sowing seeds of lettuces or herbs in diagonal rows or wide arcs takes a creative break from traditional rows.

SEED SPACING Seed packets note planting depth and spacing. Push bean seeds into soil one knuckle (an inch) deep; two knuckles apart.

SCATTER SEEDS Who says you must plant in skinny rows? Scatter seeds of lettuce or other greens in wide rows. Thin the crop for salads.

ASK THE GARDEN DOCTOR **WHEN CAN I PLANT SEEDS OUTDOORS?** The soil must be warm enough for seeds to germinate and seedlings to flourish. Seeds will rot if the soil is too cool. Use a soil thermometer or check with your extension service to determine the soil temperature. Wait until the soil reaches 55 degrees F to plant tomatoes; 65 to 70 degrees F to plant peppers, beans, squash, and other heat lovers.

TEST GARDEN TIP

SOW DIRECTLY These plants start easily outdoors from seeds; plant them after the danger of frost has passed: bean, beet, calendula, cucumber, dill, hyacinth bean, lettuce, melon, nasturtium, poppy, radish, salvia (annual), squash, sunflower, and zinnia.

1 PREPARE A BED Loosen the soil and remove any stones or large clods. Use the back of a garden rake to smooth the soil.

2 MARK ROWS Place a stake at each end of a planting row and tie a string between them, marking planting location and row spacing.

3 MAKE A FURROW Use a hoe to create a shallow furrow or a deeper trench, depending on the size of seeds you will plant in it.

4 SOW SEEDS Sprinkle the seeds in the furrow. Follow seed packet instructions for planting depth and spacing.

5 MOISTEN SOIL Cover seeds according to the seed packet instructions. Water the soil thoroughly after planting.

6 KEEP SOIL DAMP After sowing seeds water daily, if necessary, to keep the soil moist. These radish seedlings developed within two weeks.

MAKING AND PLANTING SEED BALLS

Using this method, planting seeds can be as easy and enjoyable as making mud pies.

Clay soil is the bane of many gardeners. But there is at least one good thing you can do with the sticky stuff: Make seed balls. The process is as simple and fun as patting mud into fantasy cakes or rolling modeling clay into snakes.

Making seed balls entails mixing a few easy-to-grow seeds with pinches of soft clay and shaping little balls. Seed balls make it easier to plant seeds, especially if you're sowing small ones that are difficult to see and handle. Coating seeds with clay also protects them from being washed away by rain or eaten by birds.

Seed balls keep alive a traditional planting technique. Native Americans packed seeds into bits of clay as a way to store and transport the precious resource for future crops. Modern guerrilla gardeners or gardening activists have popularized seed balls as a handy way to plant seeds on abandoned lots and vacant medians to beautify urban landscapes.

Once snuggled into soil, warmed by sun, and watered by rain or a garden hose, the clay ball gradually melts away and the seeds sprout in clusters. Continue watering as needed while seedlings develop. Soil should be damp but not wet.

IN POTS Start seed balls in pots and transplant them into the garden or large pots when they're well rooted.

IN GROUND When planting in the garden, leave a hand's width between the seed balls, allowing plants to grow in clusters.

ASK THE GARDEN DOCTOR **WHICH SEEDS WORK WELL IN SEED BALLS?** Choose plant varieties that grow easily from seed, such as borage, calendula, candytuft, cosmos, marigold, verbena, viola, and zinnia. Store dried seed balls away from heat and moisture until planting time.

1 SHAPE CLAY Roll garden-fresh clay into penny-size (about 1-inch-diameter) balls.

2 ADD SEEDS Press 20 to 30 seeds into each clay ball. Reshape the ball, working the seeds into the clay.

3 LET DRY Set your seed balls on a rack to dry and harden for several days in a warm, airy place.

4 PLANT 'EM Plant a seed ball by pushing it about halfway into loose soil in a cell pack or the garden. Do not cover the ball.

SEEDS SPROUT
Germination of the seeds may take a little longer than the usual period noted on the plant's seed packet.

TENDING SEEDLINGS

Adequate light, water, and fertilizer are the keys to growing healthy plants. Giving seedlings what they need now will help them grow strong and sturdy.

Once seeds germinate, they begin the next stage of development as seedlings. From then on, they require 12 to 16 hours of bright light per day to grow well. Fit a shop-type light fixture with one warm-light and one cool-light bulb to mimic daylight. An inexpensive outlet timer offers a handy way to turn lights on and off automatically. Encourage plants' stocky growth by keeping the tops of the seedlings within a few inches of the lightbulbs. Raise the light as seedlings grow.

Water as often as needed to keep the soilless mix damp. Initially, wee seedlings may need added moisture only once a week. As the seedlings grow, they will need more frequent water—perhaps every few days. When seedlings are big enough to move outdoors, begin adding a little fertilizer to the water.

Begin fertilizing seedlings using a water-soluble, general-purpose fertilizer weekly at one-half the listed rate (or at the rate noted for seedlings, if instructions are included on the fertilizer label).

FEEDING TIME By the time seedlings are ready for transplanting, they're also ready for a dose of half-strength fertilizer.

TRUE LEAVES Seedlings are ready for transplanting after they have at least two sets of true leaves.

REMOVE COMPETITION Gently prick out crowded plants using a thin tool. Lift them by the tips of their leaves.

GROWING UP Transplant seedlings into their own pots. Grow them there until it's time to transplant in the garden.

BIG, BIGGER Seedlings grown in cells or pots reach a transplantable size when their roots fill the container.

? ASK THE GARDEN DOCTOR **DO I NEED TO THIN MY VEGETABLE SEEDLINGS?** To avoid the need to thin, sow seeds sparingly at a wider spacing. Use a precision seeding tool to help you plant one seed at a time, and space seeds according to seed packet recommendations.

THINNING SEEDLINGS

Before seedlings become a tangled mass of leaves and roots, give them the space they need to grow in uncrowded conditions. Removing excess seedlings is vital.

Indoors or outdoors, unless seeds are sown very carefully with adequate spacing, seedlings that sprout soon become crowded. When seedlings have at least two sets of true leaves, it's time to relieve crowding. Keep the largest, healthiest seedlings.

Indoors, snip the stems of excess plants at soil level, leaving just one or two plants in each cell. Allowed to continue, crowding stresses plants and prevents them from growing properly and reaching their potential.

CROWDED SEEDLINGS Sown directly in the garden, seedlings sprout and must be thinned to give every plant growing room.

RELIEVE CROWDING Loosen the soil and gently lift out excess seedlings, leaving space between the remaining seedlings.

SPREADING OUT Transplant extra seedlings into a new row where they will have enough room to mature into productive plants.

WATER GENTLY Once you've plucked out and replanted seedlings, water gently to help them settle in and reestablish quickly.

EARTH-FRIENDLY POTS

Your choice of containers for seedlings can help protect their tender roots at transplanting time.

A variety of small biodegradable pots simplify the process of raising seedlings and transplanting them into the garden. Pots made from newspaper, paper pulp, coconut coir, peat moss, and the like can be planted along with the young plants in the garden. This way, you won't need to remove a seedling from its container before planting and risk disturbing the young roots. The container breaks down eventually, adding organic matter to the soil. Biodegradable pots are especially useful for plants such as nasturtiums that do no like to have their roots disturbed by transplanting.

MOVING SEEDLINGS TO THE GARDEN

Take a few steps to raise your seedlings to the next level: graduation to the garden.

The time comes when seedlings are ready for life in the garden. The soil has warmed, nights are getting warmer, and you can feel the sun on your face when working outdoors.

How to Protect Young Plants

A week before transplanting seedlings into the garden, set them outdoors in a partly sunny place, sheltered from wind and hard rain. Having been raised indoors, the plants won't be accustomed to outdoor conditions and will need to adjust gradually. Keeping them in a protected place or a cold frame helps smooth the transition.

This process of helping young plants become acclimated to outdoor life is called hardening off. After plants have hardened off, it's time to plant them. If you purchase seedlings from a greenhouse or indoor garden center, use this same technique to harden them off before planting. If you don't ease plants into outdoor life, the tender young things may be easily burned by sun, wind, or unexpected frosty temperatures.

If the weather becomes too chilly or nighttime temperatures drop near freezing, bring seedlings back indoors or cover them with a sheet to keep them from being damaged by frost. Cool-season plants, such as pansies, salad greens, and broccoli, can tolerate chilly weather better than warm-season plants such as tomatoes, peppers, and petunias. Cool-season plants can be acclimated and planted when the ground thaws. Wait until nighttime temperatures are above 50 degrees F to harden off summer vegetables and flowers.

GETTING ACCLIMATED Set seedlings in a protected, partly shaded place for a week before transplanting them.

KEEP WARM Move seedlings indoors at night or cover them with a floating row cover to protect them from frost.

EASY SEEDLINGS Young plants, whether homegrown or fresh from a grower, provide an easy and quick way to plant a garden.

? ASK THE GARDEN DOCTOR **HOW MUCH GROWING ROOM DO TRANSPLANTS NEED?** Read plant tags or research the plant's mature size to determine the best spacing for seedlings. Although the garden may seem sparse at first, giving young plants plenty of room to grow ensures good air circulation and helps prevent disease.

PLANTS THAT SELF-SOW

Take advantage of some plants' self-seeding ability and let them propagate themselves.

Self-sowing plants include some hardy annuals, perennials, and even vegetables that develop seeds and, when allowed, cast the ripe seeds into the soil where they will sprout and grow in the garden next year. Free plants! But be careful. Some plants sow themselves too gregariously and become weedy. Others volunteer to grow wherever they happen to germinate, such as gourds growing into an apple tree (right), on the compost pile, or in an opportune crevice.

Plants that form seedy heads typically mature in autumn and cast their seeds in time for them to germinate by spring. If you want more plants, you can help them along by breaking open fully-developed seedheads and sprinkling the seeds where you want more of the plants to grow. If you don't want more plants, snip off seedheads before they begin casting seeds, and share the seeds with other gardeners.

If you have a large area in which you want to create a meadow or similar naturalistic effect, take advantage of the self-sowing nature of some wildflowers and ornamental grasses. It takes a few years for the plants to re-create themselves freely enough to fill an area, but it is possible. You'll need to monitor the area and hand-pull weeds to keep them from taking over.

VOLUNTEER PLANTS It's not uncommon for seeds to survive in a compost pile long enough to germinate given an opportunity. These gourds sprouted in compost and grew into a nearby apple tree.

SELF-SOWING FLOWERS

Anise hyssop	Larkspur
Bachelor's button	Marigold
Blanket flower	Morning glory
Calendula	Nicotiana
California poppy	Nigella
Chamomile	Queen-anne's lace
Cleome	Scilla
Columbine	Sweet alyssum
Four-o-clock	Tall verbena
Garlic chives	Violet
Hollyhock	

LAYERING

Another way that some plants can propagate themselves is by rooting where a stem touches soil. Some shrubs and climbers are adept at making new plants this way. Encourage the process, for example, with lavender.

NICK STEM Barely cut into the stem's underside. Then gently bend the stem and push it into the soil.

AID ROOTING Cover the nicked portion of stem with soil. Hold it in place with a stone until roots grow.

SAVING SEEDS

When you harvest and save seeds, you can also save money and preserve treasured plants that might not survive otherwise.

As you clean up the garden in fall, gather seeds from favorite flowers and save them for next year's garden. The annuals, perennials, and vegetables you recognize as plants that grow easily from seed are typically the ones that will provide you with viable free seeds for the taking.

Some gardeners get satisfaction by planting seeds they have personally collected from the previous growing season. Some want to propagate a sentimental favorite passed down through generations. Others are aiming to safeguard seeds' genetic diversity.

The seeds of plants such as heirlooms and species grow reliably, reproducing the same plants. Seeds from modern hybrids are likely to yield varied results and may revert to a different plant. Harvest seeds from top-form, disease-free plants that possess the qualities you desire.

FORGOT TO SAVE SEEDS? Don't worry. By late fall, the dried remnants of plants such as coneflower (*Echinacea*) often still contain seeds that you can remove with a vigorous shake.

ASK THE GARDEN DOCTOR **HOW LONG WILL SEEDS KEEP?** Many seeds remain viable for several years or more. It's best to use them within a year of their harvest for maximum germination.

HOW TO COLLECT AND DRY SEEDS

Allow some of the season's last flowers or produce to remain until they develop seeds, then harvest the makings for next year's plants.

Many seeds can be collected in seedheads or pods, allowed to dry in a warm, airy place, and then cleaned and stored. Once dried, crumble the seedheads or pods, and separate the seeds from the remains. Sift tiny seeds through a screen or gently blow the remains away from the seeds.

Vegetable seeds that have a lot of moist pulp around them should be rinsed and dried thoroughly before storing.

SELECT SEEDPODS Air-dry fully ripe seedheads (jewels of opar). Then break the shells to release the seeds and remove the chaff.

REMOVE PULP Seeds of squash, pumpkin, cucumber, and some others need to be soaked clean and air-dried on a screen before storing them.

SET ASIDE Let large seedpods such as hollyhock air-dry. Then crack open the pods and store the seeds until planting time.

STORING SEEDS

Cool, dry, and dark are the keys to storing seeds. Place crisp-dry seeds in small paper envelopes. Write the name of the plant, variety, and date stored on each envelope. Plan to use the seeds the next year.

IN A JAR Place seed packets in an airtight jar. Store seeds away from light and heat to preserve their viability.

IN A BOX You can store seeds in freezer-weight zip-type plastic bags or a sealable box over winter.

TAKING CUTTINGS

Summer is prime time to take cuttings from plant stems and multiply your plants.

Take cuttings of young, softwood stems from late spring until midsummer, when mother plants are healthy and growing actively. Their offshoots will root readily and grow into new plants ready for transplanting within a couple of months. Next thing you know, you'll be sharing loads of free plants with friends and family.

How to Take Cuttings

Follow these steps and see how growing new plants from cuttings is easy and rewarding. Here are some tips to ensure your success: Start by filling cell packs or small pots with premoistened soilless medium. Cuttings may rot if placed in soil because it holds too much moisture. Take cuttings of the young growth of healthy plants. Keep the foliage on the top half of the stem; remove the rest. When you have filled a pot or pack with cuttings, slip it into a plastic bag and twist-tie the bag shut to create a humid, greenhouselike environment that will boost the cuttings' root growth.

SUCCESSFUL CUTTINGS Three months after cutting softwood stems of *Plectranthus* 'Mona Lavender', the new plants are ready for a larger pot.

❶ CUT STEM Using a clean, sharp knife, cut a 3- to 4-inch shoot below a leaf node (where a leaf emerges from the stem).

❷ PREPARE MEDIUM Use a pencil to poke a planting hole in damp soilless medium.

❸ PREPARE CUTTING Pinch or cut off the bottom leaves of the shoot; snip off any flowers or buds.

❹ GROWTH BOOSTER Dip the stem's cut end in rooting hormone powder. Push the stem into the soilless medium.

❺ KEEP DAMP Water as needed to keep the soilless medium damp but not wet.

 **ASK THE GARDEN DOCTOR** **HOW CAN I TELL WHEN CUTTINGS ARE READY FOR TRANSPLANTING?** A month after taking cuttings, check root development. Tip the container on its side and tap out the soil and root ball. When roots appear strong and have filled the container, it's time to transplant.

CUTTING OPTIONS

Later in the season, take cuttings to start growing new plants for next year.

Cuttings are a great way to gain more of your favorite plants, from houseplants to perennials, shrubs to trees. Snippets taken between mid- and late summer are called semiripe cuttings; new growth has begun to mature at the base but is still supple at the tips. Follow the same process as for softwood cuttings.

Early morning is the best time to take cuttings. Find a healthy, vigorous plant and cut lengths from the top and sides. Cuttings from the side of a plant have the highest rooting success rate, while cuttings from the top of the plant have the fastest growth rate. For most plants, it's best to take samples with at least three or four sets of leaves.

Hardwood Cuttings

You can take hardwood cuttings of shrubs and trees in fall or early winter, when plants are beginning dormancy. Cut 8-inch stem sections of medium thickness, rather than thin tips or fat bases. Dip the cut ends into rooting hormone. Bundle the stems, tie them together, and bury them in a 6-inch-deep trench filled with sand. Retrieve the cuttings in spring and plant them in containers or a well-draining site sheltered from drying winds.

Rooting Cuttings in Water

Some nonwoody or herbaceous plants root easily in water. Cut a few inches from the tips of plants such as coleus, geranium, scented geranium, tradescantia, English ivy, and begonia. Remove the bottom leaves, tuck the stems into a small glass of water in bright, indirect light. Change the water every few days. Depending on the plant, roots will develop within a few weeks. Pot the cuttings in soil and grow them indoors until spring.

CUTTINGS GALORE It's possible to grow an entire garden from cuttings alone. Coleus, *Tradescantia zebrina*, and begonia root easily in soilless mix or water.

BEFORE These semiripe cuttings of the chartreuse shrub *Caryopteris incana* 'Jason' were taken in midsummer.

AFTER After eight weeks in a semishaded spot, the new plants are rooted and blooming.

DIVIDING PLANTS

There's a bonus when you divide perennials: Extra plants enable you to expand your garden for free or gift to other gardeners.

After three to five years, some perennials begin to crowd their neighbors, become less vigorous, bloom sparsely, or die out in the center. These are sure signs that a plant needs to be divided into smaller sections and replanted.

Techniques and Timing

Division is the separation of a plant's crown or clump into two or more portions, each with healthy roots and shoots. How you divide a plant depends on the growth habit of the plant. It's easy to cut off sections of a plant by slicing through it with a spade without removing the entire plant from the ground. This works well for clump-forming plants, such as hostas and ornamental grasses, and mat-forming plants, such as coreopsis and thyme.

No rules exist to tell you when to divide, but gardeners usually divide plants in spring or fall. Most perennials can be divided successfully at either time, but your climate and plant hardiness may determine the best timing. Looking at a bloom-filled bed in its spring or summer glory, it's hard to think of digging up a plant and chopping it into pieces. But you know the plant will grow better, stay healthier, and bloom more freely. So you let the plant bloom, then divide it just after flowering. Fall bloomers, such as goldenrod, chrysanthemum, aster, and sedum, are best divided in early spring.

❶ HOSTA DIVISIONS
Loosen the soil around the plant or a portion of it, and lift it from the ground.

❷ SLICE PORTIONS
Use a sharp spade to slice or garden fork to pry the clump into sections.

❸ PLANT PORTIONS
Replant portions that include masses of roots and shoots, adding compost to the planting hole.

❹ WATER WELL
Water thoroughly. Shield the plant from direct sun for a few days, using a piece of garden fabric.

? ASK THE GARDEN DOCTOR **CAN I DIVIDE ANY PERENNIAL?** Not all perennials require division or benefit from it, but even those that don't ordinarily, such as astilbe and peony, may be divided merely to gain more plants. Plants with deep taproots (butterfly weed, Oriental poppy, baby's breath) should be left undisturbed.

HOW TO DIVIDE PERENNIALS

Knowing how perennials grow helps you understand how to divide them and multiply their assets. And if you don't know how to distinguish a tuber from a rhizome, this is a fine opportunity to learn about the way plants grow and what they need to improve their performance. Here are some examples.

STOLONS Some plants, such as *Verbena canadensis,* spread on their own via stolons, or aboveground stems that run across the soil's surface.

FIBROUS ROOTS Tickseed (*Coreopsis*), hybrid phlox, and black-eyed susan (*Rudbeckia*) have stringy, branched root systems that are easy to dig and pull apart.

FLESHY ROOTS After five or so years, daylily clumps become too thick. Dig a clump, split it with a spade, and replant the new, smaller clumps.

RHIZOMES Divide the underground stems of bearded iris and others every three to five years. Dig the rhizomes, discard the old ones, cut back the foliage, and replant younger pieces.

TUBERS The knobby bulbous roots of peonies and dahlias can be dug, split, and replanted no deeper than 1 to 2 inches.

CORMS AND BULBS Every few years, divide corms of gladiolus (as well as other bulbous plants) about two months after their blooms fade.

CHAPTER 11

MULCHING AND FERTILIZING

Some tried-and-true gardening techniques make a good garden better.

WHAT'S SO GOOD ABOUT MULCH?

Mulching is a timesaver for you and a lifesaver for your plants. As a finishing touch, it neatens the garden and lets plants be the stars.

The process of spreading a thin, loose layer of shredded bark, chopped leaves, or another organic material over the soil between plants is nature's way of recycling. In forests, prairies, wetlands, and hedgerows, the process works the same as it does in gardens: A layer of mulch controls weeds, conserves soil moisture, insulates soil and plant roots from extreme temperatures, prevents erosion, and attracts earthworms.

A diverse array of mulches—homemade and commercial—includes organic options (compost, grass clippings, nutshells, pine needles) that break down and gradually add nutrients to the soil and improve its structure. Ornamental or inorganic mulches (gravel, shells, recycled glass, sheet plastic) are long-lasting and effective as well as decorative.

Mulch provides one of the ultimate multitasking materials for gardens, including beds and containers. Although mulch doesn't eliminate a need for weeding, it slows the growth of weed seeds already present in soil and blocks new ones from entering. In the vegetable garden, mulch cushions ripening produce, protecting it from sitting on damp soil and rotting. In containers, mulch deters squirrels, slugs, and other animals from pestering plantings.

Mulch Isn't Perfect

During periods of wet weather when mulch is piled on too thickly, it can harbor too much soil moisture. As a result, the mulch can become matted or moldy. It may attract slugs, earwigs, and other eat-and-run insects that favor cool, moist, dark places. Straw and wood-based mulches deplete soil nitrogen temporarily after being applied.

POTTED PRACTICALLY
Tumbled stones add a decorative touch to a potted garden and preserve soil moisture.

MATERIAL MATTERS Dark-color mulches can help warm soil sooner in spring and promote plant growth.

TEST GARDEN TIP

PREVENT NITROGEN DEPLETION The soil microbes that break down organic mulches compete with plants for nitrogen in soil. Plants show signs of nitrogen depletion in pale green or yellowing leaves or stunted growth. Minimize the nitrogen loss that may occur when spreading wood or straw mulch by applying fertilizer first.

BARK SIZES Large bark mulch works well for mulching trees and shrubs. Medium bark proves less slippery underfoot and makes a nice cover for a pathway. The texture of smaller bark suits perennial plants.

COCOA SHELLS Lightweight and dark brown, these hulls have a chocolaty aroma. They break down within a growing season. The material has proved toxic to dogs.

GRASS CLIPPINGS Collect them only if the lawn is overgrown and void of herbicide or other chemicals. Spread shallowly, clippings break down quickly and add nitrogen to soil.

TYPES OF MULCH

All mulches offer some benefits, but some have greater longevity; others excel aesthetically.

The majority of mulches are organic and decompose eventually. Chopped leaves break down quickly compared with large bark chunks, for example. Inorganic mulches such as sheet plastic and recycled glass do not decompose or add nutrients to soil, and they need replacing less often than organic options.

Your choice of mulch will depend on the materials available in your region and where the mulch will be applied.

BARK Chipped or shredded, mostly pine or fir nuggets decompose slowly. Barks can float and move in heavy rain. Use it in well-draining areas.

CHOPPED LEAVES Readily available, autumn leaves should be mowed over, shredded, or composted before being used as mulch. Whole leaves can blow away or mat.

COIR Another lightweight and porous option, ground coconut husk is especially effective at holding moisture. It's sold in a compact compressed block.

COMPOST Dark and fine-textured, it blends readily with soil. Pile this free soil builder up to 4 inches deep on the garden annually.

Coordinate the texture of mulch with the size and color of plants. Large bark mulch suits trees and shrubs, for instance, while cocoa shell mulch works nicely in vegetable gardens.

When choosing mulch, consider practicalities, too. Lightweight mulches can migrate from a garden in a heavy rain or strong wind, especially if situated on a sloping or exposed site. You'll want a mulch that's easy to walk on, sweep up, or mow over.

PINE NEEDLES Creating the appearance of a forest floor, this fine-texture mulch gradually acidifies soil and works well for acid-loving plants, such as blueberries and azaleas.

GRAVEL A permanent option for rock gardens, foundation plantings, paths, and places where other mulches present a fire risk in hot, dry climates, gravel also holds warmth.

MUSHROOM COMPOST Left after mushroom harvests, this fine, high-calcium compost conditions soil when incorporated at season's end. Avoid spreading it near acid-loving plants.

RED PLASTIC MULCH This reflecting red film warms soil, retains moisture, and increases fruit production when used around tomato plants.

RECYCLED GLASS Highly decorative and permanent, the tumbled glass conserves soil moisture. It adds sparkle and color to beds and containers.

WOOD Shredded or chipped cedar and other woods fade over time and need to be replenished. Wood chips don't attract termites. Choose sustainable products.

WHEN TO MULCH

Timing varies depending on where you live and the type of plantings you plan to mulch.

Some gardeners keep their gardens mulched year 'round as a weed-beating strategy. Permanent mulches, applied any time, need only occasional tidying. When topped off periodically with fresh mulch, wood-based products, such as large bark chunks or cedar, last and last.

In warm climates where gardening continues much of the year, apply or replenish mulch as needed. Mulching at planting time is an efficient habit.

In cold climates, spring and fall mulching are typical. During the growing season, apply mulch in spring after established plants have emerged and new plantings are complete; or in summer, to suppress weeds, cool the soil, and reduce evaporation and the need to water.

Winter mulches are used in cold climates to insulate plant roots, not to keep the soil warm. Best applied after the ground freezes, winter mulch helps prevent damage to plants from freeze-thaw cycles. Spread too early, mulch can delay freezing of the ground, causing roots to go dormant later than normal and possibly damaging them. You can apply an extra-thick (6- to 8-inch) winter blanket of straw on strawberries to protect the plants' crowns from freezing; remove it in spring.

STOCK UP Packaged mulch typically goes on sale at the end of the gardening season, offering savings to gardeners who watch for this opportunity.

SUMMER MULCH Give the garden a finished, neat appearance that lasts throughout the growing season, using a 2- to 3-inch layer of mulch.

WINTER MULCH A 3- to 4-inch layer of mulch helps trees, shrubs, and perennials withstand winter's extremes.

 **ASK THE GARDEN DOCTOR** **IS THERE A BENEFIT IN USING COLORED MULCH?** Wood and bark mulches fade and appear aged after a year or two. They're now available dyed brown, red, gold, or black to make them appear fresher longer. As they are sprayed with a colorant that's possibly toxic, their use is mostly a choice based on aesthetics.

HOW MUCH MULCH?

Buying and spreading mulch is a numbers game that takes into account varying factors.

When you're ready to buy mulch, get out your calculator. But don't worry. Buying mulch isn't complicated, and it presents an opportunity to save money. Although mulch quality and type vary wildly, you don't need to pay top dollar to get the best mulch product.

Finding Bargains

You can find inexpensive or free sources of mulch. Many communities gather and compost yard waste, offering it to gardeners at little or no cost. You may also find well-composted manure free for the hauling at a nearby farm or stable. In coastal areas where there's a fish-based industry, free fish-waste compost may be available. In any case, find out how the material is composted or processed. If it is not turned, but sits and decomposes, you might be taking home compost laced with weed seeds and disease spores. In that case, the "bargain" is a problem in the making.

The cost of mulch varies, from homemade and free to permanent and costlier than most. Mulch sold in bulk is cheaper than bagged products. But if you don't have a vehicle for hauling bulk mulch, you'll have to pay a delivery fee, which can cancel out the savings. End-of-season sales make bagged mulch more economical. Store bagged mulch in a sheltered place or cover it well with a tarp to keep it dry over the winter.

By the Numbers

How much mulch will you need to cover your garden? It depends on the type of mulch, the depth of coverage, and the garden's size. Most bagged mulch is sold by the cubic foot; bulk mulch by the cubic yard.

Picture a cubic foot as a box 1 foot tall, wide, and deep. For example, a 1-cubic-foot bag of mulch spread 3 inches deep will cover 4 square feet (12 inches divided by 3 inches equals 4). A 160-square-foot garden (8×20 feet) requires twenty 2-cubic-foot bags of mulch to achieve a mulch depth of 3 inches (¼ foot). The formula to calculate this is length×width×depth: 20×8×¼=40 cubic feet.

When purchasing mulch in bulk: To cover 1,000 square feet of garden with 2 inches of mulch, you'll neeed about 6 cubic yards of mulch (two to three pickup loads or eighty-one 2-cubic-foot bags).

HOW TO APPLY MULCH

Instead of dumping bags of mulch around plants, use it like any good tool—with care and knowledge—to make the most of it.

For most mulches and soils, start with a mulch layer 2 to 3 inches deep for the growing season. Where the soil is sandy and quick-drying, go for the higher end of the range. Where the soil is heavy with clay and drains poorly, aim for the shallower depth. Rock or recycled glass works best if laid only 1 or 2 inches deep.

Thicker mulches do not increase benefits. Instead, they can lead to problems with plant rot, disease, and pests. If mulch breaks down quickly in your region's climate, it's better to apply two thin layers over a year than one thick layer at once.

Wait for a rain or deeply water plants and feed them just before mulching. Sprinkle water on a dry mulch such as shredded wood after spreading it, to prevent the material from wicking moisture away from plant roots.

When spreading mulch between plants, keep it several inches away from their stems to prevent stems from rotting and to allow moisture to reach plant roots more easily.

Pile winter mulches 6 to 8 inches deep. If you use straw as a protective mulch for cool-season crops such as kale, use only clean straw free of weed seeds. A thick blanket of snow also provides an excellent winter mulch. When shoveling snow, it's OK to toss it on the garden to help keep plants covered.

MULCH COMBOS Use different mulches—one among plants and another for pathways—if you like, as long as they don't clash.

PROPER DEPTH Spread most mulches 2 to 3 inches deep for the growing season.

STEM CLEARANCE Steer clear of plant stems when spreading mulch. Pull mulch away from stems.

 **ASK THE GARDEN DOCTOR** **DOES MULCH ATTRACT INSECTS?** Wood, stone, and any other kind of mulch may harbor insects that favor cool, damp, dark conditions. Research shows that wood mulches do not attract or promote termites. If you're concerned, keep mulch 2 or 3 feet away from your home's foundation.

TEST GARDEN TIP

TOO MUCH MULCH Piled too deep, mulch can hold excess moisture, prevent air penetration, and become sour and harm plants. Avoid piling mulch around a tree trunk, forming a volcano of sorts, that can harbor rodents and insects, stress the tree, and even kill it. Mulch wide—not deep—around trees.

NEW PLANTINGS Apply a 2 to 3-inch layer of mulch at planting time. Cover small plants with nursery pots to keep from burying them with mulch.

CONTAINER GARDEN Toss mulch between established plants, leaving a 1- to 2-inch layer of it, well away from plant stems.

COOL-SEASON CROPS A 6- to 8-inch layer of clean straw helps insulate cool-season crops (cabbage) and soil from frost, extending the growing season.

TREES AND SHRUBS Spread shredded leaves over the root lines of trees and shrubs, keeping mulch a foot away from the trunk and beyond branch ends to cover the root zone.

BED EDGES Mulch helps keep bed edges neat and minimizes erosion. If mulch drifts into the lawn, push it back into place.

DECORATIVE EFFECT Use an inch of recycled glass, shells, or what-have-you, or 2 inches of an organic mulch in containers.

FERTILIZER: THE BASICS

Plants need various nutrients in order to grow and thrive. Most soils provide many of these essential nutrients. Fertilizers supply minerals that aren't always available adequately in soil.

Plants make their own food via photosynthesis. But when a gardener adds key nutrients to soil, it optimizes plant health and improves productivity. Nitrogen is needed for growth and green leaves. Phosphorous fuels strong roots. Potassium enhances flower and fruit formation, and promotes disease resistance. Fertilizer labels indicate the percentage of the three key nutrients as a series of numbers such as 15-30-15, which means that 15 percent of the product's weight is nitrogen and potassium; 30 percent is phosphorous. The remainder consists of sand or other filler such as limestone.

Fertilizer replenishes the essential nutrients in soil, making them available to plants. Plants have different nutrient requirements. Heavily blooming sun-loving annuals require more feeding than foliage plants grown in shade, for instance. It's up to you whether you fertilize your garden according to the specific recommendations of a soil test or a more casual, plant-specific approach. Plants show signs of nutrient deficiency particularly in their foliage, alerting you to a need for fertilizer. Clues include pale or discolored leaves, weak or slow growth, and smaller leaves and flowers.

Plants also need micronutrients, including boron, chlorine, iron, and zinc Unless a soil test tells you that manganese or another micronutrient is lacking, adding excess amounts can be toxic to plants.

FORMS OF FERTILIZER

Begin to narrow your fertilizer options by choosing from two forms: dry or liquid. Although they're made for use in different situations, what matters most is that fertilizer must be dissolved to be of use to plants. You can make multiple applications of a soluble fertilizer, or fewer applications of a less soluble one.

LIQUID FOOD You'll find liquid fertilizers in concentrated or premixed forms. Water-soluble foods (crystals or liquid concentrate) are mixed with water.

DRY FOOD These fertilizers come in granules, powdery crystals, slow-release pellets, and spikes.

? ASK THE GARDEN DOCTOR **WHAT IS SLOW-RELEASE FERTILIZER?** The granules or pellets are coated with a special resin and break down slowly in soil, releasing nutrients to plants over weeks or months, depending on the product. You will pay for the convenience.

ORGANIC AND
SYNTHETIC FERTILIZERS

Understanding the differences between the
kinds of fertilizers, as well as what they can
and cannot do, enables you to give your
plants what they need for optimal health.

Organic fertilizers, made mostly from plants and
animals, include compost, manure, fish emulsion,
bone meal, kelp, cottonseed meal, alfalfa meal,
and more. Organic fertilizers contain low levels of
nutrients, but they improve soil structure, favor a
healthy population of soil microbes and earthworms,
and also contribute micronutrients that plants need.
Some organic plant foods (chicken manure and fish
emulsion) have odors that dissipate with time.

Synthetic fertilizers, made from petroleum and
natural gas, offer convenient forms of specific
formulations. The products require you to match
their nutrient content to the needs of plants. Liquid
fertilizer can give plants a quick boost.

Whether a fertilizer is formulated to be all purpose
(10-10-10) or plant specific (a 4-12-4 starter solution
for seedlings and transplants, for instance), organic
or synthetic, each is made to promote healthy plants.

**RENEWABLE
RESOURCES** Organic
fertilizers, such as
compost and rotted
manure, release
nutrients slowly and
reduce the need for
additional fertilizers.

HOW TO APPLY FERTILIZERS

When it comes to nourishing plants of any kind, you'll find a wide selection of plant foods and ways to apply them for any garden or lawn situation as well as indoors.

Your goal when feeding is to ensure that the fertilizer is distributed evenly to plants. Liquid plant foods are absorbed quickly by roots. When using dry foods, scatter them over the soil's surface between plants, keeping the fertilizer away from plant stems, then cultivate it into the soil. If dry fertilizer lands on plants, it can burn them, so brush it off plants and into the soil. Always water after fertilizing, if rain isn't on the horizon. Since all nutrients are water soluble, good soil moisture is essential.

The frequency of feeding depends on the plants, soil type, prevailing weather conditions, and the type of fertilizer. Plants growing in pots or competing in close quarters need feeding more often. Organic fertilizers can be used less often than most synthetic fertilizers (other than slow-release ones). The best time for feeding is early in the growing season. Ease off plant food late in the season, when plant growth should be allowed to slow in preparation for winter.

Container gardens require consistent feeding because frequent watering flushes nutrients out of soil. Before potting plants, mix organic or time-release fertilizer into potting soil to make feeding easy. Then use liquid food to boost plants later on, if need be.

Foliar fertilizer is an efficient means of feeding plants through their leaves. A solution is sprayed on foliage and absorbed. It is an alternative to other liquid fertilizers.

❶ FERTILIZER SPIKES
Tapped into the soil at the base of a tree or shrub, fertilizer spikes dissolve slowly.

❷ SIDE DRESSING
Sprinkle granular fertilizer over the soil between plants, then scratch it into the soil, covering the granules.

❸ ORGANIC SPIKE
Nutrients move through potting mix rapidly. A spike dissolves slowly, feeding edible plants (tomato and basil).

❹ BROADCAST GRANULES Cast dry fertilizer by hand or with a mechanical spreader, covering a lawn or other large area.

❺ STARTER SOLUTION A specialty fertilizer for seedlings and transplants, the phosphorous-rich solution gives them a boost.

ASK THE GARDEN DOCTOR **IS IT POSSIBLE TO OVERFERTILIZE PLANTS?** Yes! Don't be tempted to apply fertilizer at a higher rate than the product label recommends. There is no additional benefit for plants. Overfertilizing can injure plants and cause them to grow excessive foliage at the expense of flowers and fruit. If fertilizer is not used by plants or is spilled on an area near the garden, it will run off and pollute water supplies.

OTHER METHODS AND APPLICATIONS

Whichever type of fertilizer or application you prefer, plants need to have the nutrients present in sufficient quantities and in a form they can use. Before buying fertilizer, read the package to understand formulations and directions for use. You'll find plant foods formulated for all kinds of plants, from acid-loving blueberries to roses, bulbs, and vegetables. You can also give your plants homemade fertilizers.

FOLIAR FEEDING A soluble fertilizer (fish emulsion) is diluted in water, sprayed on plant foliage, and absorbed by the leaves.

COMFREY TEA Make this nutrient-rich brew by steeping the large leaves of the herb in water, covered, for several days. Then use it as a liquid or foliar fertilizer.

FEEDING ANNUALS Water plants with soluble fertilizer every other week during the growing season if you like a routine—but avoid overfeeding in hopes of getting more flowers.

FEEDING BULBS Feed bulbs in spring to promote next year's flowers rather than adding bone meal at planting time, which invites squirrels to dig.

FEEDING ROSES Start the season giving roses a nutritious boost by working into soil alfalfa meal (nitrogen), banana peel (potassium), and Epsom salts (magnesium).

FEEDING INDOORS A fork works well for carefully mixing granular fertilizer into the soil of potted plants.

CHAPTER 12

WATERING AND IRRIGATING

Wise gardeners find a balance between using and conserving water in the garden.

WHY WATERING IS ESSENTIAL

Water is a necessary element for the lives of all plants. But how do you know when a plant needs water? And how much water is enough?

Every plant needs water to survive and grow. Plants absorb water through their roots and lose it through their leaves. The process is affected by weather and soil as well as the plant's type, size, and age and the way you water.

Ideally, nature provides plants with sufficient rain, and the plants develop healthy root systems in well-draining soil. But with too much rain or poorly draining soil, plant roots can drown. If a hot, dry, or windy spell occurs and plants lose too much water, they wilt and may stop growing.

How Much Water

Plants' needs for water varies. Some plants require less water to survive and grow than others. Yet without water, no plant will grow. Generally, an inch of rain or supplemental water per week sustains most plants. Deep, thorough watering reaches the root zone, 6 to 12 inches deep, of most plants.

Deeper, less-frequent watering encourages plants to root more deeply, enabling them to better withstand drought. Shallow, frequent watering does more harm than good: It promotes shallow root growth, making plants more vulnerable to damage from drought, weeds, and pests.

Watering early in the day is best because less moisture will be lost to evaporation. Also, if leaves get wet, the day's light, heat, and wind will dry them and help prevent diseases that thrive on moisture.

NOT ENOUGH Wilting in early morning or evening indicates a plant's immediate need for water. Some plants wilt in the heat of midday but recover by evening.

TOO MUCH An overabundance of rain or too-generous watering can be as deadly as not enough moisture. If roots rot, plants die.

FEEL SOIL Check soil for moisture by poking a finger into it, up to the first or second knuckle. If the soil feels dry, it's time to water.

RAIN GAUGE Monitor weather reports or check the rain gauge, then water each week to make up for lack of rainfall.

? ASK THE GARDEN DOCTOR **HOW CAN I TELL IF I'M WATERING MY PLANTS TOO MUCH?** Overwatering is one of the most common causes of plants' demise. If soil is continually saturated, plant roots do not get enough air and they rot. Too-wet soil feels wet to the touch. It may smell sour and—ironically—may cause plants to wilt.

 **TEST
GARDEN
TIP**

WATERING PROPERLY Water at the base of a plant, wetting the soil, not the foliage. The goal: Deliver water to the roots where it is needed.

WATER PROPERLY
Avoid applying water faster than the soil can absorb it. A gentle, slow trickle seeps deeper, especially in dry soil. Unless applied carefully, water runs off extremely dry soil.

CONSERVING WATER

Water is among the most precious resources on Earth today. In dry regions and areas prone to drought, water conservation is essential.

Many communities restrict water use for lawns and gardens, requiring conservation. Even if you live in a high-rainfall region, your plants may not receive adequate water at the right time. Conservation methods promote healthy plants that can cope with drought. Whether or not water is scarce where you garden, it pays to conserve—you'll see an appreciable difference in your water bill.

There are plenty of ways to effectively reduce water use and still have a beautiful, productive garden. Some strategies require a change of habits, others involve choices of equipment, plants, and other landscape features, including:

Improve soil. Add loads of organic matter to help soil soak up water and stay moist longer.

Mulch. Cover bare soil with a 2- to 3-inch layer of chopped leaves, bark, or compost.

Reduce lawn area. Retain only as much turfgrass as you use. Aerate the lawn annually. Use a mulching mower and recycle lawn clippings.

Use efficient watering methods. Drip irrigation and soaker hoses lose less water to evaporation than sprinklers. Water only when needed, not automatically and regardless of weather.

Use free water. Set a rain barrel under a downspout and collect rainwater.

WATER WISELY Any place in your landscape that uses water has potential for conserving it.

WATER-HOLDING GRANULES Mixed into potted gardens or beds, polymer crystals absorb water and release it into soil as needed.

 **ASK THE GARDEN DOCTOR** **HOW DO I USE THE WATER FROM MY RAIN BARREL?** Whether you purchase a ready-made rain barrel or make one, you can add a hose spigot near the base of the barrel for easy access to the stored water. Attach a garden hose to the spigot, if you like, to route the water to plants.

HOW TO SAVE WATER WITH A RAIN BARREL

Adopt a tried-and-true practice and harvest free rainwater.

One-half inch of rain yields 300 gallons of water shed from 1,000 square feet of roof. You only have to catch it. Once you realize how much water can be saved with one barrel, you'll want one at every downspout. A 40- to 60-gallon rain barrel under a downspout fills surprisingly quickly. It collects water free of the chemicals, such as chlorine and fluoride, added to municipal water.

Rain Barrel Safety

Select a barrel that adapts for overflow, allowing you to direct excess rainwater away from the barrel (and your home's foundation) or to link multiple barrels together.

Screen any opening to keep out debris and mosquitoes.

Place a rain barrel on stable, level ground or on concrete pavers or gravel to prevent tipping and spilling.

IN COLD CLIMATES Before winter arrives, disconnect and empty a rain barrel. If water is left in the barrel, freeze-thaw cycles could damage it.

EASY ACCESS Attach a garden hose to a rain barrel via a spigot to route the water easily to plants. You can add a spigot to a purchased or homemade barrel.

HAND WATERING

Watering, like most garden tasks, is not a one-size-fits-all sort of practice. There are plenty of ways to keep your garden green and use water efficiently.

Your choice of watering method depends on the plants you are growing. Young or small plants and container gardens can be watered deftly by hand, using a hose or a watering can. A wave of a watering wand, attached to a hose, is often the best way to reach bedding plants and hanging baskets. It also helps you quench plants growing under eaves or other out-of-the-way places. The gentle shower from a can proves perfect for just-planted seeds and tiny seedlings. Why drag a bulky hose across the yard when a watering can lets you pick it up and go?

When you step close enough to a plant to hand water, you're also close enough to inspect its health, inhale its aroma, and appreciate its beauty.

Hand watering involves no soil preparation or equipment installation, but it is more time-consuming for the gardener and commonly leads to underwatering because most gardeners do not have the patience to water plants as long as needed.

ASK THE GARDEN DOCTOR **WHAT QUALITIES SHOULD I LOOK FOR IN A GOOD WATERING CAN?** A 2- to 3-gallon can holds as much water as most people can comfortably carry. Two-handled cans tilt easily with less hand and arm strain. A brass or galvanized rose (perforated spout attachment) offers longevity.

GARDEN HOSES

Look for various ways to make a hose do the work, from an efficient attachment to convenient storage.

A dependable hose requires a lightweight yet flexible material that can handle water pressure and weather extremes. The best hoses consist of multiple layers or plies of rubber, vinyl, and reinforcing materials.

Larger-diameter hoses deliver more water pressure and volume but weigh more than smaller-diameter ones. A ¾-inch hose delivers 65 percent more water than a ⅝-inch one.

RUBBER HOSE The best hoses bend easily without kinking. Brass fittings and high-quality metal (brass) attachments last years longer than inexpensive alternatives.

COIL HOSE Especially useful for watering in a confined space, such as a greenhouse or balcony, the compact 25- to 50-foot hose won't tangle or require a storage reel.

SOAKER HOSE A porous or leaky hose sweats water, soaking ground up to 3 feet away. Burying the hose under mulch minimizes runoff and evaporation.

WATER WAND Make watering more efficient with a hose-end attachment. It may have a shut-off mechanism and spray adjustments from a gentle shower to a more forceful stream.

HOSE STORAGE A durable container conceals a garden hose and keeps it handy. A hole in the container's side allows the hose to connect conveniently to a faucet.

GOOD TIMING Use a programmable two-zone water timer that enables you to use one hose for drip irrigation at the same time as you use another hose for hand watering.

HOW TO INSTALL AND USE DRIP IRRIGATION

Good for any size garden and plants that need even moisture, a drip irrigation system applies water slowly and efficiently to specific areas.

A drip- or microirrigation system saves money and water by delivering moisture to soil near plants with as little evaporation and runoff as possible. You'll save more money by installing a system over a weekend or two, starting with a garden near a spigot.

Easy to install and adaptable to most gardens, drip systems can be purchased at hardware stores. You'll find kits that include emitters, tubing, and other components. Customize your system, adding emitters on lines to it.

First, sketch a plan. Measure the tubing length needed for a simple one-zone system. Count the type of emitters (dripper, sprayer, or sprinkler) and flow rate you will need, depending on plants' needs. Match brands of tubing and emitters to avoid sizing issues.

Prevent Problems

Attach a backflow prevention device to the spigot to prevent contaminated water from flowing into the water system. Also attach a filter to trap particles before they get into the irrigation lines and clog emitters. Automate your drip irrigation with a timer. Use a Y-splitter with shutoffs so you can simultaneously use the drip system and a garden hose. Match hose thread or pipe thread when you buy parts. Check your system seasonally, especially in hard-water areas, to make sure the emitters and filter are not clogged, the lines and screens are not plugged, and the timer works.

PROPER PLACEMENT Space tubing 12 to 24 inches apart in beds to wet soil yet promote root development.

CHECK MOISTURE DEPTH
Water seeping into soil is difficult to see. After a watering cycle, use a trowel to check soil moisture.

PROGRAMMABLE TIMER
Control a watering system, turning it on and off even when you're away.

ASK THE GARDEN DOCTOR **HOW CAN I CONNECT MY CONTAINER GARDENS TO A DRIP SYSTEM?** Run a main supply line from a spigot to the vicinity of your containers. Connect each container to the main line with a branching line. Run the irrigation line up the backside of each container to hide the tubing.

TEST
GARDEN
TIP

AVOID WASTING WATER An automatic timer allows you to decide how often and how long to deliver water to your plants with a drip irrigation system. Override the timer during wet or cold weather. Turn off the system and drain the main line before freezing weather arrives.

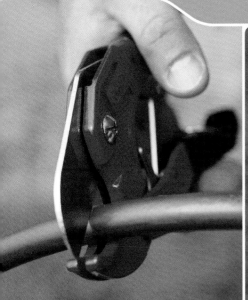

1 SNAKE TUBING Set tubing in sun to make it more bendable. Snake the line through the garden, then cut it to fit.

2 FLUSH LINE Run water through the tubing to clear debris. Crimp and clamp the end.

3 CONNECT LINES Cut the line and insert a T-fitting to connect a branching line and run the system in another direction.

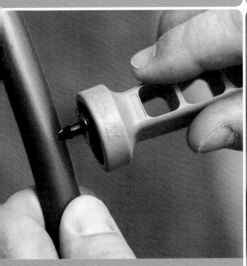

4 PUNCH HOLES Use the kit's tool to make a hole for each emitter connection. Use a "goof plug" to patch a hole.

5 ADD LINE Plug thin, flexible tubing into the drip line. Place an emitter at the end of the tubing.

6 HOLD THE LINE Use clips to hold the irrigation line in place. Use mulch to hide the line and conserve moisture.

TUNING UP INGROUND IRRIGATION

Underground sprinkler systems add convenience and the assurance that your valuable landscape plants and lawn will get the water they need when they need it.

Keep an inground sprinkler system working well with regular maintenance. Making occasional adjustments and repairs to the system will keep it working efficiently. As plants grow their needs change and equipment may fail unexpectedly. You can handle simple problems if you know how to identify them.

Monitor soil and plants regularly, checking for uniform irrigation. Adjust irrigation heads as plants grow and begin to block spray patterns.

Always drain the system to prepare for winter in a freezing area. Standing water turns to ice in the pipes and can lead to major leaks and repairs. The water must be shut off, the lines drained, and the valves cleared. The process depends on whether you have a gravity drain or compressed air system.

CHECK CONTROL Annually replace the backup battery in an automatic timer, following the manufacturer's directions.

PREVENT RUNOFF If you consistently see runoff from your lawn or garden after irrigating, the system is running too long and needs adjusting.

CLOGGED NOZZLE Fix low water flow or an uneven spray pattern by unscrewing the sprinkler head and rinsing the filter.

REALIGN SPRINKLER Depending on the type of sprinkler head, adjust it to spray water in the right direction.

CLEAR OBSTRUCTIONS Trim plant foliage or turf away from a sprinkler to remove interference with its spray.

ASK THE GARDEN DOCTOR **IS IT POSSIBLE TO HAVE A DROUGHT-TOLERANT LAWN?** Native turfgrasses and some other varieties have adapted to withstand drought and heat. Buffalograss, tall fescue, and sheep fescue are among those that need little water to thrive. Check with your extension service to identify drought-tolerant turfgrass varieties for your region.

CALL A PRO Turn to a qualified professional irrigation specialist when your efforts aren't improving the sprinkler system or you're not comfortable tackling a repair or maintenance. Not all repairs or maintenance tasks are do-it-yourself jobs.

WATERING LAWN

Portable or permanent sprinklers do the job. Choose the best system for your yard and supplement rainfall as needed.

Most people overwater their lawn. Overwatering weakens plant roots, which provides an entrance for many diseases. Water lawn deeply and infrequently. Water established lawn 1 inch every seven to fourteen days without rain. New lawn needs daily watering.

When water is scarce, during summer's peak, many turfgrasses go dormant (rest and stop growing). During a drought, it is better not to water at all than to water small amounts. Small amounts can prevent the lawn from resting and encourage weed growth. If you let a lawn go dormant, rest assured it will come back when rainfall and cooler weather return.

A portable sprinkler offers an inexpensive way to water occasionally. To cover a large area, move the sprinkler around. Be aware of the sprinkler's coverage area and pattern; compensate for uneven distribution.

In arid regions, an inground sprinkler system is an investment in maintaining lawn conveniently and efficiently. Even so, homes with a permanent system use more water than those without one.

WATERING TECHNIQUES

Effective watering is mostly about understanding plants' varying needs
for water and using an appropriate method.

Based on soil moisture, 1 inch of weekly rainfall may
or may not be enough if plants are growing rapidly
or establishing root systems. When the soil is dry,
plants need water. Heavy, clay soil holds more water;
light, sandy soil holds less. Always water right after
planting. Water the soil, directing water to plants'
roots. Avoid wetting foliage to help prevent diseases
that thrive in damp and humid conditions.

SEEDLINGS Consistent moisture is
crucial to their survival. Water deeply
when the soil begins to feel dry.

EDIBLES Many crops have shallow
roots and need water every few days
during hot weather.

PERENNIALS They may have deeper
roots but need water weekly,
especially during their first year.

WATERING TREES AND SHRUBS

MAKE A MOAT Build up a ring of soil at
least 12 inches from the plant's trunk,
forming a water-catching basin.

WATERING BAG Kept in place, a bag
slowly drips water to a tree's root zone.

SOAKER HOSE Another method uses a
leaky-hose attachment to seep water.

 **ASK THE GARDEN DOCTOR**

HOW CAN I PREVENT DAMAGE TO MY FLOWERS FROM MY GARDEN HOSE?
When you drag a hose around the garden, pulling it across a bed can crush or break plants. Place sturdy
hose guards at corners or along the perimeter of a bed to keep the hose out of the planting area.

CONTAINER GARDEN WATERING

Consistent, routine watering is vital to plants' health, especially when roots can't seek out moisture because they're confined.

Potted plantings dry out quickly, needing daily watering during hot weather. Porous and small pots dry out faster than glazed and large ones. Water when soil feels dry. If the potting mix in a container dries out completely, rewet it by standing the pot in a tub of water overnight. If a plant seems to be thirsty more often than not, transplant it into a larger container or move it to a spot with midday shade and see how its water needs change.

WATERING WAND An extended hose attachment helps you water a hanging garden without water running down your arm.

HOLDING MOISTURE Use a thick water-retentive fabriclike liner in a basket to help minimize the frequency of watering.

FILL TO RIM Water a container by filling it, letting the water soak in, and then filling it again until the water drains out the pot's bottom.

USE SAUCERS A saucer catches excess water and wicks it to plants. Empty a saucer after a day to prevent root rot.

ON VACATION Find a watering kit that includes a timer and depend on it to handle watering while you're away.

IRRIGATE A GROUP A drip system saves water and effort, targeting your thirstiest potted plants.

MAKING WATER-WISE GARDENS

No matter where you live, the simplest way to use less water is pretty obvious: Grow plants that use less water.

Creating a garden less dependent on water makes sense. You'll save money, time, and effort by taking simple steps toward a more self-sufficient garden.

Choose native plants. The plants adapted to your climate can cope with weather extremes. They may need water during severe drought.

Group plants with similar needs for water. Plant and irrigate in zones, with thirsty plants closer to the house, low-water plants farther away. Group containers too, and reduce evaporation from them.

Reduce lawn. Grass is the biggest user of water in most yards, on average. Retain only enough lawn for your needs. Replace lawn with drought-tolerant turfgrass or groundcovers.

Plant in late summer or early fall. Perennials, shrubs, and trees will need less water as they establish themselves before winter. As top growth slows with cooler weather, root growth will continue until the soil cools too.

Shelter plants. Create a windbreak or added shade with plants or a structure. Plants lose more water on sites exposed to wind or full sun.

Manage rainwater. A basin, swale, berm, or series of terraces can help catch water and guide it to planting areas. Redirect downspouts to gardens instead of letting rain run off the roof and down the street. Use permeable paving.

HARVEST RAIN
Use a downspout attachment that directs water into planting areas.

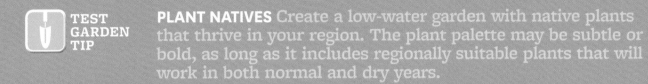

TEST GARDEN TIP

PLANT NATIVES Create a low-water garden with native plants that thrive in your region. The plant palette may be subtle or bold, as long as it includes regionally suitable plants that will work in both normal and dry years.

LOW-WATER LANDSCAPE Faced with dust and hot sun in summer, sand and salt in winter, this streetside garden features tough plants that withstand the challenges. Low-growing, drought-tolerant perennials do the trick here.

ARTEMISIA The lacy foliage of silvery artemisia blends and softens colors. Some varieties can become invasive. Zones 5–8.

LESS-THIRSTY PLANTS

In many places, water restrictions and drought have become an ongoing concern. Dealing with the situation starts with making appropriate plant choices.

Select plants that don't need much moisture to look great. Usually the plants most resistant to drought are the natives of your region. Many shrubs and perennials have adapted to environments with hot and sunny conditions or prolonged dry spells. In addition to your local nurseries, sources for drought-tolerant plants include mail-order suppliers.

DIANTHUS Old-fashioned favorites have grassy, blue-green foliage and dainty, clove-scented blooms. Plant in full sun. Zones 3–10.

FALSE INDIGO (BAPTISIA) A long-lived North American native, it has tall flower spikes and attractive seedpods. Grow it in full to part sun. Zones 3–10.

CATMINT (NEPETA RACEMOSA) The shrubby plants have fragrant blue-green foliage. The flowers beckon butterflies and hummingbirds in Zones 4–10.

LAMB'S-EARS (STACHYS BYZANTINA) Prized for its fuzzy, silvery foliage, it forms a dense groundcover in full sun and well-draining soil. Zones 3–10.

PENSTEMON, PINELEAF (P. PINIFOLIUS) A Southwest native with needlelike evergreen leaves, it blooms from summer to fall in Zones 4–10.

Where Water Is Scarce

Water shortages are already affecting a number of states, and that number will only grow in the future. Learn about drought-tolerant plants and use them to make your garden less water dependent.

New plants are especially vulnerable to dry conditions. Most perennials need regular watering in their first year to become established, but less water overall than annuals. Deep, infrequent watering encourages deeper roots.

SUNDROPS *(OENOTHERA)* A fast-growing spreader with bright yellow flowers on sturdy 18- to 24-inch stems, it grows in full to part sun in Zones 4–9.

SALVIA, PERENNIAL Plants vary from small perennials to large woody shrubs with sturdy foliage and long-season blooms in Zones 4–10.

SEDUM, SHOWY *(S. SPECTABILE)* Upright succulents are clump-forming and handsome year-round; good companions for a range of other perennials in Zones 3–10.

THYME, CREEPING *(THYMUS PRAECOX)* This ground-hugging herb forms a dense evergreen mat. It flowers in late spring and early summer. Zones 4–10.

TICKSEED *(COREOPSIS)* This low-maintenance, long-blooming tickseed needs well-draining soil and full sun. Zones 4–10.

YARROW *(ACHILLEA)* Recognized for its ferny foliage and flat-topped flower clusters, its varieties boast season-long color in Zones 2–10.

CHAPTER 13

PRUNING

Pruning is necessary, and it benefits plants in many ways.

WHY PRUNING IS IMPORTANT

Pruning is essential to plants' health, beauty, and safety. Keep all of these priorities—and a few others—in mind when you prune.

Regular and corrective pruning keeps trees, shrubs, and woody vines healthy by eliminating some problems and preventing others. Generally, pruning encourages new growth and vigor. Removing select branches lets light and air reach more parts of the plant. The ongoing priorities of pruning are the same for any plant: Remove damaged, diseased, or dead parts. When left on the plant, these parts become a harbor for pests and disease.

Prune With a Purpose

Accomplish other goals with pruning, improving the plant one way or another. Pruning is necessary when limbs create a safety issue, such as leaning precariously over a house or reaching overhead wires. These situations should be handled by a pro. When you wish to see more flowers or fruit on roses, raspberries, apples, camellias, or others, pruning is needed. Pruning also helps reveal the colorful bark of trees such as river birch and paperbark maple. And pruning prompts new colorful stems of shrubs, such as dogwood or kerria.

You can control a plant's size with good pruning, whether you have a shrub planted too close to the house, an overly assertive vine, or a shapely topiary. Similarly, pruning helps maintain a plant's natural form or creates a formal shape. It depends on the plant and your goal, whether you have a casual hedge of lilacs or a tidy border of boxwoods.

In the long run, pruning helps preserve a plant's integrity and your investment in it. Trees, shrubs, and woody vines vary in their growth habits and needs for pruning. Pruning helps you get to know your plants better and prompt them to become their best.

DEAD Removing all deadwood minimizes entry points for pests and diseases.

DISEASED Eliminate diseased parts, cutting back to a healthy branch or bud.

DAMAGED Remove broken or injured branches as close to the parent limb as possible.

? ASK THE GARDEN DOCTOR **WILL IT KILL MY PLANT IF I PRUNE IT?** Include pruning in your yearly gardening regimen. Concentrate on pruning basics and let the plant do the rest. Watch for the results of your cuts and pruning will become more of a pleasure as you gain confidence.

PRUNING SAFELY

Pruning can be hazardous. Common sense and the proper use of the right equipment will help keep you safe while pruning.

- Dress appropriately for pruning, wearing long pants, long-sleeved shirt, gloves, safety glasses, and nonskid shoes. A brimmed hat keeps the sun from obscuring your vision.
- Keep tools sharp and clean. Store a sharp tool in a protective sheath, if possible. Carry pruning tools with the points facing down.
- Choose a clear, still, dry day for pruning.
- If you must prune from a stepladder, tie it securely to the tree. Keep one hand on the ladder and one hand on your pruning saw. Station someone on the ground to help secure the ladder.

WHEN TO HIRE AN ARBORIST

Pruning a large or even a modest-size tree is a big—and potentially hazardous—job best left to a pro.

Hire a certified arborist whenever you feel the least bit uncomfortable about doing the job yourself. Leave it to a certified arborist to cut large, heavy branches, work near power lines, or prune high into a tree. An arborist is trained to work safely with a chainsaw and other equipment, even near houses, fences, and other structures.

Arborists can also evaluate trees for problems caused by insects, diseases, and nutritional imbalances and provide solutions. Problems caught early are easier and less costly to resolve. When contacting a reputable arborist, ask for references, proof of insurance, professional credentials, and a written estimate.

KNOWLEDGABLE PRO Let a certified arborist with the skills and equipment handle large, high, and precarious pruning jobs.

FOLLOW THROUGH Professional arborists clean up after themselves, removing all the debris after trimming your tree.

HIRE A PRO Pros are better equipped to handle challenging tree-trimming conditions for which the average person has neither the tools nor skills.

THE RIGHT WAY TO PRUNE

You'll avoid common pruning mistakes when you follow these simple guidelines.

Pruning is not complicated once you understand a few basic principles that will help ensure your success. These guidelines hold true whether you're pruning trees or shrubs.

Choose the Right Tool

Always use clean, sharp tools. Select the right-size tool for the branch you will prune to avoid damage to the plant and the tool. Use a pruning saw on branches larger than 1 to 1½ inches in diameter. Pruners work best on the smallest branches. Use loppers on branches an inch or so in diameter.

Choose the Right Time

There isn't a single best time for pruning. Late winter is an ideal time for pruning many trees and shrubs because they are dormant and it is easier to see what needs to be pruned. Late-winter pruning promotes fast regrowth in spring. There are exceptions.

Oaks and crabapples should be pruned in winter while they are dormant to keep diseases and insects from invading. Some trees, such as maples, birches, and magnolias, bleed sap heavily if pruned in late winter. This causes little harm but can be avoided by pruning these trees after they are fully leafed out in late spring or early summer.

Summer is the best time to remove dead branches when they stand out. Prune spring-flowering trees and shrubs right after they finish flowering in spring. Trees and shrubs that bloom during summer and into fall are best pruned in later winter or early spring as soon as their annual growth begins. Refrain from fall pruning because it stimulates new growth that could be killed by winter cold.

Prune anytime: suckers; water sprouts; branches that are dead, diseased, or damaged.

Make the Right Cuts

Holding the thinner, upper cutting blade nearer to the trunk or main stem, make a clean cut without tearing the bark. Avoid leaving a stub, which is unsightly and provides an entry point for pests and diseases. Cut just outside the branch collar, the swelling where the branch begins.

RIGHT TOOL Use short- or long-handled shears to cut small branches. Switch to a pruning saw for larger branches.

RIGHT TIME Pruning in late winter allows you to see the shape of a dormant (not growing) plant.

RIGHT CUT Prune with the blade held next to the branch collar (the swelling where branch meets trunk).

DISINFECT SHEARS Clean shears between pruning jobs. Rub the blades with a disinfectant to prevent the spread of disease.

 **ASK THE GARDEN DOCTOR** **WHAT SHOULD BE DONE TO REMEDY A STORM-DAMAGED TREE?** You can depend on a certified arborist to evaluate the tree for its species, location, and contribution to the landscape, as well as estimate the cost for pruning, repair, or replacement.

PRUNING TREES

Pruning is necessary at certain times in a tree's life.

Pruning young trees encourages strong natural forms and leads to less work for you later in their lives. There's no need to prune a newly planted tree unless it has damaged or dead branches. Give it a year to establish itself before pruning. Over the next few years, prune annually to remove poorly positioned branches (crossing or competing) and help the tree develop its ideal form.

Established trees need occasional pruning to remove dead branches. If the tree has been neglected, it may be necessary to control its size, reduce excess shade, or prevent branches from rubbing against each other, wires, buildings, or vehicles.

As a rule, cut no more than one-fourth of the tree's branches in one year. If a tree needs extensive renovation, spread the task out over two or more years. Cutting more than 25 percent of any tree's branches can compromise its viability.

PRUNED YOUNG TREE It's easier to prune a tree when it is young. Removing a low branch allows freer movement such as mowing beneath it.

COMPETITIVE BRANCHES Sometimes parallel or sharply angled to a main branch, competing branches weaken a maturing tree.

CROSSING BRANCHES Limbs that cross or rub may lead to decay or death. Leave the branch that best fits the overall structure.

WATERSPROUTS These soft, fast-growing branches often rise from the trunk or large limbs, taxing the tree's strength.

SUCKERS Shoots from the trunk base or roots compromise the tree's natural shape and drain its energy.

ASK THE GARDEN DOCTOR **HOW OFTEN SHOULD I PRUNE MY TREES AND SHRUBS?** After their first or second year in the garden, prune most trees and shrubs annually; prune slow-growing evergreens once every two years. Even small plants and dwarf trees need regular trimming to stay small and tidy.

CUTTING LARGE BRANCHES

Big branches are best removed in steps to avoid damage to the tree—or to you.

Remove a branch too large to hold in one hand with three separate cuts, using a bow saw. Make the correct cuts using a three-step process instead of trying to do it in one cut, which can rip the bark from the tree. Also avoid leaving a stub, which will decay eventually and may become a harbor for pests.

The first cut should be made on the underside of the branch within 6 inches of the trunk. The second cut should be made on the top of the branch 2 to 3 inches from the initial cut. Make the third cut just outside the branch collar to remove the stub. Leave the branch collar; it contains chemicals that speed the formation of callous, healing the wound.

Let pruning wounds heal on their own. Applying tarlike wound dressings is no longer recommended. The treatment does not benefit the tree or speed healing in most cases.

Although it may a take a number of years, some trees that have been pruned incorrectly can be improved. When you start to correct a poorly pruned tree, begin by looking for hidden decay in branch stubs. Prune stubs back to healthy wood.

CUT JUST RIGHT Cut just outside the branch collar or swelling near the trunk to speed healing. Do not cut flush with the trunk.

INITIAL CUT Saw from the bottom and cut halfway through the branch.

TOP CUT Just beyond the undercut, saw into the top of the branch. Eventually, the branch will break at the first cut.

FINAL CUT Just outside the branch collar, saw from the top and let the branch stub fall.

PRUNING EVERGREENS

Needled and broadleaf evergreens require minimal pruning and different techniques.

Most evergreens need pruning only to remove dead, damaged, or diseased limbs and to preserve the plants' natural forms while limiting their size.

Needled Evergreens

The pruning schedule is less rigid than the timing for other trees and shrubs. Ideally, prune needled evergreens in winter when plants are resting or in late spring or early summer after new growth stops.

One option is to prune your plants and use the trimmings for holiday decorating.

Pines and others that have three or more branches at each node (the spot where buds develop and form new foliage or stems) grow new branches from the tips of each branch. Prune only their new growth, called a candle. Arborvitae, juniper, yew, and others grow from random buds and can be pruned or sheared anywhere along their stems.

PRUNING BROADLEAF EVERGREENS

Flowering broadleaf evergreens, such as azalea, pyracantha, and camellia, are best pruned right after the blooms fade. Prune broadleaf evergreen shrubs without flowers (boxwood) and with berries (holly) in late winter or early spring.

BOXWOOD Shearing as shown mutilates foliage. Use hand pruners instead of hedge shears to snip stems.

RHODODENDRON Remove faded flowers by snipping or gently snapping off the spent blooms.

ASK THE GARDEN DOCTOR **HOW CAN I REJUVENATE AN OVERGROWN EVERGREEN?** In early spring cut one-fourth of a shrub's older stems back as far as green growth is present (over four years) to encourage new growth and side-shoot development. Avoid severe pruning on pines or other evergreens that produce new growth only from branch tips.

PINCHING This easy method of pruning young pine tips involves no equipment, just a thumb and forefinger to ensure denser growth.

HOW TO PRUNE NEEDLED EVERGREENS

The type of plant dictates the pruning technique and the right tool for the job.

SPRUCE Prune select branches to gently shape the evergreen and to allow balanced exposure to sunlight.

YEW Shearing creates a formal shape. It also prompts denser, more vigorous growth.

JUNIPER Selectively prune branches to maintain the evergreen's natural shape while opening it to more light.

PRUNING TOPIARIES

An evergreen topiary, nipped into an ornamental shape, adds personality to a garden.

Ordinarily, careful annual pruning of a young tree—or training—is done to help the tree grow up strong and develop its natural shape. Sometimes gardeners want their tree to take a more formal shape or to fit the confines of a small garden.

Topiary elevates pruning to an art form. With regular snipping, common evergreens become living sculpture—from spheres, spirals, and cones to animals, birds, and other imaginative shapes. Topiary is all about being creative with pruners.

Fine-textured evergreen shrubs and trees, such as boxwood, myrtle, and juniper, work especially well for topiary. For the patient, it can take five years to sculpt a holly or privet into a

double-ball form, starting with a regular shrub. Start with an already shaped tree or shrub for the easiest topiary.

Maintaining a shape is surprisingly simple, with monthly trimming of any shoots that stray from the decided form. Snipping here and there throughout the growing season keeps the lines of the design sharp. Use a straightedge or other guide to help you make a geometric shape. Work slowly and gradually, standing back and viewing the topiary as you trim to see more clearly where cuts need to be made. Rounded forms are typically easier to make and maintain than sharp-edged geometric shapes.

POTTED TOPIARIES Trimmed boxwood and rosemary shapes flourish in containers year-round in zones where they will not freeze.

PRUNING BOXWOOD Keep slow-growing boxwood in shape with seasonal pruning. For best results, snip each branch by an inch or so using pruners.

ASK THE GARDEN DOCTOR **ARE THERE OTHER PLANTS THAT WORK WELL FOR TOPIARY BESIDES EVERGREENS?** As candidates for topiary, evergreens work well because they have small needles or leaves, dense foliage, and compact or columnar growth habits. Other plants with similar characteristics that work well for this art of shapely pruning include herbs, woody shrubs, and small trees that are evergreen: rosemary, lavender, santolina, privet, laurel, viburnum, and holly.

MAINTAINING A TOPIARY

The easiest way to achieve a finished topiary is to start with a ready-made shape such as a spiral juniper from a nursery or garden center. Maintaining the shape with monthly or seasonal snipping is super simple. From the start, you'll have an artful evergreen for a garden bed or pot that will give you a continuing opportunity to practice your pruning skills.

For a spiral juniper like the one shown, start with a precut 5- to 6-foot dwarf variety that will grow slowly. A younger, smaller tree will cost less but take more years to mature.

In Zones 7 and warmer, the tree can grow in a pot year-round. In colder regions, transplant the tree to the garden in early fall. Or move the potted tree to a protected place over winter.

FOLLOW THE LEADER Using the original shaping as a guide, cut, then stand back to see the effects.

BEFORE
By late winter or early spring, a Hetz juniper is ready for a trim.

AFTER
It takes only minutes to refine the tree's shape each season.

PRUNING FRUIT TREES

Follow basic pruning steps to encourage healthy branches and loads of fruits.

All fruit trees need annual pruning to ensure their proper shape and optimum harvest. Young trees benefit from shaping of their developing structures. Keep in mind the main goal when pruning any fruit tree: to let light into the canopy. Also let standard pruning rules guide you to remove any dead, damaged, or diseased wood.

Prune fruit trees in late winter when their branches are bare and you can see a tree's structure. Several pruning strategies produce strong branches capable of supporting loads of fruit, yet leave the tree open enough to allow light and air to reach all of the branches.

The example shows a free-standing apple tree pruned with a central leader (trunk). The overall shape resembles a Christmas tree, with a narrow top and broad-reaching lower branches. This technique suits pear, cherry, and plum trees too.

Thinning Fruit

Fruit trees naturally produce excess fruit. Remove (thin out) overcrowded, small, diseased, or damaged fruit before it reaches 1 inch in diameter. Thinning helps produce larger fruit for harvest.

ESPALIER This technique trains a tree or shrub to grow in a two-dimensional form on a trellis, wall, or fence.

APPLE TREE Before (left side) and after (right side) pruning, a 20-year-old semi-dwarf apple tree has a central leader shape.

TEST GARDEN TIP

NEGLECTED TREES If you have an established fruit tree that has been pruned little if any, just trim it a little at a time as part of a pruning plan. Cut 25 percent a year over the course of four years to help the tree reach its optimal form.

RIGHT CUT Cut just outside of the branch collar (swelling where a branch begins) at a slight angle outward, without leaving a stub.

BEST ANGLE Maintain branches growing at a 45-degree angle. Branches growing horizontally or downward are less productive and best removed.

REMOVE CONFLICTS Prune out crossing branches. Also remove a branch growing directly above another and shading it.

CUT VERTICALS If a branch grows straight up or down, remove it.

REMOVE PROBLEMS Damaged and dead branches, and those growing nearly straight down, should be pruned.

MINIMIZE CUTS Remove no more than 25 percent of a tree in any one year. Make the fewest cuts to accomplish the same effect.

PRUNING SMALL FRUITS AND BRAMBLES

Fruiting shrubs and vines are among the easiest to tend.

BLUEBERRIES

Even bad pruning is better than none. Without pruning, blueberries can become overgrown and unfruitful. Prune dormant mature shrubs annually in late winter, after the threat of severe cold has passed but before the plants resume growing. Buds will have become clearly visible on the branches. Remove dead or damaged branches. Cut out one or two old, poorly producing branches each year; remove no more than one-fourth of the branches. Cut to an upright shoot or low bud. This selective trimming helps stimulate the growth of new branches.

GRAPES

Without annual pruning, the woody vines become tangled and fruit production will become diminished.

There are different methods for pruning grapes, which fruit on year-old wood. Consult your fruit stock supplier or extension service to determine the best method for the type of grapes you have. Your goal will be to develop a strong framework, then train the vines to keep a supply of year-old fruiting side branches. Begin by planting grapes on a trellis, with 6-foot-tall posts and galvanized wires stretched between them at 2½ and 5 feet high. This way, you can prune the plants to a main trunk with four main side branches, two to each side.

Each spring, cut the shoots back to spurs with two buds each, leaving 12 to 15 buds per vine. Remove the remaining vines, which is usually quite a bit.

PRUNING VINES Choose from various methods of pruning grapes, whether complicated or simplified.

ANNUAL TASK Thinning and harvesting grape clusters are also forms of beneficial pruning done each year.

ASK THE GARDEN DOCTOR **HOW DO I PRUNE MY KIWI VINE TO ENCOURAGE MORE FRUITING?** When growing kiwi for fruit, train the vine to an arbor or a 6-foot-tall trellis with three to five wires strung between T-shape supports. Like grapes, kiwis bear on one-year-old wood. Encourage a strong main stem, pruning to keep a continual supply of year-old fruiting side branches.

RASPBERRIES AND BLACKBERRIES

These fruiting shrubs are easier to tend than tree fruits because they are easier to reach and prune.

Bramble fruits need pruning to keep them from turning into a thicket where only birds can reach the best berries. If you combine pruning with a system of support that keeps the canes off the ground, the plants will be neater, less susceptible to disease, and more productive.

Blackberries

Blackberries have biennial canes that emerge from the crown and grow a year before bearing. After harvest, remove the spent canes. Thorny blackberry canes can be wicked, so wear gloves and rugged long sleeves. Thornless varieties tend to have fewer canes and less foliage than thorny ones.

Begin a pruning regimen for blackberries at planting time. Cut all the canes to ground level. As new upright canes grow, train them to a trellis and pinch off their tips to encourage branching. After harvest, cut back the portion that fruits. In late winter, trim the lateral branches to 18 inches.

Raspberries

Raspberries bear fruit either once in summer or twice, in summer and fall. Cut spent stems of summer-bearing types right after harvest. Leave the new canes that grew this summer, cutting them back by one-third to one-half—they will produce next year's crop. Prune twice-bearing types after the second crop.

Once you plant raspberries, look out! The plants spread by suckers and pop up wherever they please. This is a good thing when you want to fill a bed with raspberries; not so good if they appear in the midst of nearby flowerbeds or the lawn. Pruning will keep them under control and improve fruiting. Remove any spindly or errant canes.

PRUNING SHRUBS

Begin pruning a shrub when it is young and you'll have a much healthier, better-looking plant as it matures. Established shrubs may need annual pruning to control their size and maintain their vigor.

Many shrubs grow rapidly, becoming overgrown and excessively twiggy with leafy top growth and bare bottom branches. This top-heavy bushiness eventually obscures the shrub's structure, reduces flowering, and invites fungal disease.

As with trees, annual moderate pruning to maintain a good framework of well-spaced branches works better than severe pruning to rescue plants after years of neglect (see Restorative Pruning on page 284). Control the size and shape of shrubs with selective pruning up to one-third of the plant, heading or cutting back individual shoots with pruners. Larger woody branches should be cut back to a side branch using loppers and leaving no stub.

Prune the shrub to its natural growth habit and shape, from upright to rounded.

Each year, remove some top growth or entire branches to allow more light into the plant, resulting in dense, spreading growth at the bottom.

HYDRANGEA PRUNING Repeat-blooming *Hydrangea macrophylla* varieties bloom on last year's growth. Wait till they leaf out in early spring to prune out deadwood.

PRUNE SUCKERS Remove suckers (vigorous upright growth from roots) to redirect the plant's energy.

DEADHEAD FLOWERS Snipping off spent flowers of lilac and other bloomers as soon as they fade is another form of pruning.

? ASK THE GARDEN DOCTOR **MY BUTTERFLY BUSH DIED TO THE GROUND. NOW WHAT?** Some shrubs, such as *Buddleia*, are marginally hardy in cold climates. Roots survive harsh winters but branches do not. Cut the wood close to the ground using loppers in early spring. New growth will follow.

PRUNING SPRING-FLOWERING SHRUBS

The bloom time of flowering shrubs determines when to trim them.

Spring bloomers flower on branches that grew the previous year, so winter pruning removes limbs that would produce flowers. Prune spring bloomers right after they finish flowering. Pruning encourages new growth on which more buds can grow for best flowering next year.

LATE WINTER Leaf and flower buds are ready to go.

EARLY SPRING Blooms usually appear first, followed by leaves.

LATE SPRING Prune these shrubs as soon as the flowers fade.

SUMMER Next year's flower buds develop on the new stems.

PRUNING SUMMER-FLOWERING SHRUBS

For best results, prune in late winter into early spring.

Pruning in fall or midwinter leaves open wounds that lose moisture. Pruning cuts made during these times commonly cause dieback, resulting in more pruning in spring to remove stubs. Pruning cuts made just before or during active growth heal quickly and allow time for new growth for summer blooms.

LATE WINTER By spring, leaf buds, but not flower buds, have formed.

EARLY SPRING Prune the shrub before it begins growing.

LATE SPRING Each cut results in at least two new branches.

SUMMER The new branches produce a wealth of blooms.

RESTORATIVE PRUNING

When faced with a neglected or overgrown shrub, you may wonder whether the only solution will be to dig it up and replace it.

Give a shrub a new lease on life—instead of a death sentence—if it outgrows its space, looks unkempt and shabby, or produces few flowers or little fruit. When lilac branches reach more than 2 inches in diameter, for instance, remove them and allow suckers to develop into new branches.

Renewal pruning

This method of pruning removes some older stems to promote new growth. Plan to accomplish the process over three years, pruning out one-third of the old stems each year. Eventually, you end up with an almost entirely new plant.

Renewal pruning encourages new growth on an otherwise leggy, bare-bottom shrub. Some plants, such as lilac, honeysuckle, and spirea, respond well to this method of pruning. New growth fills in at their base, and more profuse flowering occurs.

AFTER RESTORATION Several years of restorative pruning prompt a lilac to bloom as much as—or more than—ever.

1 BEFORE Each year, over three years, remove one-third of a neglected lilac's old stems, cutting at ground level.

2 PRUNING Removing one-third of the old shrub's stems begins the renewal process.

3 AFTER One-third of the old stems have been removed, and the old shrub looks better already.

? **ASK THE GARDEN DOCTOR** **HOW CAN I IMPROVE THE APPEARANCE OF MY OVERGROWN HEDGE?** If a broadleaf shrub or group of shrubs hasn't been thinned to control height and width, you may have to resort to a three- or four-year renovation. Cut one-third to one-fourth of the oldest stems to the ground each year in early spring. New growth and side shoots will develop. This method may not work if the shrubs need to be replaced.

REJUVENATIVE PRUNING

This method of cutting back all the stems of a shrubs works best on some fast growers.

Another way to renovate some overgrown shrubs entails cutting all the stems to within 1 or 2 inches of the ground. It may take a few months for the entire shrub to produce new growth, and a year or more to regain an attractive shape.

This severe pruning method works well for some shrubs, such as *Cornus* (red-osier and yellow-twig dogwood), with multiple shoots. But it can kill some shrubs. When in doubt, use renewal pruning to determine whether the shrub produces new stems.

In warm-climate regions, less severe cutting back to 6 to 12 inches works well for these shrubs: abelia, azalea, burford holly, camellia, crape myrtle, heavenly bamboo, and privet.

❶ PRUNING NEEDED Some shrubs, such as butterfly bush, become overgrown unless pruned severely.

❷ MAKE CLEAN CUTS Use loppers or a pruning saw to accomplish rejuvenative pruning.

❸ PRUNING COMPLETE Cut all the stems to within 1 to 2 inches of ground level. They'll resume growing within a few weeks.

REJUVENATE THESE SHRUBS

Shrubs that benefit from rejuvenation:

Butterfly bush *(Buddleia)*
Caryopteris
Cinquefoil *(Potentilla)*
Dogwood *(Cornus)*
Forsythia
Hibiscus
Honeysuckle *(Lonicera)*
Hydrangea, 'Annabelle'
Lilac *(Syringa)*
Privet *(Ligustrum)*
St. johnswort *(Hypericum)*
Sumac *(Rhus)*

Hibiscus

Forsythia

Butterfly bush

SHEARING AND TRIMMING A HEDGE

Shrubs grown in a hedge need regular pruning to maintain their size and shape.

Too many gardeners shear all their shrubs, attempting to turn everything in the yard into some sort of geometric shape—gumdrops and lollipops. Many shrubs withstand shearing, but that doesn't always make it desirable. Restrict shearing to hedges, borders, topiaries, and other design elements suitable for aggressive shaping.

When you shear or head a shrub to control its size, you'll get a fast flush of growth that will require more pruning. A hedge may need trimming several times during a growing season, depending on the plantings.

Uniform shearing results in a formal appearance with straight sides and a flat top or a geometric shape. Removing one-third to one-half of individual branches produces a more natural form. Older deciduous hedges can be rejuvenated if they have grown too large or become bare bottomed.

Formal hedges trimmed properly are narrower at the top and broader at the bottom, allowing sunlight to reach more of the plants and snow to shed.

OLDER SHRUB An overgrown forsythia shows a tangle of branches and sparse blooms. Rejuvenative pruning—not shearing—will improve its appearance.

YOUNG SHRUBS If you want to trim boxwood or another shrub into a hedge, start pruning in the plant's second season.

ASK THE GARDEN DOCTOR **HOW CAN I KEEP A HEDGE LOOKING GOOD WITHOUT TONS OF WORK?** Opt for an informal hedge, which grows to its natural form and requires less maintenance. Thin the shrubs almost any time of year, removing a portion of the oldest branches and stems annually for uniform growth. Use hand pruners or loppers to remove branches and allow light into the center of a shrub.

LEVEL HEDGE When shearing a formal hedge, make a guideline for trimming. Run a string between two stakes and use it to help you cut the top of the hedge in an even and level horizontal.

IDEAL SHAPE A properly shaped hedge has a narrow, tapered top and a broad base with dense foliage. Dwarf Korean boxwood makes a hardy hedge for Zones 4-8.

PRUNING ROSES

Begin each growing season by pruning to enhance roses' health and flowering. Seize the opportunity to encourage vigorous, well-shaped plants.

It's easy to see quick results from pruning roses—more so than with many shrubs. Here are the basic necessities: In early spring, prune dead, damaged, and diseased canes from established plants. Cut back to healthy, green wood. Also cut out crossing canes, weak suckers sprouting from roots, and canes growing into the center of the plant. Opening up the plant's center improves air circulation and lets in more light, preventing disease.

Snipping off spent flowers throughout the growing season prompts more blooms. Let the last roses of summer wither on the canes. This allows plants to prepare for winter by developing hips. Different types of roses have specific pruning needs.

Modern roses, such as floribundas, grandifloras, hybrid teas, and miniatures, bloom on new wood and benefit from removing one-half to two-thirds of the plant's height, and all but three to five of the canes.

Climbers bloom on old wood, so wait until after the flowers fade to cut back some canes older than two years. Prune for a balance of old and new canes to ensure a good display.

Shrub and old garden roses need only light pruning to remove weak, old stems and shape plants.

CUT FLOWERS Snipping roses, whether fresh or spent, is another form of pruning. It benefits the plant.

MASTER THE CUT Prune like a pro, cutting ¼ inch above a bud or five-leaflet leaf at a 45-degree angle.

ROSE HIPS The fruits of roses develop at the end of the flowering season.

ASK THE GARDEN DOCTOR **DO I NEED A SPECIAL TOOL TO PRUNE ROSES?** Use sharp, clean bypass pruners to cut most canes. Cut thick canes with loppers or a pruning saw. After pruning, clean blades with a weak bleach solution or comparable disinfectant to minimize spreading disease.

ROSE PRUNING TIPS

In late winter or early spring, when a rose resumes growing, its green stems, buds, and foliage will help you see where pruning should occur.

ANGLE CUTS Make all cuts at a 45-degree angle outward (away from the plant's center).
WEAK GROWTH Remove canes thinner than the diameter of a pencil.
FROST DAMAGE Cut back frost-damaged or winter-killed canes (brown or black) to healthy green wood.
REMOVE SUCKERS Cut off weak suckers growing from roots.
CLEAN UP Remove debris that can spread disease from around the bush.

PRUNING VINES

Unless woody vines are disciplined by regular pruning, they become too much of a good thing. Vigorous vines especially need annual cutting back.

Guide a perennial vine's growth from the beginning, cutting all but the sturdiest stems and tying them to their support at planting time. At the opposite end of the spectrum, if a vine has grown into a huge tangle, renovate it in late winter or early spring. Remove the vine from its support, lay it on the ground, and cut all the old woody stems; leave one or two young stems at the base. Vigorous new growth will take off in spring. Pruning vines on a regular schedule helps keep them in check.

General Maintenance

Prune vines to curb their size, bolster flowering, and remove weak or dead growth. Vines that bloom on current season's growth (coral vine, trumpet vine) need pruning in early spring, just before they begin growing. Wait until after flowering to prune vines that bloom on the previous year's growth (mandevilla, which also blooms on the current year's growth).

Aggressive vines need to be cut back two or three times a year to keep them from taking over. Frequent pruning will make them more enjoyable and less of a pain. Wisteria, trumpet vine, Virginia creeper, and others can be pruned during the dormant season and again during the growing season.

BEFORE/AFTER
A fast-growing trumpet creeper uses a house for support, *above*, but it requires annual spring pruning to keep it from taking over, *right*.

ASK THE GARDEN DOCTOR **AFTER PRUNING AN OLD, OVERGROWN TRUMPET VINE, NEW PLANTS HAVE SPROUTED ALL OVER MY LAWN. HOW CAN I GET RID OF THEM?** Trumpet creeper activates dormant roots when the parent plant is threatened. You may continue to see sprouts appear for another year or two. Repeated mowing or pruning will kill them. Continue to cut any sprouts. You'll eventually starve the roots of energy.

PRUNING CLEMATIS

Some of the vines thrive with a good cut; others should be left alone.

Clematis are divided into three groups. The type of clematis you have dictates how and when it should be pruned.

Group 1: First-to-bloom varieties, including alpine, montana, and macropetala, flower on old wood. If it flowers before the end of June, don't prune. Tidy plants after flowering.

Group 2: Flowering on old and new wood, the large-flowering types need little pruning. Do it in winter.

Group 3: The late bloomers should be cut back to 8 to 12 inches in autumn, after flowering.

LATE WINTER Many clematis need little if any pruning. Your goal in pruning will be to remove dead or unproductive wood, minimize tangles, and increase flowering.

PRUNING WISTERIA

Keep growth in check and stimulate flower production.

Blossoms develop on spurs or short side shoots off the main stems. In winter shape the plant overall; avoid cutting the spurs. In spring remove leafless shoots and shorten laterals by half. Cutting back severely each year causes excessive foliage growth at the expense of flowers.

LONG SHOOTS Cut the long shoots of current-season growth after flowers fade.

MAJOR PRUNING Do major pruning right after flowering finishes.

CHAPTER 14

GARDENING IN CONTAINERS

For easy-care plantings that suit any lifestyle, potted gardens provide infinite possibilities.

BENEFITS OF POTTED GARDENS

Do you dream of a beautiful garden but face constraints of time, energy, money, or space? Container gardening offers many ways to overcome limited resources.

Although contained plants rely on gardeners for their needs, you can devise a container-tending routine that's enjoyable and suits your everyday life. Before long, potted gardens will contribute to the daily use of your surroundings as well as the appearance of your home—indoors and outdoors.

Count on your potted gardens to generate pleasure and make their setting more appealing. Containers make the ultimate garden accessories. They're colorful, portable, and changeable. Potted plantings encourage creative expression and reward it with cheerful displays that can extend the growing season and even keep going year-round.

Wherever you live, container gardens allow you to experiment with new plants and combinations. Containers enable you to enjoy plants that don't ordinarily grow in your location's climate or soil.

Wherever you put containers to work, they'll provide solutions—filling dull or bare spots, marking an entryway, creating privacy, decorating for a party, keeping produce handy, or adding flowery fragrance.

Indoors, you can turn windowsills, floors, and tables into garden spaces with a few plants. Plants add lush green life to any room and improve the air quality.

CONTAINER GARDENING STRATEGIES

Practice strategic planting and use containers where they'll provide the most benefits. Versatile and portable, potted gardens let you stage them where they will put on the best show.

As long as you give potted gardens adequate light, water, and food, they'll serve you well. Match plants to the available light conditions, whether growing single plants or grouping them. It takes only a few plants or pots to accomplish your mission.

Greet guests. Framing an entryway or lining steps, containers soften the hard edges of architecture and create a welcoming vibe. They guide traffic when lining a walkway or make a small balcony seem more inviting.

Provide garden space. Create a garden where there is not enough room or sun for a conventional one. Containers give you lots of options for planting on a small patio or stoop, or a sprawling deck or terrace. Potted plants add instant color and interest. They let you grow edible plants nearer the kitchen. In addition, containers place plants within comfortable or easy reach.

Use vertical space. Where containers can hang or plants can climb, you'll make more efficient use of an area—and maybe even create more privacy in the process.

Unify the decor. Employ a strategy most often used indoors, where repetition of color unites the decorating scheme. Use similar or identical containers or plants throughout an area to pull it together visually.

GARDEN INDOORS
Group plants and pots with contrasting leaf shapes, colors, and textures, enlivening the dullest room.

EASY DRAMA Combine an edible plant (Swiss chard) with ornamental ones (tufted hairgrass and pansies) for a lasting show.

PICK A PEPPER Raising fresh produce in pots adds to family meals throughout the growing season at a low cost. Dwarf or compact varieties of peppers and tomatoes suit containers.

IVY LEAGUE Growing in roomy planters and climbing on trellises, ivy creates privacy for a patio. Flowering plants add color; candles in staked holders create ambience after sunset.

ASK THE GARDEN DOCTOR

IS IT SAFE TO MOVE HOUSEPLANTS OUTDOORS FOR THE SUMMER? Many plants, including an array of tropicals more commonly known as housplants, can move outdoors for the summer and back indoors for fall through spring. The same plants create a vacationlike setting outdoors, then move back indoors healtheir and stronger for the respite. Set plants in a shaded, protected place when you move them outdoors to help them adjust to stronger light.

START WITH A CONTAINER

Selecting an ideal pot for your container garden helps ensure its success.

The best potted gardens start with well-chosen containers. Begin by matching the container to its use as a home for plants that will help deliver enough space, moisture, nutrients, and air to nurture them. The most-suitable containers also express the style of your home and garden.

Pick a Pot

You'll find containers available in a huge range of types and materials, from classic terra-cotta and concrete to contemporary lookalike and self-watering planters. Synthetic pots (resin, plastic, fiberglass) last longer and shake off weather better than most natural types (wood, woven, fabric).

Colorful pots create instant garden accessories. Plain or decorative, lightweight or heavy, there are plenty of prospects to suit any garden. Improvised containers also complement many garden designs.

Picture an ornamental grass in a rustic bucket or an iron urn or a tall sleek cylinder—each metal container creates a different effect.

When choosing containers that appeal most to you, buy the best quality that you can afford. Balance the size of the container with the potential size of mature plants and their combined presence where you plan to place the garden. The larger the pot, the more room for roots and the slower soil dries. A shallow cast-concrete trough proves perfect for low-profile succulents, while a lightweight wall pot holds a precious begonia at eye level where you can notice it daily.

Good drainage is a container's most important feature. Unless a pot has a means of releasing excess water, plant roots can suffocate and die. If your pot doesn't have a drainage hole, use it as a decorative cachepot instead, hiding a drainable pot inside it.

GLAZED ALIKE If you plan to group containers, select ones with something in common, such as color or material.

SHAPE OF THINGS Big and deep (at least 12×12 inch) pots can host an assortment of plants and those with long or extensive roots.

BY THE BUSHEL Gently used baskets or wooden crates work well to raise a veggie garden in a small space.

ASK THE GARDEN DOCTOR **HOW CAN I WEATHERPROOF A CONTAINER?** Baskets, wooden crates, and other containers quickly disintegrate when exposed to continually wet soil and weather. Protect the exterior with several coats of waterproofing sealant. Plant in a plastic pot that fits inside the container.

MEASURE UP Containers seem big enough at the store when you decide to purchase them. But when you bring them home, they appear smaller than the surroundings. Prevent this common problem by taking along measurements when shopping.

THE ANATOMY OF A POT

All pots are not created equal. But good containers include essential characteristics that help plants thrive.

CLAY DIFFERENCES
Terra-cotta is reliable and easy to find. Unfired clay is heavy, rough-textured, and porous. It breaks more easily than high-fired clay. In a freezing climate, store pots in a sheltered place over winter.

ESSENTIAL MOISTURE
Soil dries out faster in clay pots than in plastic or fiberglass ones. Large planters hold moisture longer than smaller ones.

A SPACIOUS CONTAINER
Your garden's success depends on the container's ability to provide an adequate growing environment where roots can develop and flourish.

KEEP IT LIGHT
Lighten the weight of larger pots (more than 12 inches in diameter) to make them easier to move. An upside down plastic pot or packing peanuts will do the job. Fill smaller pots with soil for good root growth.

CRUCIAL DRAINAGE
Pots must have a drainage hole for excess water to pass through. A saucer catches the water and helps prevent staining on a tabletop or deck.

PLANTING A CONTAINER GARDEN

Think of a container garden as a miniature version of an inground garden. Your goal is to make the finished container look good, fulfill its intended function, and thrive in a site you have selected.

Use a few guidelines and you'll be creating container gardens like a pro in a snap. Effective design starts with a container. Choose one that is aesthetically pleasing and practical. Think big to save time and effort. The bigger the pot, the less you'll need to water and the better your plants will perform.

Ready to Plant

Choose healthy plants and a planting strategy. The simplest scheme includes a single variety or color. Combining different plants may entail balancing heights and forms with a tall star, a medium filler, and a trailing accent.

Also group plants with similar needs for light and water. Grouping is accomplished with multiple plants in one container or with multiple containers in a pleasing arrangement. Mix foliage textures and bloom colors as you like. Choose long-blooming annuals or feature perennials, edibles, or houseplants.

Round up everything you will need for planting, including a clean container with adequate drainage. Choose a premium potting mix (see page 61) and other ingredients such as plant food based on the plants' needs for nutrients, moisture, and drainage.

Once planted, leave 2 inches between the top of the soil mix and the container rim for mulch (if desired) and water.

A note about the long-season container garden shown: The scheme features a shrub that can be transplanted into a garden bed in late summer or early fall. As a bonus, the variegated foliage plants can be transplanted into their own smaller pots, saved over winter indoors, and replanted in fresh container gardens for the next season.

❶ GATHER ROUND Plant a large container in place so you won't need to move it.

❷ HALF-FILL POT Use high-quality potting mix. Plant the centerpiece, snuggling the the shrub's root ball into the potting soil.

❸ FEED NOW Sprinkle continuous-release plant food on top of the soil mix. This fertilizer will last for months.

❹ ADD SOIL Remove other plants from their nursery pots. Set them in place; fill in between with soil mix.

❺ ALWAYS WATER Sprinkle plantings thoroughly. Water as needed throughout the summer.

? ASK THE GARDEN DOCTOR **HOW MANY PLANTS WILL I NEED FOR MY CONTAINER?** First consider the size of the container, then determine the number of plants needed depending on their nursery pot size and their potential at maturity. When shopping for plants, set them on a cart to see how they might work together. When you bring plants home, arrange them in their nursery pots at first. At planting time, adjust their position in the container, considering how large they will grow.

MIXING PLANTS IN A CONTAINER

Underplantings complement a young tree-form Quick Fire hydrangea (*H. paniculata* 'Bulk') in a 20-inch-diameter plastic pot. The grouping grows steadily, providing a lively display all season.

ANGELONIA This sturdy annual blooms throughout summer if deadheaded consistently.

SCENTED GERANIUM (*PELARGONIUM*) 'Lady Plymouth', a rose-mint variety, has a pleasant fragrance and a unique leaf shape.

SPIDER PLANT (*CHLOROPHYTUM COMOSUM*) 'Variegatum' grows easily and adds a graceful accent to groupings.

SWEDISH IVY (*PLECTRANTHUS COLEOIDES*) This fast-grower has trailing stems and a spicy scent.

GROWING A THREE-SEASON GARDEN

This potted garden goes with the flow, changing with the seasons, and epitomizes spring, summer, and fall with a few changes.

Start with a roomy pot such as a 16-inch urn or the pot of your choice. Anchor the planting scheme with an upright evergreen tree or shrub that remains as the centerpiece throughout the growing season. The constant in this scheme is a golden juniper (*Juniperus communis* 'Gold Cone'), a dwarf variety that reaches 3 to 5 feet tall when mature. It moves out of the pot and into the garden in fall.

Highlight it with annual flowers and foliage, starting with a spring combo. Replace the annuals for a fresh display as spring turns to summer, and again

as summer turns to fall. It takes a dozen or fewer annuals in 3- to 4-inch pots to fill the planter each season. Relegate the passé plants to garden beds if you can't bear to compost them.

Help keep a long-season container garden going strong by fueling it from the start: Plant with a premium potting mix that contains time-release plant food and moisture-holding granules, or add these ingredients to your custom soil mix.

When changing the annuals, scoop them out of the pot, using a trowel and avoiding the shrub's roots.

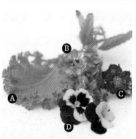

SPRING: COOL-SEASON PASTELS
- **A** Ornamental kale
- **B** Verbena 'Quartz Waterfall Mix'
- **C** Stock
- **D** Viola

SUMMER: WARM-SEASON CHANGEOUTS
- **A** *Helichrysum petiolare* 'Lime Light'
- **B** New Guinea impatiens

FALL: BRIGHT
REPLACEMENTS
A Chrysanthemum 'Dawn'
B Liriope muscari ' Variegata'

A

B

**ASK THE
GARDEN
DOCTOR**

CAN I KEEP A POTTED GARDEN GOING ALL YEAR? If you live in a climate that allows it, you can grow plants in containers year-round for the most sustainable schemes possible. Many woody plants and hardy perennials will thrive in containers for several years in a large-enough pot. If freezing weather threatens the survival of potted plants in your region, transplant them to the garden in early fall and return them to the container the following spring.

PLANTING A HANGING BASKET

Take a simplified approach to creating a beautiful hanging garden in minutes.

Garden centers commonly offer standard 10- or 12-inch hanging baskets. The plants are usually lush and beautiful, but the plastic pots and hangers that come with them are not. Plenty of pretty woven-basket options also exist that give plants more growing space and create satisfying displays.

Hanging baskets often go on sale before summer reaches full swing, making this an economical container gardening idea. Planting is a breeze. A few tricks ensure the garden's success.

Ruffly petunias bloom and cascade, making them ideal for hanging baskets and other containers. A sweet-scented, double-flowering variety puts on a colorful summerlong show. Monthly fertilizing helps keep the show going strong.

JUST PLANTED
A new hanging basket looks great from the start and will only get better.

❶ SET UP Set the 14-inch basket in a heavy pot to hold it. Remove the plastic liner.

❷ BETTER LINER Line the basket with moisture-holding fabric to let air reach plants' roots.

❸ ENRICHMENTS Add fertilizer and moisture-holding granules to the lightweight potting mix.

❹ GET PLANTS Release the plants' root ball from the nursery pot, keeping it intact.

❺ REPLANT Set the root ball in the basket half-filled with potting mix. Fill in with more mix. Water.

? ASK THE GARDEN DOCTOR **HOW CAN I KEEP FROM HAVING TO WATER HANGING BASKETS SO OFTEN?**
Start with the largest container possible, giving the plants' roots room to spread. Two special materials available to gardeners will make a difference if added at planting time: moisture-holding granules and a thick fabric-type basket liner. Then hang the basket where it will get needed light without baking in too much sun.

GROWING POTATOES IN A BAG

Grow bags made of fabric enable you to grow potatoes and other crops in almost any sunny place, such as a patio, deck, or balcony.

Growing potatoes or other edibles in a fabric bag available from a garden supplier couldn't be simpler. The lightweight, porous container allows the drainage and air circulation essential to healthy roots. You can also plant in burlap bags. Once planted, you only need to water regularly. A full-sun site is best for potatoes and other edibles, but 6 hours of sun daily can suffice.

The 18-inch-diameter grow bag shown holds well-draining potting mix amended with compost. Planted in spring, five seed potato pieces will produce a pleasing crop by early fall. Empty the grow bag into a wheelbarrow to harvest your potato crop.

ADD SOIL MIX As the potato plants grow, cover the stems with soil mix, adding more mix every few weeks.

SPUD SEEDS Seed potatoes are ready for planting when buds form. Cut and plant lime-size pieces that have at least two buds.

PLANTING Half-fill the bag with soil mix and compost. Cover the planted seed potatoes with soil mix. Water.

HARVEST TIME Potatoes are ready for harvest when the plants wither and turn brown.

GARDENING IN A SELF-WATERING CONTAINER

A container with a built-in water reservoir helps ensure that plants receive consistent moisture and minimizes watering chores.

A self-watering container holds a limited water supply. Moisture is wicked to plants' roots as the soil dries. You still need to water plants and refill the reservoir regularly, but less often, saving you time and effort. Various self-watering containers are available.

The planter shown (40×17×32 inches) holds 100 quarts of potting mix and has built-in overflow drainage. Once the reservoir is full, excess water drains out, which is especially helpful after a rain.

BUTTERFLY GARDEN PLANT LIST

A Butterfly weed 'Silky Deep Red'
B Salvia 'Fuego'
C Pineapple sage
D Marigold
E Pentas 'Ruby Glow'
F Lantana 'Landmark Blaze'
G Dill
H Parsley

WATER RESERVOIR Moisture is drawn up to the plant roots as needed.

FILL 'ER UP The water reservoir is refilled periodically.

WILD BEAUTY A swallowtail butterfly is one of the garden's winged visitors.

ASK THE GARDEN DOCTOR **DOES A BUTTERFLY GARDEN REALLY ATTRACT BUTTERFLIES?** Even when planted in a container, a garden designed to lure and sustain butterflies can serve all of butterflies' life stages. They need places to lay eggs and form a chrysalis; leaves, stems, and buds for caterpillars to feed on; and nectar for adults. The self-watering container garden shown offers an irresistible stop for nature's brightly colored winged beauties.

BUTTERFLY GARDEN Grow butterfly-friendly plants in a container garden and place it on a deck or patio, or in an opening in the garden where there is a need for color. Choose nectar-rich flowers, such as salvia, marigold, zinnia, and verbena, for your potted display.

1 **MATERIALS READY** A rot-resistant cedar planter on legs lets you garden without bending over.

2 **PREPARE SOIL** Premoisten a premium lightweight potting mix; blending until it's fluffy, not soggy.

3 **ADD FERTILIZER** Mix slow-release plant food into the potting mix, following the product's suggested quantity.

4 **FILL PLANTER** Add prepared potting mix to the planter. Fill the container to within 2 inches of the rim.

5 **ADD PLANTS** Ease one plant at a time out of its nursery pot, nestling its root ball into the potting mix.

6 **WATER PLANTS** Water the soil mix to thoroughly moisten it and ensure root-to-mix contact.

ANNUAL COLOR For a pot full of portable color, plant six Wave petunias in a lightweight 18-inch container. Apply liquid fertilizer every other week.

GREAT PLANTS FOR POTS

Most plants will adapt to life in a container outdoors during the growing season. Single plants in single pots make it easy to group plants effectively. Simplify plant combos by including only three elements—vertical, filler, trailer—for an effective design.

As you plan to plant a container garden and acquire plants, mix and match your selections depending on your garden conditions (sun, shade, or both) and goals. Depend on tried-and-true varieties or experiment with new and improved

BULBS FOR SPRING Plant prechilled bulbs (available at garden centers) for a concert of daffodils, tulips, and grape hyacinths plus annual violas, as an early-season treat.

DELICIOUS DUO Harvest spring lettuce, then let the 'Patio' tomato take over for summer pickings.

EVERGREEN TRIO Dwarf evergreen trees and shrubs thrive year-round in spacious individual pots and form handsome groupings.

FRAGRANT PLANTS Favorite herbs pack a planter with sensual delights, including lavender, basil 'Pesto Perpetuo', scented geranium, rosemary, and thyme.

GRASSY TEXTURE Even ornamental grasses do well in containers. Annual ruby grass teams with sweet potato vine for a marathon display.

ones. Explore the array of plants particularly adaptable to life in containers.

Choosing plants for containers is as easy as picking up a flat of petunias at the garden center. You might shop with a color scheme in mind, or just be drawn to delightful plants. Almost any plant can grow successfully in a container, at least for a limited time. Simplify the selection by focusing on plants' strengths and the practical advantages they provide. Drought tolerance or slow growth are pluses, for instance. You'll discover gradually which plants are most rewarding for you.

ROSY REALITY A shrub rose blooms all summer as it grows in this deep container with annuals at its feet.

HOUSEPLANTS' HIATUS Give houseplants a summer vacation outdoors, where they'll thrive with filtered light, increased air circulation, and refreshing showers.

PERENNIAL FARE Yes, you can grow perennials in containers, too. This one features gooseneck loosestrife and coral bells with lemongrass.

SIMPLY SUCCULENTS A collection of young succulents prefers warm, bright light, and careful watering (on the dry side).

SUMMER SHOW Canna and other summer-flowering bulbs grow well in a pot with annual accents (geranium, calibrachoa). Keep the bulb in the pot indoors over winter.

VERTICALLY INCLINED Pair a climber (black-eyed susan vine) with a trellis in a pot for a small-space solution. Annuals (calibrachoa, zinnia) add color.

MAINTAINING CONTAINER GARDENS

Routine tasks accomplished consistently keep potted plants healthy, whether outdoors or indoors.

Good basic gardening techniques promote lush, vigorous container gardens. Make a container garden where it's most convenient for you to maintain it—along an often-used walkway or near a favorite sitting area—and you'll enjoy it even more.

Watering is essential to plants' health. When plants' roots are confined to a container, water is vital to their survival. Check soil moisture by poking a finger into it; water if soil feels dry. Watering frequency depends on the time of year, size of container, plant needs, and soil mix. Outdoor containers require watering daily during summer; less often during cool weather. Small pots dry out faster. Indoor potted plants need less water during winter.

Mulching potted plants has multiple benefits: Besides conserving soil moisture, it insulates plant roots and keeps them cooler on the hottest days. Mulch deters squirrels, slugs, and other creatures from pestering container plants. Organic mulches, such as chipped bark and cocoa shells, decompose and gradually add nutrients to soil. Decorative mulches include gravel and recycled glass.

Fertilizer, available in various forms, provides essential nutrients to plants growing in the confines of a pot throughout the growing season outdoors. Indoor potted plants require little if any feeding over the winter—a rest period for them.

Groom potted plants regularly year-round to remove spent flowers or foliage. Watch for signs of pests and diseases, such as disfigured or discolored foliage or visible insect pests. Take action right away.

PLANT FOOD Add fertilizer to potting mix at planting time, following the product package directions.

TOOL TIME Short-handled and scaled-down tools work best within the tight space of a container.

ENOUGH WATER You've watered potted plants thoroughly when water runs out the bottom of the pot.

MULCH HELPS Polished stones, shells, or other mulch cover the soil surface and add ornamental value.

? ASK THE GARDEN DOCTOR **MY CONTAINER GARDENS GET SCRAGGLY AND BEDRAGGLED BY MIDSUMMER. WHAT CAN I DO?** Keep your plants growing beautifully throughout summer with regular grooming. Remove spent flowers and discolored or damaged foliage. Trim 1 to 2 inches from annuals every other week. Replace plants past their prime.

SEASON'S END

Protect the investment you've made in containers. Although some are made to withstand weather extremes, others should be sheltered over the winter.

When chilly nights signal an end to the garden season, it's time to move tender container plants indoors and protect other containers that remain outdoors. You'll be ready to grow in the spring with clean pots.

Over the winter, moisture from rain or snow held in a pot can freeze, expand, and crack or break the vessel. Weatherproof containers, such as resin or plastic, can be left outdoors year-round, but they require good drainage. Potted perennials, shrubs, and trees can remain in the garden. The plants will need regular watering.

Many container tropicals and annuals can move indoors for the winter. Give them extra attention before and after you move the plants indoors to help them make the transition. Most container plants thrive and grow considerably over the summer outdoors and may need repotting into a larger pot with fresh soil before they migrate back indoors. Inspect plants for insect problems and spray with insecticidal soap if you spot any.

HEAVY LIFTING Use the leverage of a two-wheel dolly or hand truck to lift and move hefty pots.

STORE POTS Protect containers from the ravages of winter by storing them under cover in a garage, shed, or such.

FORCEFUL SHOWER Before moving a plant indoors, give it a strong shower, using the hose to chase off insects.

SCRUB POTS Empty pots and scrub them clean to prevent spreading disease to new plants next season.

FALL CLEANUP Emptying, washing, and storing containers maintains them and helps you be ready to garden when the next growing season arrives.

INDOOR GARDENING: THE BASICS

Growing plants inside your home involves an exchange. An understanding of what a plant needs to flourish yields green, healthy growth.

Plants require light to grow well and flower. What's more, plants have different needs for light, and light levels vary throughout most homes. Place plants that need full sun in a south- or west-facing window for optimal bright light. The brighter the light, the stronger the shadows. Eastern and partly obscured western exposure provides medium light (partial shade). A north window offers low light (shade). To grow sun-loving plants in a low-light situation, use an artificial light source, such as fluorescent or halide lights that imitate sunlight.

Houseplants grow more slowly in winter as light levels diminish and days shorten. Stop fertilizing indoor plants then, except for those that flower or fruit in winter. Resume feeding in early spring to support new growth.

Indoors, most plants need only minimal care beyond adequate light, water, and humidity. Set containers on saucers, coasters, or casters to protect furniture and other surfaces from water damage.

INSTANT LIGHT Plants benefit from supplemental lighting where natural light is lacking.

BOOST HUMIDITY Set plants on a gravel-filled tray in winter to add humidity to dry indoor air.

REPOTTING A HOUSEPLANT

Periodically, a plant outgrows its container and needs to be repotted. When roots fill the bottom of the pot or reach through the drainage hole, it's time for a bigger pot.

❶ LARGER POT Give roots at least an inch of growing room on all sides.

❷ FRESH SOIL Fill one-third of the new pot with fresh soil mix. Add time-release plant food.

❸ WATER WELL Set the plant in place and fill around it with fresh soil mix.

 **TEST GARDEN TIP**

RIGHT LIGHT Give pots a quarter turn clockwise every few weeks to help them receive even light. They'll grow more evenly and lush.

BETTER LIGHT Grow sun-loving plants in a low-light situation using an artificial light source, such as a fluorescent or halide bulb, which imitates sunlight.

MOISTURE METER A water meter or sensor takes the guesswork out of the when-to-water dilemma. You can also use your finger as a dipstick.

BEGONIA A wide variety of showy leaf varieties as well as bloomers need medium to bright light and warmth. They're fun for collectors.

EASY-CARE HOUSEPLANTS

Each houseplant has its own preferences for light and water. Getting to know them is part of the fun of growing houseplants. Understanding the plants' needs will help you grow varieties that are just right for your home.

Plants bring the pleasures of nature indoors. With their lush, green beauty and ability to grow and change, houseplants offer varied charms. Some plants thrive with little tending—only watering and grooming—whereas others reward you with exotic flowers in return for ideal conditions and conscientious care.

FITTONIA, RED-VEIN This plant suits a terrarium because it prefers warmth and humidity. Give it medium light and damp soil

FOXTAIL FERN *(ASPARAGUS DENSIFLORUS* 'MYERS'*)* Among the wide range of ferns that grow marvelously well indoors, this one needs medium light and high humidity.

MADAGASCAR DRAGONTREE *(DRACAENA MARGINATA)* Given evenly damp soil and medium light, this variety and other dracaenas grow easily.

PEACOCK PLANT *(CALATHEA)* Varieties of this beautiful foliage plant grow easily in medium light and evenly damp soil.

PEPEROMIA CAPERATA 'BURGUNDY' Clumping, upright, and trailing varieties are easy to grow in medium light as long as you avoid overwatering.

Whether you line up plants on a windowsill or group them to create a gardenlike scene, they will enhance your quality of life as well as the air you breathe. Choose plants for their aesthetic appeal, but also take advantage of their ability to remove pollutants such as formaldehyde and carbon monoxide from indoor air. Some of the best air-purifying plants include spider plant, pothos, peace lily, and umbrella tree.

Learn what plants need by observing them: If humidity is too low, leaf edges will turn brown. If soil feels dry, it's time to water. If soil feels wet but the plant is wilted, it is being overwatered—let the soil dry. If sticky sap appears on the leaves or tabletop, an insect pest has likely invaded and merits action.

SNAKE PLANT (SANSEVIERIA) This plant survives neglect. It likes low light, little water, and high heat; will not tolerate cold or frost.

POLKA-DOT PLANT (HYPOESTES) Pinch growing tips to promote bushiness, and give plants medium light. Allow soil to dry slightly.

POTHOS (EPIPREMNUM) This vigorous, vining plant does best in medium to bright light and benefits from annual pruning.

SPIDER PLANT (CHLOROPHYTUM COMOSUM) A long-lived, easy-care plant, it produces baby plants on long, wiry stems in medium to bright light.

TRADESCANTIA ZEBRINA Break off a piece of the plant, push the stem end into soil, and see how easily it grows in bright light.

WAX PLANT, VARIEGATED (HOYA CARNOSA) Hoyas like to be potbound, with little extra growing room. They trail or climb a trellis in medium to high light.

EASY INDOOR GARDENING PROJECTS

Most indoor plants have few needs, but some plants require so little, they're practically self-sufficient.

In the time it takes to make a cut-flower arrangement, you can create an indoor garden that brightens your home no matter what the weather. Just use these ideas for inspiration.

Like other potted gardens, indoor plants need a generous container and enriched potting mix that provide good drainage. But there are exceptions: A group of plants called epiphytes or air plants survive without soil. As desert plants, cacti and succulents growing indoors over winter need water only occasionally. The soil mix should be allowed to dry between watering.

A terrarium defies the usual challenges of gardening. As an enclosed and sheltered environment, it resists pests and diseases, rarely sprouts a weed, and needs only periodic watering and grooming.

Adequate light and air help plants thrive within the confines of a glass or comparable container.

Also, as with other potted gardens, grouping indoor plants with similar needs for light and water will help you tend them more efficiently. The plants' health will reward you as a result.

SUCCULENT SUCCESS Bright light and dry periods ensure the survival of water-storing cacti and other succulents.

VIOLET SHOW A collection of plants makes a natural display, such as these African violets grouped in a birdbath. Grouping similar pots works too.

GLASS HOUSE Humidity-loving plants live happily inside a terrarium. A glass jar, soil, and moss provide an ecosystem that fends for itself.

 **ASK THE GARDEN DOCTOR** **WHAT KIND OF POTTING SOIL IS BEST FOR HOUSEPLANTS?** Inexpensive potting soil may be too dense and heavy for many plants. Improve it with a simple addition of perlite or vermiculite, or customize potting mixes suited to particular plants. Make a mix for African violets, for instance, using equal parts peat moss, perlite, and vermiculite. For cacti and succulents, combine equal parts sand, perlite, and crushed gravel, plus a handful or two of garden limestone.

TEST GARDEN TIP

TRY AIR PLANTS Often called *Tillandsia*, these fascinating plants comprise the largest and most varied genus of bromeliads, with hundreds of epiphytic species. The plants have few roots and don't need soil. They absorb moisture and nutrients through their leaves. Some air plants blossom.

AIR PLANTS Also known as bromeliads, these interesting plants need only daily misting and a weekly plunge into a sink partially filled with tepid water.

GROWING HERBS ON A SUNNY SILL

Keeping a bit of green life on a windowsill bolsters gardeners through the winter. Herbs offer extra-special pleasures with their fragrances and flavors.

Among the traditional outdoor plants that fare well indoors, herbs grow well on the sunniest windowsill. Small to medium-size pots of favorite culinary herbs provide fresh, convenient crops for use in preparing meals.

Start with young transplants in late summer or early fall, or sow seeds directly in a container. You can dig up herbs from the garden in early fall, transplant them into pots, and bring them indoors. But you'll get the best results from bringing in herbs that have been growing in containers all summer or starting with new plants. In addition to the herbs shown, plants that grow well indoors include rosemary, cilantro, chervil, and dill.

Pinch off herbs' stem tips often to keep plants growing lush. Plant growth slows naturally through the winter, but progresses and quickens in spring. Plants can be moved outdoors for the summer.

Avoid overwatering herbs by allowing the soil to begin to dry between waterings.

CULINARY HERBS
Thyme, basil, oregano, and parsley grow in small pots on the sill of a south-facing window.

READY TO PLANT To make an herb garden, you'll need terra-cotta pots and saucers, potting mix, and plants.

TRANSPLANT Remove plants from their nursery pots and slip them into the terra-cotta pots, adding fresh soil.

WATER Give each plant a deep drink, until the water runs from the bottom of the pot.

? ASK THE GARDEN DOCTOR **WHEN AND HOW SHOULD I FERTILIZE MY POTTED HERB?** Eat your herbs but do not feed them. Most herbs do not need fertilizer to grow well indoors and outdoors; in containers and in the garden. What's more, fertilizer promotes growth at the expense of flavor.

TEST GARDEN TIP

AWESOME ORCHIDS Few plants intrigue gardeners as orchids do. Their extraordinary blooms and growth habits make them fascinating and adaptable houseplants. If you think you cannot grow them or need a greenhouse to do so, bring home an orchid and see how undemanding it can be.

POTTING AN ORCHID
Chopped bark provides an ideal, well-aerated potting medium. A bit of added moss holds moisture.

GROWING ORCHIDS

Brilliant orchids create an intriguing presence indoors. They'll grow and rebloom with attention to their basic needs.

FOR STARTERS The types of orchids easiest to grow include *Phaiocalanthe*, cattleya, lady's slipper, and *Phalaenopsis*.

WATERING Keep the potting medium damp for most orchids (not cattleyas). Run water through the pot and pour off the excess.

REFRESH PLANTS Repot orchids once a year in fresh bark. At that time, clip off roots that are dead, shriveled, or broken.

STAKE PLANTS The tall, delicate flower stalks need support to avoid breaking. Secure stems using slender bamboo stakes and small clips.

MAKING THE MOST OF BLOOMING PLANTS

Flowering and foliage plants make welcome gifts, especially popular around holidays. Enjoy them as part of a seasonal indoor garden and don't worry about keeping them from year to year.

KALANCHOE This succulent prefers high light (full sun). Allow the soil to dry between waterings. Snip off spent flowers.

OTHER EASY FLOWERING HOUSEPLANTS

AMARYLLIS Varieties of the tropical bulb grow easily into large blossoms in medium light. Keep the soil barely moist to induce growth.

CYCLAMEN Keep the plant in a cool spot, away from direct sun and heat sources. Water at the soil's edge when it feels dry.

AZALEA Some greenhouse-grown azaleas and other shrubs are more tender than their cousins bred to survive outdoors in the garden.

HOLIDAY CACTI

These popular flowering plants grow easily indoors year-round. Cultivars are available for an annual bloomtime around Thanksgiving, Christmas, or Easter.

The plants are worth keeping from year to year. For colorful displays in fall, early winter, or around Easter, grow *Schlumbergera* varieties in bright indirect light most of the year. The season prior to your plant's annual bloom (late summer for Thanksgiving cactus, fall for a Christmas cactus, winter for Easter cactus) cut back on watering and move the plant to a cool room (about 65 degrees F) away from a window. When buds appear in four to six weeks, move the plant into bright but indirect light. Water when the soil begins to feel dry.

POINSETTIA

Colorful and evocative of the holidays, *Euphorbias* are ideal as long-lasting winter houseplants.

Of all the houseplants that bring a festive holiday touch, showy *Euphorbias* are the most popular living gift. Their colorful bracts (comparable to leaves) in varied hues from red to white and bicolors can hang on for months indoors. Remove a potted poinsettia from a florist sleeve, if it comes in one, and set the pot on a saucer to prevent the plant from standing in water. Set your plant in bright light away from drafts. Water only when the soil feels dry. The display shown includes 'Diamond Frost', a variety of *Euphorbia* with tiny flowers.

 **ASK THE GARDEN DOCTOR**

I RECEIVED A CHRYSANTHEMUM AS A GIFT. HOW CAN I MAKE THE FLOWERS LAST LONGER? Most homes do not offer the ideal conditions of a greenhouse where the plant was raised, but it can fare well indoors given proper care. Set the plant in a cool spot, away from direct sun, heating vents, and cold drafts. Water it only when the soil begins to feel dry. It should bloom for about one month.

FORCING SPRING-FLOWERING BULBS

Chill bulbs and trick them into blooming as if it were spring. This process, called forcing, provides a fun annual ritual.

In fall, purchase plump, firm bulbs. Hyacinths, daffodils, grape hyacinths, and others force well. Place the bulbs in paper bags and chill them in the refrigerator for 12 to 16 weeks. Keep the bulbs away from apples and other fruits (they produce a gas that retards bulb growth). Or chill bulbs in a cool (35 to 45 degrees F) frost-free garage or shed.

Once chilled, plant bulbs in pots filled with soil, leaving the tips above soil level. Water to moisten the soil. Or set bulbs on gravel or marbles in a watertight container. Add water to barely touch the bottoms of the bulbs. Place the bulbs in a cool room. Check the moisture level of the container weekly and add water as needed. After a month, move the developing bulbs to a warmer room. They'll bloom in another month.

SEEING CLEARLY A glass cylinder makes a perfect home for hyacinths, with glass marbles and a splash of water.

FORCING IN WATER
The traditional means of forcing hyacinth bulbs entails suspending each above water in a shapely glass vase.

LASTING BLOOMS A bulb blooms within about eight weeks after chilling. Flowers last best away from sun and heat.

FORCING IN SOIL
Hyacinths and other forced bulbs also grow well in soil.

CARRY ON Forced hyacinths and other potted bulbs can be enjoyed indoors or outdoors.

ASK THE GARDEN DOCTOR | **I FORGOT TO PLANT MY SPRING-FLOWERING BULBS IN THE FALL. WHAT CAN I DO?**
Hardy, spring-flowering bulbs require chilling in order to bloom. As long as the bulbs have not dried out or frozen and become mushy, they're salvageable. If you place them in the refrigerator in late fall or early winter, they'll be ready for forcing after three to four months of chilling.

TEST GARDEN TIP

FORCING BLOOMS Hardy bulbs can be forced into bloom only once. After that, commit the bulbs to compost or plant them outdoors with a handful of bulb food and let the foliage wither naturally.

FAVORITE BULBS FOR FORCING INDOORS

SUPER SIMPLE
Paperwhite narcissus bloom without prechilling. Their pungently fragrant flowers mature in about five weeks. They will not bloom again.

PAPERWHITE NARCISSUS Pot the tender bulbs in soil or water-covered pebbles from mid-October through February for indoor blooms.

TÊTE-À-TÊTE NARCISSUS One of the easiest hardy daffodils to force indoors, this one has bright blooms on 6-inch stems.

FRITILLARIA MICHAILOVSKYI This 8-inch-tall Turkish native has intriguing bellshape flowers for an unusual display indoors.

CHAPTER 15

MANAGING WEEDS, PESTS, AND DISEASES

Safe and effective methods of dealing with common problems often boil down to resourcefulness and persistence.

RECOGNIZING PROBLEMS

Knowing that something is amiss and knowing what to do about it are very different.
Begin by observing and learning to identify pests.

Pests, including insects, animals, weeds, and diseases, are inevitable in a garden. Their presence is an opportunity to test your mettle without turning your yard into a war zone. Savvy gardeners learn how to work with nature to promote healthy plants with healthy soil and to manage the garden ecosystem through observation, identification, and prevention.

A daily walk in the garden, with a careful look at leaves, stems, flowers, and the ground around plants, helps you spot signs of a problem in time to try effective controls. With practice, you'll learn how to recognize a problem and identify its cause.

Pest Detective

Garden pests and environmental challenges cause a staggering range of symptoms: discoloring, wilting, stunting, curling, and deformation, to name a few. Use the general categories of poor plant growth, damaged foliage, damaged fruit, no fruit, or plant death to begin defining your plant problem and finding a solution.

Many plant problems cause only cosmetic damage; little or no control is necessary for plants to be productive. Although some insects can cause major damage to plants, an amazing number of them are beneficial because they eat the bad bugs. Too often, people reach for a can of spray at the first sign of any critter.

IS IT AN INSECT PEST? Look for the pest or identify it by the damage done. Decide if intervention is required.

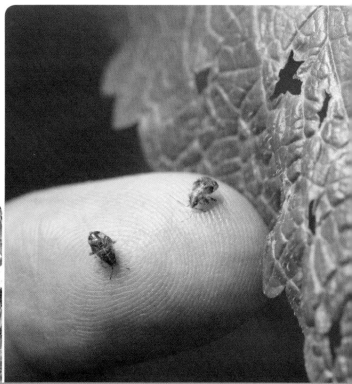

IS IT A DISEASE? If the affected part of a plant is limited, snip it off and trash it. Identify the problem and possible solutions.

IS IT A WEED? Early spring is prime time to wipe out weed seedlings before they grow deep roots.

ASK THE GARDEN DOCTOR **WHAT SHOULD I LOOK FOR WHEN DIAGNOSING A PLANT PROBLEM?** Your examination of a plant should first sort out if it has a pest-related problem or something going on in the plant's environment. Consider the type of plant, its age, size, condition, location, relationship to other plants, weather, recent care, soil conditions, and symptoms.

IDENTIFYING INSECTS AND DISEASES

The most common garden problems fall into two categories: insects and diseases. If it's not one of these, the problem may be related to weather, soil condition, or other common situations. A weak or stressed plant is more susceptible to pests. Look for answers on the Internet. The local gardening hotline or extension office can help you too.

MARRED LEAVES Leaf miners are immature stages of flies, wasps, beetles, or moths. The larvae make winding or blotchy mines on foliage.

CHEWING INSECTS Damage from caterpillars and other insects includes holes and chewed marks in leaves.

SUCKING INSECTS Damage from spider mites and other insects comes from them sucking plant sap and spreading diseases.

DISEASE SYMPTOMS Viruses, fungi, and bacteria are responsible for a range of plant problems, from spotted foliage to wilting.

LAWN PROBLEMS Brown or dead patches of lawn may be due to disease, insects, dog urine, weather, or chemical spill.

ENVIRONMENTAL FACTORS Blossom end rot is caused by inadequate calcium. Dry conditions or excessive nitrogen can make calcium in soil unavailable to plants.

CLEAN GARDEN Remove
spent flowers, dead leaves,
fallen fruit, and other debris
that can harbor pests
and diseases.

PREVENTING PROBLEMS

The adage "an ounce of prevention is
worth a pound of cure" certainly rings true
in the garden.

More often than not, it is much easier to prevent a
pest, weed, or disease from infiltrating your garden
and causing a problem than it is to eliminate the
problem and its cause. In nature, a balance of natural
predators and a healthy environment keeps most
pests, weeds, and diseases under control. One of a
gardener's most essential tasks in gardening is to
manage problems with a preventive approach. When
problems occur—and they do—a knowing gardener
helps the garden to help itself and turns to earth-
friendly solutions when necessary.

Simple Strategy

You won't make your garden 100 percent free of pests
or weeds, but you can take steps to make it a less
inviting target. Many problems are avoided simply by
using good gardening practices, promoting healthy
soil and plants, and keeping the garden clean. A weak
or stressed plant is more susceptible to pests.

Keeping a close eye on the garden enables you to
spot problems in the making. A problem caught early
is easier to resolve, whether the early stages of a
disease, weed seedlings, or a bit of rabbit damage.

Preventive practices become a way of life when
gardening. Watering in the morning gives plants a
chance to dry during the day, minimizing a damp
haven for disease. Spacing plants with plenty
of growing room also allows for air circulation.
Overcrowding can cause weak plant growth and less
air movement, resulting in more problems with insect
pests and diseases. Rotating crops minimizes pests
and diseases.

Avoid injury to plants. Broken or dead limbs,
cuts, bruises, cracks, and insect damage are common
sites for infection by disease organisms. Remove and
dispose of damaged or dead plant parts.

**ASK THE
GARDEN
DOCTOR**

HOW DOES WORKING IN A WET GARDEN PROMOTE PLANT DISEASE? When plants are wet
with rain or dew, diseases can be spread easily. Adequate spacing of plants and careful watering (of soil, not foliage) help
prevent disease problems.

PRACTICING PREVENTION

The best thing you can do to prevent pests and diseases is to grow diverse, healthy plants that can resist challenges. Provide the sun exposure, soil conditions, moisture levels, and nutrients that plants need.

RESISTANT VARIETIES Choose disease- and pest-resistant plant varieties. For example, plant only tomato varieties bred to resist wilt diseases.

HEALTHY PLANTS Start by purchasing the healthiest plants you can find, if you don't grow them from seeds.

HEALTHY SOIL Have your soil tested and amend it accordingly. Healthy soil can prevent most insect and disease issues.

FEWER WEEDS Keep weeds out of beds. Removing them when they're young is easier than wrestling with weeds' deep roots or when they've gone to seed.

PROBLEM PLANTS If a plant shows more stress, diseases, or other problems than most, get rid of it. Roses and other plants harbor disease or pests.

PLANT DIVERSITY Attract beneficial insects with a mix of flowers, vegetables, herbs, fruit trees, shrubs, and vines. Plant diverse and dissimilar species.

BENEFICIAL CREATURES

In this bug-eat-bug world, your garden will get by with a little help from some insect friends and wildlife allies.

When dealing with insect pests, it is more efficient, economical, and earth-friendly to support the web of life shared by humans, plants, insects, and other creatures. You don't have to take on pests by yourself. Enlist allies.

How to Welcome Beneficials

If you encourage beneficial insects and others (birds, bats, toads) to visit and stay in your yard by providing food, water, and shelter, nature will take its course. Most adult beneficial insects need nectar, pollen, or plant sap that is available in a diverse flower garden.

Similarly, insect-eating birds, bats, and toads are attracted by a habitat that includes a wide range of plant types, including sources of food and shelter, as well as water. Providing simple housing for birds and bats also encourages them to stick around.

Observe the garden regularly and get to know its residents. Of the 1.3 million identified insect species, less than 1 percent are pests. The rest are harmless, or better, they're beneficial. A beneficial insect (green lacewing, ladybird beetle, and praying mantis) preys and feeds on pest insects. Beneficial nematodes and other good parasites lay eggs on or in a host to feed on it. They do not harm humans or their pets. Likewise, most wasps and bees provide benefits.

Learn to identify beneficial insects of your region and watch how they behave. The delicate green lacewings that are attracted to your outdoor lights at night are one of the best suppressors of aphids and other soft-bodied insects by day. If you're concerned that your yard lacks a balanced insect population, you can purchase and release helpful insects in your yard. They may or may not stay.

PRAYING MANTIS A highly effective insect predator, the mantis preys with strong, quick forelegs.

LADYBIRD BEETLE Also known as a ladybug, this aphid-eating insect may be red or orange.

GARDEN SPIDER Harmless to humans, the yellow-and-black garden spider is an important garden insect predator.

HONEYBEE Bees and wasps, the irreplaceable pollinators, are among the garden's most important workers.

ASK THE GARDEN DOCTOR **HOW ARE BEES BENEFICIAL?** Gardeners depend on bees and other insects to pollinate plants grown for their fruit, seeds, and other edibles. More bees in the garden means a more bountiful harvest. What's more, bees transform flower nectar into honey—what a sweet reward.

TEST GARDEN TIP

WELCOME WILDLIFE Providing food and water sources in your yard encourages birds to visit, feast, drink, and bathe. Trees, shrubs, and vines also create shelter and nesting places.

WINGED ALLIES
Enlist the aid of birds in pest control. Add to your garden fruitful plants (serviceberry, crabapple, viburnum) and a source of water that will attract birds.

MINIMIZING INSECT PESTS

Some pest problems are mainly cosmetic; others can kill plants. Coordinated pest management uses gardening methods of damage control.

Not so long ago, chemicals were the standard approach to controlling garden pests. Today's world of environmental awareness and health consciousness spurs gardeners to avoid using chemicals and seek alternatives.

Determining your best management strategy entails decisions: Is the problem unsightly or serious? Is it worth the time, effort, or expense to take action? Consider the alternative controls and evaluate consequences before you act. Combine different control tactics to develop your strategy for maintaining a healthy garden.

Physical Controls

The least toxic ways to deal with insect pests are simple: Pick troublesome insects or eggs off plants and squish them. If you spot Japanese beetles feasting on your roses, knock them off into a bucket of soap-sudsy water to their demise.

You won't eliminate pests from your garden, but you can control their numbers with a variety of traps and hinder their access to plants with physical barriers such as row covers.

Biological Controls

Encourage or even add natural predators and pathogens such as ladybird beetles against scale insects, parasitic nematodes against cucumber beetles, or the bacteria Bt (*Bacillus thuringiensis*) against caterpillars. Biological controls target specific pets and won't wipe out other insects.

Chemical Controls

Newer botanical chemicals developed from plants provide effective pest controls with fewer harmful side effects to the environment. If you use a petroleum-based chemical pesticide as a last defense, you will kill beneficial insects along with pests. Read product descriptions and labels carefully. Products made for use on ornamental plants may not be safe for use on edibles.

Keep in mind that most steps taken to manage pests of all kinds require repetition. Insects, weeds, and diseases have life cycles: Repeating a method of pest control several times within a month helps minimize the problem and successive generations.

❶ INSECTICIDAL SOAP A variety of insecticidal soaps, including organic options, are available from garden suppliers to spray on pests.

❷ PHYSICAL BARRIERS A cloche made from a tomato cage and window screen lets in light and moisture but keeps insect pests away from a tender plant.

THE SAFEST SPRAY: WATER

Start with the least-toxic control. Nudge the system, instead of hammering it, to reestablish a healthy balance.

If you feel compelled to spray something on plants infested with aphids or a similar pest, reach for the garden hose. Attach to your garden hose a nozzle that will spray water in a forceful jet. Use a blast of water to chase off aphids and other soft-bodied insects. The force of the water, as well as the water itself, will work quickly to knock off the fragile insects. Do this early in the day, allowing the sun and wind to dry plants afterward.

MAKING STICKY TRAPS

Traps let you know where certain pests are active and when it's time to start putting controls to work.

Traps lure pesky insects onto a sticky surface using an attractive color or insect sex pheromones. A variety of insect pests are attracted to yellow, including whiteflies, aphids, cucumber beetles, flea beetles, fruit flies, fungus gnats, and leaf miners.

It's easy to make yellow sticky traps for use among garden plants or houseplants. This is a nontoxic way to snag the pests. They stick to the surface of the card.

You can achieve the same effect using a yellow plastic drinking cup, coating the inside with Tanglefoot, and turning the cup upside down over the end of a garden stake. Stand a few stakes with sticky traps among garden plants. Gently shake nearby plants from time to time to dislodge insects, encouraging them to fly off and into the traps.

❶ YELLOW CARD Cut yellow cardstock into 6x8-inch pieces. Attach each card to a stake or hook.

❷ MAKE IT STICKY Brush petroleum jelly or Tanglefoot (from a hardware store or garden center) on both sides of each card.

PROBLEMATIC INSECTS

You don't want to see your garden ravaged by hungry insects.

The first sign of an insect pest rarely means that a devastating infestation is about to settle on your garden. Most gardens have a small amount of insect damage, and it does not affect the garden's overall appearance. Get out your magnifying glass and have a field day: Learn to identify common insect pests and the damage they cause.

APHIDS They suck plant juices, causing shriveled leaves and wilted flowers. Control: Spray with water or soapy water; release ladybird beetles.

CABBAGEWORMS/MOTHS Tan or white moths lay eggs that hatch into leaf-munching caterpillars. Control: Bt *(Bacillus thuringiensis)*.

CUCUMBER BEETLES Striped or spotted, they feed on crops and spread wilt disease. Control: carefully timed release of parasitic nematodes; floating row cover.

FLEA BEETLES The tiny hopping insects cause shot-hole damage in leaves. Control: horticultural oil; pyrethrum.

GRUBS The larval forms of Japanese and June beetles burrow under lawns. Control: parasitic nematodes.

JAPANESE BEETLES Look for green and coppery wings. They devour edibles and ornamentals. Control: handpicking; horticultural oil.

Unwanted Insects

Keeping plants as healthy as possible is the first line of defense against insect pests. The next step is learning what the culprits look like and how to control them. Decide how much damage to a plant you can tolerate and then act. In the process, don't let pesky insects get you down.

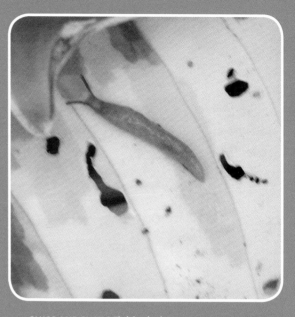

SLUGS AND SNAILS Thriving in damp areas, they rasp holes in leaves and flowers. Control: minimal mulch; traps; bait; diatomaceous earth.

ROSE SLUGS The larval stage of sawfly wasps chew holes in leaves, leaving veins. Control: Pick off leaves; apply insecticidal soap.

SCALE INSECTS Different types of these sap feeders may be cottony, soft and waxy, or hard and shellac-like. Control: horticultural oil; dormant oil.

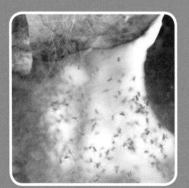

SPIDER MITES Minuscule arachnids (not insects) sap plants, leaving stippled foliage and tiny webs. Control: Spray with water, citrus oil, or insecticidal soap.

SQUASH BUGS The sap suckers injure squash, pumpkins, and cucumbers. Control: garden hygiene; crop rotation; handpicking; traps.

WHITEFLIES The tiny sap suckers raise havoc indoors and outdoors. Control: sticky traps; horticultural oil.

COMMON ANIMAL PESTS

Once you've extended a welcome to the wildlife in your area, you may find some animals less desirable than others.

Watching backyard wildlife can be enjoyable, but some animals quickly wear out their welcome when they treat your garden as an all-you-can-eat buffet. Deer have no regard for the hours of loving care you lavish on the roses or the fortune you spend on tulips; for them, the plants are just another meal.

Wild animals known to coexist with people and pets can damage gardens and homes, carry diseases, or pose a health threat to pets or family members. When the damage is serious enough to warrant your intervention, it's important to identify the cause of the problem and determine your coping strategy.

A rabbit can devour seedlings or sprouting lilies overnight, chomping off stems near ground level. Deer can decimate just about any plants, yanking roots right out of the ground and leaving their uneven bite marks on shrubs and flowering plants. Woodchucks and gophers inflict damage lower to the ground, nipping stems neatly with their sharp teeth.

Can you tell the difference among the tunnels of different rodents? Gophers leave a fan-shape pile of earth around half an entry hole. Moles excavate a perfect circle of soil around the hole. Voles tunnel close to the soil's surface without leaving mounds of earth. If one of these rodents is tunneling in your yard, it is also feasting on your garden.

Find a humane way to discourage an animal pest or trap it for relocation. For assistance, call your local animal control office, a local wildlife sanctuary, or a professional pest control specialist.

DEER A widespread pest, deer damage all kinds of plants. Tall fences slow the agile jumpers.

RABBIT This rodent favors tender shoots and young plants. It gnaws bark, twigs, and buds in winter.

RACCOON Foraging at night on compost, fruits, and vegetables, raccoons can be deterred by a dog or an electric fence.

SQUIRREL This pest raids birdfeeders, eats bulbs, and nests in attics and garages. Trim tree branches away from rooflines.

WOODCHUCK A strong rodent (or groundhog) digs big holes. It eats shoots, flower buds, and fruit.

ASK THE GARDEN DOCTOR **WHAT CAN I PLANT THAT DEER WON'T EAT?** Hungry deer will eat almost any plant. But they tend to avoid plants with toxic foliage (daffodils, foxglove, rhubarb); fuzzy foliage (lamb's ears, black-eyed susan); prickles (yucca, barberry, pine); and fragrant foliage (artemisia, lavender, catmint).

TEST GARDEN TIP

TRAP AND RELEASE You can catch small critters, such as moles and gophers, in baited traps, then relocate them—but check local regulations before turning to this method. First try to repel, exclude, or otherwise deter the rascals before resorting to trapping and releasing them elsewhere.

DEER DAMAGE During breeding season, bucks aggressively rub their antlers against trees. Deer severely damaged these aspen trees.

RABBIT DAMAGE Rabbits devour garden plants, especially tender young growth in spring. Fencing deters them.

DETERRING ANIMAL PESTS

Instead of taking action after the damage is done, protect your garden from hungry critters.

You have plenty of options when taking a preventive approach to animal pests. Some methods are more effective than others. A combination of a barrier and a repellent often produces better results, because the methods by themselves have limitations. Repellents must be reapplied after a rain. Fencing select areas or plants may be possible, but enclosing an entire yard may not.

Some gardeners have dogs to keep deer and other wild creatures at bay. Put your faithful friend to work in your yard, especially after dusk and in the spring when deer and others are most active.

There are also ways to make your property less hospitable to deer. Plant the most-vulnerable plants closest to the house, protected by fencing. Avoid planting fruit trees and susceptible ornamental plants such as roses along your yard's periphery. Deer dwell at edges of woods, graze their way into the open from the periphery, and retreat to the woods for safety.

Deer fencing—at least 8 feet tall or electric—works, but it is not always suitable, especially in suburbia. Installing two parallel 5-foot fences about 5 feet apart, and planting shrubs in between them, is effective. It's also a more attractive alternative to an 8-foot barrier.

KEEP OUT DEER Set a sturdy fence tall enough (at least 8 feet). It can be pretty as well as practical.

PROTECT FRUIT Heavy-duty garden netting shields a cherry crop from hungry birds.

ASK THE GARDEN DOCTOR **HOW CAN I CONTROL MOLES THAT ARE TUNNELING IN MY YARD?** It is a common misconception that controlling grubs in your lawn will get rid of moles. Although moles do eat grubs, their number one food source is earthworms. Unless the grub population is high (more than 10 per square foot), control isn't needed. Trapping moles is the most effective way to eliminate them from your yard.

PEST-CONTROL OPTIONS

Discouraging deer, rabbits, raccoons, voles, and other pesky creatures requires gardeners to be proactive and resourceful. Use homemade or commercial deterrents such as these. Alternate repellents throughout the year for maximum effect because deer and others lose their fear of the familiar.

TREE WRAP Wrap a sturdy shield around young trees, from below soil level to above the snow line. Remove it by summer.

REPELLENT SPRAY A smelly or distasteful spray, formulated to thwart rabbits, deer, and others, works until it must be replenished.

LOW FENCING A barrier such as waffle fencing deters rabbits, but 24-inch-tall wire excludes them, especially when buried in 6 inches of soil.

WIRE CLOCHE A portable and temporary device covers a tender young plant such as a lily, protecting it from grazing rabbits.

TALL FENCING Stakes and mesh combine to make an economical 8-foot-tall enclosure for a vegetable garden in a neighborhood rife with deer.

WIRE WRAP Hardware cloth, cut to form a simple wrap, keeps animals away from a young blueberry plant.

STAYING AHEAD OF WEEDS

Don't let weeds rob your garden or lawn of its health and beauty.

It's often said that weeds are uninvited plants growing in the wrong place. Although weed seeds lurk in almost any soil, most weeds don't become a problem because they never get the light needed to germinate. But when you cultivate soil, weed seeds inevitably surface and sprout among your more desirable plants.

Weeds compromise the health and welfare of edible and ornamental plants as well as turfgrasses, competing for nutrients and moisture. Weeds harbor disease pathogens as well as insects and their eggs. Left unchecked, weeds can take over.

Understanding the Pests

It helps to know the difference between annual and perennial weeds, and to understand how they grow, because this determines the best approach to weed control. Most weeds are shallow-rooted annuals that complete their life cycle in one growing season, but produce masses (even thousands) of seeds. They germinate in spring or fall and can be prevented. Annuals include crabgrass, foxtail, and ragweed.

Perennial weeds, such as dandelion and creeping charlie, grow tenaciously in ever-expanding patches. Spreading by seeds or roots, they live for years once established.

Remove weeds before they bloom and make seeds for another crop; or remove the entire root system.

TAPROOT Carefully dig weeds with long, deep, or assertive roots, such as wild grapevine, to eliminate them.

FIBROUS ROOTS Soil-clinging roots of foxtail and purslane can be pulled easily en masse.

SEEDHEADS Pull weeds such as plantain before they develop seeds and grow into obnoxious hordes.

ASK THE GARDEN DOCTOR **HOW CAN I TELL A WEED FROM A GARDEN PLANT?** Learn to recognize weeds common in your region, distinguishing between their appearance as seedlings and mature plants. If you're stumped in IDing a weed, send a sample or photo to your extension service. Sometimes weeds are a matter of opinion: One gardener's wildflowers (sweet violets, dandelions, oxalis) are the bane of a neighbor's weed-free lawn.

TEST GARDEN TIP

OUTGROWING WEEDS Some vegetable crops take care of weeding chores for you by shading the soil so much that they prevent weed seeds from germinating and leaving no room for weeds to grow. Notice how weeds are suppressed by the dense canopy of these crops: bean, corn, cucumber, melon, pumpkin, and squash.

VIOLET (VIOLA) Common or meadow violets bloom in spring. They can become troublesome in lawns and gardens, reproducing by seeds and by creeping roots and rhizomes. Pick the flowers or pull the plants to minimize them.

COMMON WEEDS

Weed species number in the hundreds, but a relative handful are responsible for most problems.

If you could do just one thing to control most of these common weeds, it would be this: Prevent them. Use mulch. Avoid allowing weeds to develop seedheads. A single mature weed can produce tens of thousands of seeds in one season. Different weeds produce seeds at different times. Getting to know their life cycles helps you time your weed-control practices. Eliminate small patches of a weed before it gets a foothold in your garden or lawn.

BINDWEED This perennial climber has small white trumpet flowers. It twines tightly around garden plants.

CRABGRASS Spreading easily by growing roots where stems touch soil, this annual lawn bully requires careful pulling.

CREEPING CHARLIE The creeping stems of perennial ground ivy root where they touch soil, spreading across lawns and into gardens. Dig the roots.

DANDELION Lobed leaves and yellow flowers grow from the perennial's long taproot. The flowers turn to puffy seedheads.

FOXTAIL Dense, fuzzy seedheads appear on this 2- to 3-foot-tall annual at summer's end.

LAMB'S-QUARTERS Yank the annual plants, taproot and all, before they mature at 3 to 4 feet and cast thousands of seeds.

Practice other weed-control methods shown on the pages ahead. Otherwise, keep your expectations realistic: There is no such thing as perfect weed control.

Weeds can grow anywhere and they do—in lawns, gardens, cracks in sidewalks, gutters, and wherever their roots can survive. Some of the most noxious weeds around, such as kudzu, poison ivy, and Japanese knotweed, grow up into trees, only to make eradication more difficult.

PURSLANE This drought-tolerant annual thrives in poor, compacted soil. Pull the taproot carefully.

OXALIS With cloverlike leaves and tiny yellow flowers, this perennial grows a taproot in sun or shade.

PLANTAIN The wide leaves of this perennial smother turf. Its presence signals compacted soil.

RAGWEED, COMMON This 2- to 4-foot-tall annual with ferny foliage grows from a taproot and tortures allergy sufferers.

SPURGE, PROSTRATE Seeds of this ground-hugging annual sprout all summer. Pull the entire taproot.

THISTLE Known for its prickly leaves, this fast-spreading perennial has underground stems that colonize.

STUBBORN TAPROOT The
reason dandelions and
some other weeds are
difficult to pull is that they
have a long taproot. If you
don't remove every bit of
the root, the weed will
soon grow back.

CONTROLLING WEEDS

This unending task begins as soon as the
ground thaws or plants begin growing in
the spring.

If you are diligent in weeding throughout spring,
summer weeding chores may not be overwhelming.
As summer progresses, different weed species crop
up, prompted by warmer soil. Opportunities continue
for you to uproot weeds and their seedlings and
banish their seedheads.

Different Tactics

Many gardeners think of weed pulling as a meditative
or therapeutic task: simple, repetitive, productive. For
best results, remove weeds as soon as they appear,
while their roots are undeveloped. Pull weeds after
rain or irrigation, when soil is damp. Gather and trash
weeds to prevent their seeds and roots from sprouting.

Turn to a few trusty tools designed to make
weeding easier. Some tools are specialized; others are
multipurpose. Your choice will depend on the way a
weed grows and how you like to remove them. Use
mulch as a tool too: Spread 2 to 3 inches of mulch on
open ground, especially after weeding, to prevent new
weeds from getting started.

Herbicides or chemical weed killers act on some
weeds. Preemergent herbicides prevent annual weeds
but interfere with all seed germination. Applying
them in the fall is best. Post-emergent herbicides act
on plants that already have leaves.

Less-toxic Solutions

Resourceful gardeners practice other weed control
methods, including:

Scalding them. Pour boiling water carefully from a
teakettle onto tenacious weeds.

Eating them. Many weeds are otherwise known
as wild edible plants. Dandelion, purslane, lamb's-
quarter and others have long been foraged for spring
salads. Other weeds (nightshades) are toxic—beware.

**ASK THE
GARDEN
DOCTOR** **WHAT CAN WEEDS TELL ME ABOUT MY GARDEN SOIL?** Some weeds (purslane, plantain) indicate
compacted soil and a need for aeration. Excessive weeds may tell you that the soil is high—maybe too high—in nitrogen.

WEED-CONTROL METHODS

With so many different weeds sprouting in lawns and gardens, there isn't one simple solution—there are many. To keep on top of weeds, various control methods are usually necessary on a regular basis throughout the growing season. Discover which methods and tools work best for you.

DON'T TOUCH A warren hoe does the dirty work of uprooting a painfully prickly thistle.

DIG AND PULL A hand-weeding tool helps loosen soil and roots at once with a little leverage.

WITHOUT A TRACE It isn't easy to get all the roots of creeping charlie, but a cultivator helps get the job done.

MANUAL LABOR Rainy weather brings on lush weed growth. Pulling weeds is easiest after rain.

DIGGING DEEP A well-designed hand weeder reaches deep to pop out the whole taproot of a weed such as purslane.

ORGANIC OPTION Corn gluten meal is an organic preemergent herbicide that controls some grassy and broadleaf weeds.

COMMON DISEASES OF PLANTS

Protect your plants from debilitating diseases. Learn to recognize the symptoms and practice prevention.

Diseases are caused by bacteria, fungi, and viruses. Bacteria are single-celled organisms that live on various kinds of organic matter. Unable to survive in the open, bacteria live inside plants and are transferred plant to plant by insects, water, and hands. Fungi are minute organisms that live on plants and cause visible symptoms. They spread most often via water, wind, and insects. Viruses are the smallest of disease vectors and the most difficult to control. They are typically spread by insects, but some are spread by seeds and tools.

Generally for a disease to occur, organisms must be transported to a susceptible host, such as a stressed plant. Ideal conditions (humid, dry, cloudy) make it possible for the disease to thrive.

Prevention is the best defense against pathogens. Above all, start with disease-resistant plant varieties and practice garden hygiene. A disease-prevention strategy includes these:

- Site plants far enough apart to allow air circulation.
- Manage susceptible plants, growing them in the recommended amount of sun, keep them well-watered, and don't over- or underfertilize.
- Spray healthy leaves of susceptible plants with a homemade fungicide (see recipe below).
- Remove and trash affected plant parts.

EASY TARGETS Some plants are susceptible to disease, such as powdery mildew on this phlox. Other vulnerable plants include rose, iris, tomato, lilac, and zinnia.

EARLY ON Use a fungicide as a preventive, rather than a cure for disease.

 **ASK THE GARDEN DOCTOR** **IS A HOMEMADE FUNGICIDE AN EFFECTIVE WAY TO PREVENT DISEASE?** Yes. Spray healthy leaves of particularly susceptible plants with a solution of 1 teaspoon of baking soda and 1 teaspoon of horticultural oil in a quart of water. Adding one of these antifungal ingredients to your spray can boost its effectiveness: 2 crushed cloves of garlic or 2 tablespoons of neem oil (derived from the tropical neem tree).

NOTORIOUS DISEASES

Leaf spots are one of the most common symptoms of disease, whether caused by bacteria, fungi, or viruses. Other symptoms of disease include sudden wilting, ragged or curling leaves, deformed flowers or fruit, and generally discolored or mottled foliage.

MOSAIC VIRUS Peonies and other plants affected by this or other viruses should be destroyed to prevent spread of the incurable disease.

BACTERIAL SPOT Most common in damp, humid weather, the disease can be controlled by avoiding working among wet plants.

BLACK SPOT Especially common on roses, the fungal disease causes dark splotches on leaves and leaf drop.

RUST Spread by several fungus species, rust deforms leaves with orange, gold, or brown-red spots and weakens plants.

POWDERY MILDEW A fungus resembling white powder on foliage thrives during dry, humid weather.

ROSE ROSETTE This viral disease spread by a minuscule mite cannot be prevented or cured.

RESOURCES

PLANTS AND SEEDS

BONNIE PLANTS
Bonnie Plant Farm
1727 Hwy 223
Union Springs, AL 36089
334/738-3104
www.bonnieplants.com

BRENT AND BECKY'S BULBS
7900 Daffodil Lane
Gloucester, VA 23061
804/693-3966; 877/661-2852
www.brentandbeckysbulbs.com

HEIRLOOM ROSES, INC.
24062 NE Riverside Drive
St. Paul, OR 97137
503/538-1576
www.heirloomroses.com

HIGH COUNTRY GARDENS
2902 Rufina Street
Santa Fe, NM 87507
800/925-9387; 505/438-3031
www.highcountrygardens.com

KLEHM'S SONG SPARROW NURSERY
13101 E. Rye Road
Avalon, WI 53505
800/553-3715
www.songsparrow.com

LOGEE'S TROPICAL PLANTS
141 North Street
Danielson, CT 06239
888/330-8038
www.logees.com

MILLER NURSERIES
5060 County Road 16
Canandaigua, NY 14424-8904
800/836-9630
www.millernurseries.com

NICHOLS GARDEN NURSERY
1190 Old Salem Road
Albany, OR 97321-4580
800/422-3985
www.nicholsgardennursery.com

OLD HOUSE GARDENS
536 Third Street
Ann Arbor, MI 48103
734/995-1486
www.oldhousegardens.com

PARK SEED
1 Parkton Avenue
Greenwood, SC 29647
800/845-3369
www.parkseed.com

PROVEN WINNERS
111 E. Elm Street, Suite D
Sycamore, IL 60178
877/865-5818
www.provenwinners.com

RENEES GARDEN SEEDS
6060A Graham Hill Road
Felton, CA 95018
888/880-7228
www.reneesgarden.com

RICHTERS HERBS
357 Highway 47
Goodwood, ON L0C 1A0 Canada
800/668-4372
www.richters.com

SPRING HILL NURSERY
110 West Elm Street
Tipp City, OH 45371-1699
513/354-1510
www.springhillnursery.com

STARK BRO'S NURSERIES & ORCHARDS CO.
P.O. Box 1800
Louisiana, MO 63353
800/325-4180
www.starkbros.com

TERRITORIAL SEED CO.
P.O. Box 158
Cottage Grove, OR 97424
800/626-0866
www.territorialseed.com

UNDER-A-FOOT PLANT CO.
4742 Liberty Road S #326
Salem, OR 97302-5000
503/581-8915
www.stepables.com

WHITE FLOWER FARM
P.O. Box 50, Route 63
Litchfield, CT 06759
800/503-9624
www.whiteflowerfarm.com

TOOLS AND SPECIALTY SUPPLIES

ALLSOP HOME & GARDEN
660 North Main Street,
Suite #220
Ketchum, ID 83340
866/425-5767
www.allsopgarden.com

A. M. LEONARD, INC.
241 Fox Drive
Piqua, Ohio 45356-0816
800/543-8955
www.amleo.com

ARBORVANTAGE
515/402-8662
www.arborvantageinc.com

A RUSTIC GARDEN
RR3, Box 4C
Mount Sterling, IL 62353
866/514-2733
www.arusticgarden.com

BOUNDARY FENCE AND RAILING SYSTEMS, INC.
131-02 Jamaica Avenue
Richmond Hill, NY 11418
800/628-8928; 718/847-3400
www.boundary-fences.com

COW POTS
324 Norfolk Road
East Canaan, CT 06024
860/824-7520
www.cowpots.com

ESPOMA CO.
6 Espoma Road
Millville, NJ 08332
888/377-6621
www.espoma.com

GARDENERS SUPPLY CO.
128 Intervale Road
Burlington, VT 05401
888/833-1412
www.gardeners.com

GARDENS ALIVE!
5100 Schenley Place
Lawrenceburg, IN 47025
513/354-1482
www.gardensalive.com

GEOHUMUS INTERNATIONAL
www.geohumus.com

JAMALI GARDEN
149 W. 28th Street
New York, NY 10001
212/996-5534
www.jamaligarden.com

KINSMAN CO.
P.O. Box 428
Pipersville, PA 18947
800/733-4146
www.kinsmangarden.com

LEE VALLEY TOOLS
P.O. Box 1780
Ogdensburg, NY 13669-6780
800/267-8735
www.leevalley.com

LIQUID FENCE CO.
P.O. Box 300
Brodheadsville, PA 18322
800/923-3623
www.liquidfence.com

MAGNIMOIST BASKET LINERS
Think Mint, Inc.
P.O. Box 487
Northfield, MN 55057
800/713-6188
www.thinkmint.net/liners

MUD GLOVES
26 Computer Drive East
Albany, NY 12205
866/916-1563
www.mudglove.com

PLANET NATURAL
1612 Gold Avenue
Bozeman, MT 59715
406/587-5891; 800/289-6656
www.planetnatural.com

RAIN BARREL SOURCE
Hayneedle, Inc.
9394 W. Dodge Road, Suite 300
Omaha, NE 68114-3319
888/880-4884
www.rainbarrelsource.com

SIMPLE GARDEN JR.
Fertile Earth
877/883-2784
www.fertileearth.com

THE GARDENER'S HOLLOW LEG
1442 A Walnut Street #59
Berkeley, CA 94709
510/735-6165
www.thegardenershollowleg.com

INDEX

Looking for more gardening inspiration?

See what the experts at *Better Homes and Gardens* have to offer.

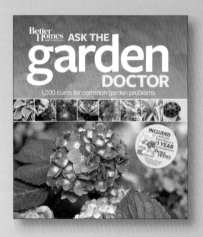

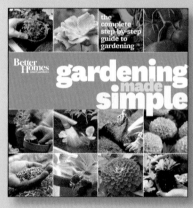

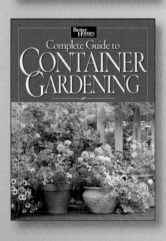

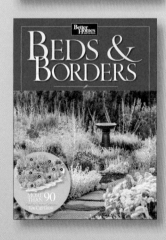

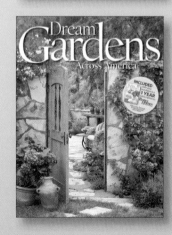

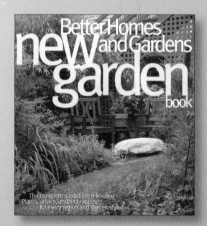

Available where all great books are sold.

WILEY